GOLD RUN

A novel by: Anthony J. Machicoté

Copyright © 2021 Anthony J. Machicoté

All rights reserved. In accordance with the U.S. Copyright Act of 1976, the scanning, uploading, and electronic sharing of any part of this book without the permission of the publisher constitute unlawful piracy and theft of the author's intellectual property. Any resemblances to real people, living or dead, actual events, establishments, or locales are intended to give the fiction a sense of reality and authenticity. Other names, characters, places and incidents are either products of the author's imagination or are used fictitiously. Those fictionalized events that involve real people did not occur.

Cover Design: Muniquedesign

ISBN:

Publisher: Royalty Writing Services LLC

Disclaimer: The publisher is providing this book and its contents on an "as is" basis and make no representations or warranties of any kind with respect to this book or its contents. In addition, the publisher assumes no responsibility for errors, inaccuracies, omissions, or any other inconsistencies herein.

CHAPTER ONE

It all started because I ran out of milk! I woke up that Friday morning in my steamy, shoe-box sized, one bedroom apartment absolutely starving. It was July 1st and blazing hot at 9 in the morning. I knew this because the fan in my bedroom window did nothing but move sticky, heavy air around the tiny space. I rolled out of my twin bed lazily, and walked the few steps to the connected bathroom, where I drained myself of fluids. Leaving the bathroom, I walked through my bedroom and into the living room, which connected to the kitchen and dining room.

I grabbed a mixing bowl and filled it with my favorite cereal; Apple Jacks then sat the bowl on my card table which doubled as my dining room table. I put a spoon into the bowl then opened the door of my miniature refrigerator, and snatched the half-gallon carton of milk. Immediately I knew it was empty, but still shook it and looked inside. Not more than a sip was within.

"Shit!" I spat under my breath, irritated that I had not gotten more when I saw it was low.

I tossed the carton into a small trash can beside the fridge and walked to my bedroom, hating how I could be such a procrastinator! I had only worn socks and boxers to bed so I grabbed a pair of shorts from my floor, a muscle shirt from my dresser, and slid both the items on. Being 6 feet tall, 200 pounds with an athletic build, creamy brown skin, braided black hair that fell just below my shoulders, made me mildly attractive. Add to that my deep brown eyes plus a Colgate smile, and it was easy to see why the ladies tended to fly to me almost magnetically! But, being a less than flashy dresser and 22 without a car, the ladies who desired a man with major paper did not stick to me that long.

I worked in a factory five days a week, making just over $12.50 an hour, which kept me housed, fed, and clothed, but left my pockets slimmer than an anorexic at a swimsuit pageant. I snagged a couple bucks in change from my basket of coins, because I was void of paper money and hours short of snagging my check later that day. I stepped into some Nikes that sat near a bedroom wall and scooped my keys from a wall hook on my way out the apartment door. I walked down the musty, unkempt hallway, passing three other apartment doors before reaching the stairs down to the front door.

I opened the front door to a blast of A.M. sun and heat, shading my eyes with my left hand because of the onslaught of sunshine. The busy street that held my house was alive with vehicles moving east and west on the slanted avenue. It was the first of the month in the hood, plus, the start of the weekend before the 4th of July, so people were already in motion. I turned right, walking towards the corner store at a leisurely pace. Across the street from my apartment was the edge of Washington Park, one of the historic parks in Milwaukee. Kids were in the grassy area next to a fenced in baseball diamond, playing as youngsters do on beautiful days in the summer. I passed a single-story building beside mine, an empty lot with overgrown grass and litter of all varieties before coming upon the back of the cinderblock-painted-white store on the intersection.

A pair of pretty black girls, late teens in short shorts that showed off sexy, slender legs and baby tee's that accented their upper curves passed me saying in unison. "Hey sexy!" followed with girlish giggles.

I smiled, eyeing the two as I replied, " What up gorgeous ladies?" They both laughed as dames do, then one blew me a kiss as we passed.

I turned to watch them walk away, adding "Later love!" Both waved while staring back over their svelte shoulders. I rounded the edge of the store, entering into the parking lot. A teenage black boy, scrawny but freshly fitted stood posted on the side of the door, leaning back with one foot on the wall, his left hand in his pocket.

He saw me and asked, "You need some weed homie? I got that bag!"

"I'm proper right now, but later we will holla, a'ight?" I told him

He nodded as I entered the store. I went right to the cooler on the far-right end of the store and grabbed a carton of milk. A few other people were in the 3-aisled store. A pair of little girls haggled with each other about chips, a teen boy with a box of chicken nuggets stood in an aisle snagging something from a shelf, and an older lady perused a shelf of cereals. Milk in hand, I went to the counter and dropped exact change, literally, on it with the Arab behind the plexiglass ringing up the purchase. A pudgy-faced cutie, with rich brown skin, in her 20's smiled at me as she reached the counter.

I shrugged, smiling unabashedly before saying, "Gotta use what you got on hand, feel me?"

She laughed single-syllabled, replying, "I already know how it is sometimes boo, believe dat!"

I chuckled while slipping past her and out the front door, hiding hints of shame from having a chunk of change but no paper money.

While languidly walking out of the parking lot, I heard sirens off in the near distance. This was nothing even slightly unusual, my zip code being one of the worst in the city, crime-wise. I turned the corner of the store, squinting from the sun's brightness as I headed east. At the next corner, 40th street, rounding a bend in Lisbon Avenue was an old school Chevy flying up the street. It was heading my way. At the lights, 3 quarters of a block away, a bag was tossed out of the vehicle into a small crowd of people who watched things from the sidewalk. A tad surprised by the sight, I continued towards my place.

As the Chevy, all candy painted and chrome wheeled neared me, I saw the passenger hoist a duffle bag up to the window. Behind them, half a block back, a police cruiser, all noise and lights screamed around the bend, kicking up dust in its wake. A masked man in the Chevy pushed the bag out the window, staring directly into my face. The bag hit the pavement in a space between two parked cars, a heavy metallic clunk and rattle sounding as the bag rolled to a stop just a few feet away from me. Intrigued, I walked to the bag as a trio of cop cars zipped past in high gear pursuing the Chevy. I scooped the duffle by its handles, glancing to see if anyone was eyeing me.

The kid who peddled weed was watching me from the side of the store, his cellphone up to an ear, but I ignored him. I took the heavier-than-expected bag into my apartment swiftly. Inside, I dropped it on my ragged, black synthetic leather sofa. I sat on my coffee table facing the place, I laid the bag. With my mind relaying images of treasures and crazy stacks of money, I unzipped the duffle bag immediately. Dumping the contents, I found 2 handguns, a bag of loose cash, and a pile of small gold bars the size of an iPod. I grabbed a face towel, and put the guns on my coffee table, not much interested in them. I examined the gold blocks. There were 15 in total, and on their sides were an engravement. It read "1kg". My public-school education left me clueless as to what that equated to in pounds, so I pulled out my Galaxy and looked it up.

"2.205 pounds." I said out loud, a wave of shock crashing over my senses as I realized that I had over 30 pounds of gold in my possession.

Swiftly I moved to my bedroom, returning with my bookbag, where I put everything inside. I tossed the duffle bag into my trash can, intending to take the bag out when I left. I took a fast shower and dressed, my head running through scenarios of splurging on luxurious things and having a lovely life from then forward. I didn't have a solid plan on what to do with the newly acquired windfall that had been tossed at my feet, but I knew that holding it in my lousy apartment was not an option. I lived smack dab in the ghetto, so I knew anyone could come seeking the loot. I put on my bookbag and stepped out of my place, heading towards the front door. In the street beyond my building's door, I saw people crowded around yellow police tape, which stretched from 40th to 42nd street, though only on the westbound side of the four-laned two-way street.

That happened to be the side of the street my apartment was located on, exactly the side where the duffle bag had been tossed. I was sure that wasn't coincidental! Policemen and detectives conversed with people who milled about. I turned west, headed towards the corner store, weaving my way through people. I had on blue jean shorts, a gray T-shirt, gym shoes and a ball cap pulled low. The boy trying to sell weed was leaning beside a payphone in the store's parking lot. He saw me and threw a look my way I did not like at all. I kept moving up the angled avenue somewhat hurriedly, not enjoying the heavy police presence with what I had inside the bookbag on my back!

"Hey!" someone called out in my direction from behind me as I walked.

I looked over my shoulder and saw a husky, white detective a few steps behind me as I crossed from the east to west side of 41st street. He beckoned me to wait, and I did, with my heart pounding like the rabbit Thumper in that old Bambi movie.

"W-what's the issue officer?" I asked as he neared, trying to remain as chill as possible outwardly.

"No issue, just wanted to know if you saw something that could help us out." he answered when we were face-to-face.

I feigned absolute ignorance, saying, "What happened?" while praying my face was not betraying me.

"High speed chase of some robbery suspects. It ended in a foot chase, where a few of my men took some rounds."

That caught me by surprise, so I didn't have to show an Oscar winning performance. When my head whipped back in shock, it was legit! "Damn! I'm sorry to hear that, sir. I heard the sirens, but I was in the shower. Plus, sirens in the summer 'round here are as normal as birds chirpin', kids yelling' and gunshots." I added an apologetic shrug before continuing, " I can't help you."

I felt the gold and guns shift slightly in my bookbag, which spooked me a bit. I tried remaining nonchalant as he studied me. He watched me a bit longer than I liked, and I readied myself to bolt like Usain, at the slightest inkling of trouble.

The dick dug into his pocket and handed me a business card, saying "Well, if you hear anything..."

I nodded and smiled, saying, "I got ya officer, no problem!" I then turned, walking westward without looking back. Relief rained from the crown of my head down to my ankles.

"Aye, you!" I heard the detective yell again.

I had to actually fight the immediate urge to sprint like a runner out of the starting blocks. Instead, I simply turned my head casually.

"I gave you my old card." he said with a sheepish grin, jogging into my direction. "This one has all my current info on it. Sorry." he finished with an embarrassed titter.

I smiled, wordlessly accepting the second card. I continued walking west, releasing the breath I did not realize I was holding. I was still trying to center and calm myself from the shakiness of the police encounter, when I reached the intersection of North Avenue and 43rd street, a crazy busy conjunction about 5 blocks north and west of my apartment. I was on a corner awaiting a westbound city bus that would take me up North Avenue. Walking past about one hundred cops with one portion of their query on my back felt like I was swimming in a tank of tiger sharks with a blood-soaked carcass strapped on my back.

I lit a Newport 100 as I stood by the bus stop, scanning the foot and street traffic while doing my best to get my heartrate below 180 beats per minute. I decided to go directly to a storage facility, put the gold bars away, then get my check and do some shopping. I had a bag of cash find me and I figured it was my luck finally turning! I pulled out my Galaxy and did a google search to get the current price of gold. It stated $1,763.04 per ounce. I almost dropped my phone upon seeing that. Thoughtlessly, the calculation was computed in my head and out of pure disbelief I used my phone to double-check my math.

CHAPTER TWO

The bus pulled up with a screech of brakes then hiss of hydraulics. Stepping onto the bus, in my bookbag I carried a life-changing $934,411 and change in the gold bars. I found an open seat in the ¾ full bus trembling internally, excitement coursing through my veins right beside oxygen and red blood cells. The bag sat on my lap, my arms atop it as I rode westwardly, watching the scenery. My mind was spiraling through images of trips to exotic lands, flashy cars and drop-dead gorgeous dames on my arms in pairs.

I was simply ecstatic but still I wanted to put things in a safe place immediately to see what may be trailing it all. I stepped off the bus on 76th and North Avenue, crossing the busy intersection. I stood on a small island on the northwest corner, impatiently waiting for a southbound bus. I watched the steady stream of cars passing me in all four directions, with an unshakable smile on my face. I surveyed the area, first glancing at the bank on the southeast corner, where a pair of patrons walked out of the glass doors. A library was directly across the street on the western side of the intersection, where kids could be seen through the windows playing on computers.

Behind me was an elementary school closed for the summer and directly in front of me, on the northeast corner was a large retirement home, with balconies on the exterior walls that I could see. I felt euphoric standing there. I lit another cigarette, wondering what I should do that night. I had to work the following day, which was Saturday, but it wasn't until 10am, which was late enough to recover from a good time, something I was damn sure intent on having! I had no clear idea of my plans, but I did know that I would have the freshest of fits I could find using the bag of cash I had come across.

After about 20 minutes that felt like 20 years, the bus halted alongside the curb a step away from where I stood. Traffic was getting thicker as the bus took me south, through the center of Wauwatosa and then into the northern edge of West Allis, two western suburbs of Milwaukee.

The storage units were located about 3 miles south of North Avenue, across the street from the Wisconsin State Fairgrounds and the Pettit National Ice Center on 84th and Walker Street. I stepped off the air-conditioned bus and moved casually to the office of the storage facility. It was located in a parking lot with a driveway that led up to wrought iron gates. The heat was a bit oppressive, but I didn't much mind, my focus only on getting the gold bars into a safe place.

Inside the bathroom-sized office, a wrinkly white woman greeted me not too cheerily but that was fine because fans inside the tiny space made it about fifteen degrees cooler. I asked for a very small unit, and she handed me papers to fill out, asking for my ID so she could photocopy it. I gave it to her and when all the formalities were taken care of, she presented me with a keycard and a package with a new master lock inside once I paid the fees.

"If you go one month without paying the rental fee, we charge you double to get your stuff back or continue storing. Two months and it quadruples. Two months and one week, your stuff gets auctioned " she said in a monotone voice just as shriveled as she was. "Got me?" She added, emphasizing her point as if it was the key to the universe.

I nodded while smiling and said, "Yep, don't forget to pay up!"

She returned a solemn nod, and I was out the door. I let myself into the area that housed the different storage units, my key card opening a gate door about 10 feet to the left of the opening for cars. The space was basically a fenced-in area with different sized garage-like door openings, all a reddish-brown brick build. I walked up to a plaque showing where the different units were by numbers. I walked leisurely, the lanes lined with what seemed like a countless number of units, giving off the feel of a never-ending alleyway. With every step I was spending money in my head, ten thousand at a time, smiling as I painted a picture of luxury for my future.

My stall was very tiny—basically a closet with a sliding metal door that rolled up like blinds. I opened it and saw a single lightbulb hanging in the center of the depressing space, a string limply dangling beneath. The space had a concrete floor and cinder block wall. It was clean and nearly airless. I turned the light on after stepping inside, and with a click the space was illuminated.

I slid the door closed behind me. I kneeled, sitting my bookbag on the floor, and pulled out the bag of cash. I counted out five thousand in 20's, 50's and the ever popular, always trendy, Mr. Benjamin Franklin. Dismissing a notion to count the remaining figures in the stifling, claustrophobia-inducing box, I put the still puffed-up bag of money into the bookbag. Pocketing the cash I had picked out, I opened the lock packaging, went by the door, and set the bookbag on the floor. I lifted the door after turning out the light and walked into the beaming sunshine.

I closed and locked the door, putting one key in my sock, the other on my keyring. I left, taking a cab to my job which was located in the northwest side of Milwaukee, about five miles from the storage facility. I went into the factory, a nondescript, two-story, cream colored concrete building with windows only on the bottom floor. Basically, it was the American version of a sweatshop. I saw my boss outside his office, talking to an older woman who worked in a different part of the leather production factory. I waited patiently, and when they finished conversing, he motioned for me to come over as the lady walked away, not looking happy at all.

A fat, bald guy, with lemon drop colored teeth, and colorless, nearly translucent skin, the boss carried an air of sleaziness and never contradicted that in his actions. He was in no way admired by any of his employees and any one-on-one time with him was about as pleasant as a tooth extraction.

"Chris, my boy." He began in a fatherly way that made my creep-o-meter hit 'weirdo' asap. I snipped a laugh from escaping when an image of my boss trying to explain to Chris Hanson why he had come to the home of a 14-year-old boy with wine coolers, condoms, a whip and handcuffs.

"S'up Mr. Whalt?" I asked, wondering why he was being chummy and giving me his politician grin.

"I ah, wanted you to know that I had to dock your pay 1½ hours." he said with the limpest show of remorse I had ever heard, while walking me into his dingy office.

"What? Why?" I inquired, pissed and momentarily confused, even though this was one of his many shows of abject shadiness.

"Sorry son, but my records show that you were late 3 times this pay period." He stated with even more faux remorse.

"Not even Mr. Whalt! I made a point to be on time, with multiple alarms on my phone because we had this same issue before!" I told him, a bit of venom in each vowel. "I do everything to make sure I get here early so that I will avoid this situation since I need all the funds I can make!"

Obviously unmoved, my boss shrugged and said, "I'm only going by the time clock. You know, these computerized gizmos can't be tampered with, and I cannot argue with them son. Sorry."

I took a deep breath to hold back from spazzing out on my crook of a boss, and said, "Whatever man, just gimme my check."

He lent me another phony look of sorrow as I signed the book.

"Its policy. Even I have to answer to higher ups." He said in a way that only made me dislike him that much more.

I noticed that my check was just under 20 dollars short but ignored it, reminding myself that my financial future was secure as I headed out the door. From work I walked the nine blocks on the slanted Fond Du Lac Avenue, headed southeast from 69th to 60th, where the Midtown Shopping Center was located. My stomach let out a beastly roar, reminding me that I had not eaten a single thing all morning, just as I reached the commercial area. I walked into the spacious triangular shopping space which was a strip mall composed of a community of stores on both sides of a few streets that dissected the plaza.

The place was alive with patrons, with it being the first of the month and a Friday. I decided to indulge in my favorite breakfast spot, an IHOP located on the southeast corner of the shopping complex. Never really having much excess funds left me rarely able to afford the delicacy of many restaurants. That day, I ordered a huge breakfast and devoured it, savoring every single forkful like I had not eaten a more flavorful food in my life.

Stuffed and feeling that much happier with the current scope of my life, I walked to Playmakers, an urban clothing store not far from the eatery. The store had hundreds upon hundreds of all the latest outfits and shoes, hats, glasses, and any other accessory required to look like the folks in all the hip hop magazines and tv shows aimed at the urban communities of our beloved country. I purchased four head to toe outfits which included tops, bottoms, belts, hats, shoes, shades and all! I would have spent my check five times over had that been the source of my funds. Thank God I had stumbled upon that treasure like a pirate. I left with three bags and went to a jeweler that was located closer to the center of the shopping district.

Inside, were walls and cases full of different jewelry, all looking quite sparkly and fresh. I saw an Asian lady standing off in a corner and approached her. When I neared, she threw me a weak smile, but I flashed her a sincere one as I asked, "Do you buy gold?"

"Shure. What you got for sale?" she replied in a mild accent that let me know she was not originally from the country. Her voice turned sweet and friendly, as her eyes did a quick scan of my hands for something not there.

"I have a few gold bars my grandpa willed to me. What do you pay?" I explained, conveying that with a relaxed smile.

"We pay 90% of market value. So, if price is 15 hundred per ounce, we give you 1350. It is a good deal. Other places, they like to take more. We just wanna make customers happy!"

I nodded, then changed the subject, asking about some diamond earrings I saw in black. She let me take a closer look at them, then showed me more jewels she swore would look good on me. I copped a pair of black and white diamond earrings and a fly ass watch. Smiling vibrantly, I left very happy with my purchases. I spent more in the jewelry store than I did in two years of rent.

There was a Currency Exchange across the busy 4 lane Fond Due Lac Avenue, and I jogged through the speedy traffic to not become roadkill. I cashed my check, then took a bus down to 43rd street. From there, I rode a crowded, standing room only bus southbound to a bus stop across the street from my apartment! It was well after 1pm and everyone seemed to be out in motion, preparing for whatever they had planned that night.

    Police seemed to have moved on with their investigation. All the police tape was gone, and traffic was heavy in both directions. I jogged across the 4 laned street, eyeing the people while feeling like a million bucks...well, close enough to it! I threw a smile at a pair of girls who came out of the store just as I stepped on the sidewalk. They waved, fingers moving like it played an invisible piano. I winked back but did not speak. I kept on until I reached my building and opened the door. Inside the hallway, I ran up the stairs three at a time, then moved in long strides to my apartment.

    Inside my place, I chuckled at the bowl of Apple Jacks on the table before trashing it, even though prior to that day I would never have violated the sanctity of my beloved cereal—nor wasted the money. I hopped into the shower for the second time that day, singing like I was auditioning for THE VOICE, and feeling just jubilant. I got dressed in all new everything, down to socks and boxers. I was looking impeccable, spending extra time in front of my full-length mirror, grinning at the dapper cat I saw staring back at me. I took a few selfies just to make a record of my flyness.

Following my moment of vanity that lasted for about ten minutes and didn't really stop—I simply mustered the strength to pull myself away from reflective items and put my phone away—I placed my check stub on my entertainment center and put the clothing I had purchased into my bedroom closet. I returned to my bedroom and decided I would get new furniture and a place that wasn't so small I could sneeze in the living room and spray every wall in the apartment!

CHAPTER THREE

I plopped onto my soon-to-be "old" sofa and pulled my phone out to check Facebook and IG to see how those pics I had posted were doing, when someone knocked on my apartment door. I paused at the odd event, seeing that you needed a key to enter the building and I didn't interact with any of the other tenants. Phone in hand, I walked to the door believing it to be my landlord to converse about who-cared-what. He only made house calls over important things like overdue rent or major complaints.

I unlocked the door and turned the knob, my focus on the phone until the door was completely opened. I was wrong about the visitor. Two black men, one bulky and tall, the other thin and a head shorter than me stood at my threshold, both looking at me with grins that had an ominous vibe to them.

"What's the deal?" I asked, my eyes sliding from one face to the other while awaiting an answer. I felt myself trying to remain calm while looking at the guys.

The short guy's grin turned a tad more menacing as the muscle-headed cat waved a thick, shiny pistol in a manner that was the universal message for, 'I got a gun stupid, move aside!' I obliged, never being one to test a gun-toting goon's temper, and they both walked in as the short one said, "You got my shit!"

Taking languid steps, the men made their way to my couch, the pistol carrying cat never removing his eyes from me. I simply stood at the door, watching them, spooked half to death. Both my heart and mind raced like Matt Kenseth, Bubba Wallace, or any of those other NASCAR nuts. "What you talkin' 'bout yo?" I quizzed, hoping I was exuding a calmness that did not live within me that very instant.

The smaller cat, who scanned my garage-sized abode with a look of disgust said, "That bag you picked up this mornin' with the money, gold and straps." He looked at me while I stood by a semi-partition that separated my itsy-bitsy kitchen and living room. He added with a wider grin that reminded me of those evil ass hyena's from THE LION KING. "All that shit belonged to me!" he added.

I did my damnedest to show calm on the surface while inside I was computing every possible exit strategy which kept me from having to share the story about how I got a bullet in my ass years down the line. "Yo, seriously, I have no clue what you talkin' 'bout bruh."

The shorter cat pulled a black pistol from under his arm and sat it on my coffee table while still giving me a wicked grin. The larger brother sat his pistol on the table too. The duo looked at each other and laughed.

"Nigga, you got on crisp ass clothes right now!" He stopped, looked at his ace and said, "Train, he is scared to death! I gotta get a picture of his ass!" With that, he pulled out an iPhone and snapped a few pics of me. Then he finished, saying," My little homie saw you scoop the bag. I saw you as I threw it out the car window. You STILL don't know what I'm talkin' 'bout?"

I was trying to think swiftly but fear was making ideas fuzzier than five shots of Patrón, when all I needed was clarity. I pushed panic slightly to the rear and said, " Yo bruh, that was NOT me! I got these clothes because today was payday." Lifting my hands up, palms facing forward, I pointed towards my entertainment center, adding, "I'll show you my check stub."

The cats looked at each other and shrugged. "Go 'head money!" The smaller goon said, both eyeballing me again.

Calmly, I moved towards the entertainment center, and as I did, I thanked God for my marvelous mother. Beside her picture was a small canister of pepper spray she had gotten me as a gag gift that year. Smoothly I grabbed the canister and check stub. I turned to face the unwelcome visitors, holding my check stub sheet wide as I said, "See fam, I just got paid!"

They both leaned closer to examine the paper, and unhesitantly, I squeezed a stream of burning liquid into the larger cat's eyes. He screamed, rubbing at his eyes as I kicked over my coffee table, causing both guns to clatter to the wooden floor and slide under the couch. Without pause I sprayed the smaller guy. He was trying to get his hands on me as the stream hit him in the face, causing him to yell in agony. At full speed, I ran out my apartment door, turning left in the hallway and heading towards the back steps.

I jumped down the winding stairwell five steps at a time, my only desire being to put as much distance between myself and my new friends with the guns who probably wouldn't be interested in talking if they got ahold of me. As I exploded out of the building's backdoor, a dark-skinned teenager sat on the hood of a gorgeous Infiniti G35, his radio thumping in the tiny parking space for residents of my building. When he saw me, he hesitated then reached for something on his hip, but I was still in motion and caught the guy with a solid right punch. He rolled over an edge of the front bumper and landed on the blacktop.

People watched the wild situation as I sprinted across the street headed for the alleyway that led north between 40th and 41st. I heard a trio of gunshots crack from behind me just as I hit the mouth of the alley. I kept my head low and ducked alongside a few trashcans, turning the corner of a garage just as 4 more pistol pops rang out behind me. I slipped into a gangway, scared to death and not daring to look over my shoulder as I raced south through someone's backyard, bursting onto 40th street from between two houses. People on the street were moving for the safety of their homes or getting low as they located which direction the gunplay came from. I didn't stop, only hesitating mildly to see that no cars were coming down the block as I flew across the street. I ran up a few concrete steps and through a gangway between two duplex apartments, blowing past a dog that jumped at me, and hopped a rear fence with an athleticism that would have made Olympic hurdlers envious!

At the alley I turned left, heading north as I passed garage after garage, still not looking back, only focused forward. I ran for about half a block, never slowing down. A few houses from the alley's opening, I jumped a chain-linked fence into a huge backyard, sprinting towards the front of the house and 39th street, leaping the front gate as well.

I dashed north on 39th, passing Lloyd Street, avoiding cars on the slender two-way road. I dodged kids who played on the sidewalk and women of all ages who called out to me as if I was navigating a human obstacle course. Just shy of Garfield Street, the next intersection, I shot across the one-way street and cut through an empty lot beside a church's fenced in parking area. That open space was mirrored by another across the alley, coming out on 38th. I dashed across the one-way street and continued through another houseless plot, into the next block's alley. I ran a bit through the alley, then cut across another empty area of grass between two houses and came out on 37th street.

Having run six city blocks in a time that would have gotten me to qualifiers for a track meet minus so much as a glance behind me, I slowed to a jog as I moved north on 37th street, passing Garfield Street. I ran through another open lot to the alley where I paused to catch a breather between a pair of garages. I surveyed the space around me, peeking around the corner towards the mouth of the alley 30 feet away while taking deep suctions of air. I saw no one who seemed intent on turning me into a human sprinkler, so I cautiously walked north to where the alley split east and west. I turned right, walking east alongside a white house that had what looked like bullet holes in it's siding, coming out on 36th street, my head on a swivel. Seeing nothing ominous, I walked diagonally across 36th street headed towards North Avenue about 40 feet from the alleyway. On the busy avenue, I saw an eastbound bus coming and jogged to the nearest bus stop, which was at the lights one block east on 35th street.

    I waited for the eastbound bus with absolutely no clue as to my destination, simply sure that being anywhere else was the best idea! I watched all angles of the bustling intersection as the bus neared, not really sure how I would spot danger with enough time to get away but still staying hypervigilant. No one seemed to pay me any added attention except for a pair of precious teenie-boppers a few years below the cut-off age for me to entertain with more than a kind smile. I boarded the bus still winded, as I walked to the rear seats.

    I paid little attention to the passengers I passed until I saw a thin, chocolate-toned dame with a pink baby-T and white short-shorts that looked quite delectable on her, sitting all alone. I sat directly across from the ebony beauty and caught my breath. I still watched the street for any sign of trouble nonchalantly, my eyes roving like a panning camera.

    I noticed the chocolate cutie eyeing me and when our retinas connected a second time, she smiled. I shot her a smile in return, then went back to making sure I was still in the clear. "Hey." she said, catching my attention again.

    I looked at her, a smile still on my face. "Yeah ma?"

"Why are you panting?" she questioned with a grin that was so beautiful it mesmerized me momentarily.

I let out a single-syllabled chuckle before answering honestly, "Just got chased by goons with guns hoping to make me holier than Jesus!"

She laughed a laugh so warm she could melt the polar ice caps instantly, then asked, "What?" An eyebrow raised inquisitively.

"Ignore me sweetheart, I'm just being silly! I had to run a few blocks for this bus." I explained with a smile as the bus moved east down North Avenue. "I'm Chris." I added, reaching across the aisle separating us.

"I'm Tatiana." she returned, shaking with a soft, slim hand all French-tipped gorgeously.

"Hmm...'Chris and Tatiana'. Sounds nice together, doesn't it?" I said with the purest smile I could muster.

She let out a melodic laugh that carried an air of sweetness sugar couldn't compete with. She looked away shyly, then focused on me again with a glistening smile. "It sounds alright." Was her response and the coyness made her eyes sparkle like sunlight rippling off waves on a lake. I loved it. "Maybe!" She added, which made me chuckle.

"Maybe huh?" I teased with a grin, enjoying her jousting.

"Yep, maybe." She confirmed, toying with me.

"Where are you headed, beautiful Tatiana?" I quizzed simply to further the conversation until I could come up with another clever quip.

With a straight face she inquired, "Why? You plan on stalking me?" We were just pulling past the intersection of 27th and North Avenue, but my whole focus had turned to the darling dame a few feet away from me.

"Stalk you? Me? Not even sweetness. I was actually going to ask if you wanted to get some ice cream with the man of your dreams and your future hubby." I told her. She laughed way too loud, throwing her head back and all, which made me wonder if I had been too cocky.

Tatiana composed herself before asking, "You actually know him? God, I've been waiting forever for him to pop up! What does he look like?" She mocked me but did it with a warm smile. A pair of teenage girls who sat on the back row of seats listened and watched our interactions intently, enjoying the banter as much as Tatiana and I.

"You wanna see his photo?" I asked, smiling with confidence on blind like high beams.

"Definitely!" she answered, with a curious grin.

I pulled my phone from my pocket, happily realizing that I went on autopilot while under duress and put it into my pocket. I made a show of preparing for a selfie, took one then made it seem like I did not like the shot and took another one before handing her the phone. She laughed as I said, "Here he is." The girls behind us giggled adorably. I looked at them and winked.

"You are too much, you know that?" Tatiana told me while smiling superbly and looking at my picture. I shrugged in response, enjoying the way she bit her lip while studying my photo. She looked up and handed me my phone. "How old are you, Chris?"

"22. How 'bout you?" I returned as I put my phone away.

"Just turned 23 in May." She answered.

"Happy Belated Birthday mama, but I need to see some ID because there is no way a youngin' like you can be 23. Maybe 20! Maybe!"

"I am!" She protested, a look of defense on her darling face. She fished through her tiny little handbag adding, "Why would I lie?" She pulled her ID out, showing me.

"I have no clue why you would lie. I just wondered if you would show me."

She blocked all but her birthday from view as I smiled her way. "See!" she said then pulled it away. We both shared another smile. The bus sat at the intersection of Fond Du Lac and North Avenue, waiting for the lights to change.

"Where you headed?" I again asked her, wondering if she would be willing to share that now.

"To my girl's house. We plan on sitting around and being bored together for a while. Why?"

I shrugged then said with a straight face, "Sounds hella...boring."

Tatiana laughed, then said, "Shut up!"

"Okay but then you won't know what I'm thinking, which would be a true travesty!" I said, pretending to be disheartened while dangling the bait like a fishing line.

"What are you thinking Chris?" she quizzed with an edge, as if she dared me to come up with a grand idea.

"I'm thinking you should change your plans." I answered with a smile as I stared into her Hershey kisses colored eyes

She looked interested but hesitant and asked, "What shall you do to keep me entertained?" The way she laid her words out actually felt like she was challenging me.

"Change your plans first!"

"What?!? Blind?! Nuh-uh!"

I laughed then asked, "Why not?"

"Because I want to...wait! Are you even single?" she inquired completely out of nowhere.

I chuckled, saying, "Here you are on the cusp of allowing me to take you on a fantastic, always-to-be-remembered first date and you're just now asking if I'm single?"

"Yeah, so...are you?"

"Yes Tatiana, I am single. I've never been married, nor engaged, and I have no kids. I've been riding solo for about 2 months. You?"

"4 months." she said with sadness below her cool facade! She looked out a nearby window to further mask her feelings.

"Wow, 4 months. Ready to date. Again?" I joked, hoping to entice her smile once more.

It worked. She laughed and placed her eyes back on me, saying "Shut up! You say it like I said years, not months."

"Well, may I take you out Tatiana?"

She gave me a penetrating gaze, all seriousness before asking, "Where?"

I paused, absolutely clueless of an answer. "Ice cream!" I said, blurting out the first thing that came to my head.

She laughed, tossing me a skeptical glance. "Really?"

"Yeah sweetheart. You game?" I asked with a daring smile.

"Okay. Hold on a second." she said, then pulled out her phone and dialed someone. She began to speak, and I took that as my cue to search for ice cream shops located on the Lower East Side of Milwaukee, which was the direction the bus was heading. I found a Cold Stone Creamery and mapped it out.

Tatiana ended her call and said, "Okay, we are having ice cream!"

She smiled at me brightly and I realized that her face was one I would love to see on the regular.

"Bet!" I said, matching her smile with my own.

CHAPTER FOUR

"Where were you headed? Not to get ice cream, I expect." Tatiana asked as the bus passed Humboldt Drive, continuing east on North Avenue, nearing the bridge that crossed the Milwaukee River. The river was the unofficial border between the east side and the "Lower East Side" of the city. The "Lower East Side" was ritzier, with a new age hippy vibe and multiple college campuses.

I chuckled as I stepped across the aisle and slid into the seat alongside Tatiana. "Nah mama, I was going to the lakefront actually! Figured I would relax and enjoy the weather." I told her, not lying nor being completely honest. I did not have a destination before meeting her, and the bus took you about 4 blocks from the lakefront, so I could have ended up there.

"Oh, okay. What is the plan...where are we headed?" She inquired as we crossed the river, passing factories on both sides of the street. With a mischievous smile I said, "You'll see soon enough my dear!" I almost added a spooky cackle but held off because I didn't want to push my luck with this lovely lady I had just met.

Tatiana and I stepped off the bus at the intersection of Oakland and North Avenues. Traffic was heavy with North Avenue being the main artery from the northwest sides of the city leading to the lakefront.

"Do you want to walk or take another bus? It's only 5 blocks from here and it is lovely out." I stated while we stood on a corner of the hectic crossroads.

"That's fine!" she answered with a smile.

In the heavy heat, Tatiana and I walked south, staying under trees for shade. "Why are you single?" She asked as we headed towards Brady Street, where the Cold Stone Creamery was located. We crossed a bridge covering a bike path that was once a railway that led down to the waterfront.

I inhaled deeply as the memory of my last romance came to mind, "My ex... she shattered me in ways I don't even like looking at." I didn't want to be considering the emotionally stunted shortie I had last dated, but I continued: "I've been focused on other things lately like...absolutely nothing actually!" A nervous, nearly embarrassed titter fell from my mouth when I finished. It caused me to look away.

"Awww, that's so sad!" Tatiana said, which felt lovely coming from a lady as proper as she seemed. "Seriously?" she added, with compassion in her sexy voice.

"Yep! I've been focused on absolutely nothing." I said with a straight face.

Tatiana laughed, bumping me with her slender hip as she said, "I mean the heartbreak" part.

I broke into a laugh, saying, "I know. I'm being silly." I was quiet for a few ticks, before taking a deep breath and continuing; "Yeah, she crushed me like an empty soda can."

"Do you mind my asking why?" she said softly, her brown eyes shining with warmth.

"Not at all. Go ahead, ask." I told her, simply being cute. She tossed me a look that made me chuckle. I averted my eyes while laughing before going forward, "We were about 19 months strong and really in what I thought was a great place. I was starting to think about kids, and the future, but she just wanted to have fun. Then she decided that our ideas for the future were never going to be the same and left."

"Awww!" Tatiana cooed once more, though this time she grabbed my right arm and weaved her thin arms around it while laying her head on my bicep.

"That is sooo sad! How old was she?"

"20 at the time."

She sucked her tongue in a way that made a tick like sound, then stated, "That explains it!"

I didn't speak for a few steps, allowing the pain from the past to pass. Memories I had deaded tried to return like romance zombies.

"My ex," Tatiana began, unprompted after a few seconds of silent steps except for the passing of traffic. "He was not my type in the slightest." She finished when I looked down at her.

"How not?"

"He was 26, mean-spirited, and very self-centered." she elaborated.

"Ah, a winner I see!" I joked, enticing a laugh from her. She emphasized that by pressing her side into mine and played with the fingers on my right hand.

"Exactly! He was so wrong for me, and I knew it!"

"Must've been quite a charmer, huh?" I said, earning another chuckle.

"Don't tease. He actually was at first, and I just fell! Then..." she stared ahead, going silent.

I began to sing a line from an old Phil Collins song 'True Colors', saying, "You saw his true color shine through!" Tatiana emitted a laugh so beautiful it made my stomach flutter.

"Precisely, but he had some positive traits, and I was set on keeping them on the surface." she said.

"Cause that ALWAYS works!" I pointed out, making her laugh again. I added, "And even the whack job Charles Manson was a good dude in the eyes of some ladies he dated."

She clicked her tongue, then said, " He wasn't bad like that! He just sold dope and I hate drug dealers!"

"Oh." I stated, simply allowing her to continue as we walked beside a long field with lush grass and trees spaced around the area.

"I asked, then begged him to quit. He had lots of money, multiple cars, property all over the city...I told him he could go to college, start a business, and we could just enjoy life. He said he would, but always had an excuse not to. One day it just hit me that he was never going to let go of that life! It was his business, so I walked away from it and him." She shrugged, then sighed, adding, "A few months later, after I had completely cut him out of my life, I got a message on Facebook. He was locked up in a federal holding facility facing many years from an indictment. He said he should've listened. I begged him for 2 years, but he ignored me.

" 'That's life!' was all I said in the message I sent back, even though I was so sick about his plight". She shrugged and went silent. We crossed an intersecting street, continuing south as we continued our conversation. We passed a small yellow church that had its front doors open, then some nice, antique Victorian homes.

"Do you, or have you ever sold drugs Chris?" she posed as we walked.

I let out a chuckle before answering, "I earn 12.50 an hour in a factory making pieces for leather products ma! The only thing I do is smoke weed sweetness!"

She stopped me unexpectedly, stepped in front of me and looked directly into my eyes. A bit confused, I asked, "What?" As she studied me.

"Just seeing if you are being honest. My granny said that most people can't lie and stare you in the eyes without having some other reaction that lets you know not to trust them." She explained. As she stood, trying to soul-search through my iris', I had to push away a notion to lean in and kiss her sexy, flawlessly sculpted lips.

After her eyes danced back and forth across my face, I said, "Ma, I promise that if I sold any kind of narcotics, I'd not be walking with you to an ice cream parlor as a first date."

She smiled, moving back to my side, now holding my hand like we were kids, while we walked. "You never know, you could be lowkey, not out to make your moves at all known. And, you are looking especially clean in this outfit you have on!" she noted.

"Thank you for the compliment. Chalk that up to my having a mother who never allowed her baby boy to leave the house looking less than dapper, no matter the price tags torn from them." I explained, adding, "You are looking fly as hell yourself!"

She smiled bashfully, then gave me a darling look asking, "You really like my cheap clothes?"

"Definitely mama, on you anything would look priceless!"

She giggled girlishly and blushed a bit. Then she looked at me with her face lit up and said, "That's just because it was 'priced less'!"

Though the joke was kind of lame, I loved how quickly she came with her play on words. It was cute and deserved the slight laugh I gave her! "Nah," I began, shaking my head, "You're just so beautiful that clothes can't help but accentuate your externals!" I told her as we passed another intersection, still going in a southern direction.

The light in her eyes as she looked over at me was like a flash of lightning and followed a heartfelt smile that was quite heavenly.

"You are adorable Chris!" was her response.

All I could respond with was, "Thanks!"

A strip mall was located at the corner of the next intersection, which was at Brady Street and Oakland Avenue. We cut through it, heading westward as we conversed.

"When is your birthday, Chris?" Tatiana asked me as we passed a Papa John's pizzeria.

"9th of September. You?"

"May 17th." she shared as we passed a used electronics retailer. She still held my hand, and I had no intention of letting hers go. Shoppers and others who passed Tatiana and I smiled at us, which only made me like Tatiana more because obviously outsiders liked how we looked as a couple.

"Where do you work?" I questioned as we passed an ATM machine. In the shade of the overhang, the weather was just perfect! We passed a video rental place that specialized in adult movies as she answered.

"I don't! I'm in my senior year at Marquette University."

"Wow, really?" I asked, a tad shocked by this revelation. We passed a Walgreens and came out of the strip mall on Brady Street.

"Yep, I'm getting a degree in Preschool Education." She elaborated, leaving me sincerely impressed!

"Oh, that's so great that they would have college courses where you could have a second chance at learning all the things you didn't conquer as a toddler. Good for you sweetheart, gone 'head!" I said.

She laughed, tossing her head back so joyfully that I could not help but be enamored with. "What? Shut up!" she said, pushing me but not letting go of my right arm.

When both of our laughs subsided, she said, "I am going to be a Daycare Specialist. I love kids and I have wanted nothing more than this my whole life! It is my dream."

Sincerely I said, " That's actually a beautiful thing! Truly, Tatiana!"

"Thank you!" she said with a twinkle in her eyes. "You like kids?"

"For sure ma! I got 2 adorable 'nieces' I call them though they are my cousin's kids. I love kids and want a few of them. I just have to find a lady who is good for me, feels the same and voilà—babies shall rain from our loins!" I expressed with a bit of dramatic flair at the end, waving my free hand haughtily.

Tatiana looked at me with a smile that carried something I couldn't quite decipher at that moment. "You are a character, you know that?"

"That's a compliment or an insult? I'm a tad dense at times, so..."

"It's a compliment. I love character." She said as we crossed at the intersection of Brady and Jefferson streets, holding hands.

Tatiana and I entered the bustling Cold Stone Creamery and stepped into a rope guided line, waiting for our turn to order. We were hugged up, talking about small things, and sharing smiles constantly as if we knew how to do nothing else. We purchased interesting bowls of candy, fruit concoctions with an ice cream base, then sat on stools by a counter lined up against street-facing windows. We watched the traffic, both foot and vehicle pass heavily beyond the glass as we learned more about each other.

"You from Wisconsin?" Tatiana asked me as she scooped a spoonful of chunky ice cream yumminess.

"Nah ma, I was born in the Bronx. My mom moved here when she and my dad divorced. I was 6. I stayed with my dad in New York for the school year, but spent the summers, Christmas and New Year's break here. At about 10, my dad decided he and his new wife would start their own fam' and I didn't fit the picture they had in mind, so he sent me to live with mom for good."

"I thought you had a mild accent. Sorry to hear about your parent's divorcing, and your dad sending you off. That was wrong of him." Tatiana said, her tone solemn and sincere.

I shrugged as my spoonful of vanilla-banana-chocolate-crunch dissolved in my mouth, "Don't be. My dad was a topnotch scumbag! I'm lost as to what my mom saw in the fucker." I told her.

"Oh," Tatiana said, before quickly transitioning to her next question like a DJ mixing two songs seamlessly. "You and your mother close?"

"Yep. She moved back to Chicago, her hometown, two years ago, but we talk on the regular! I loved it here, so I stayed. Where were you born?"

"Here, but I don't know my parents. My mom..." Tatiana paused, and I noticed a sadness slip over her face like a film. She continued. "She put me up for adoption as a newbie. My granny took me in. Granny passed away 3 years ago from cancer, so it is only me left now."

Immediately I wasn't sure what to say, so I put my spoon in my bowl, then leaned over and wrapped Tatiana in my arms from beside her. I hugged her and said softly, " I'm sorry to hear about your grams' passing. She is most assuredly in a better place and based upon what I've been exposed to of you, I am positive that she is smiling down upon you, proud of the woman you are!"

Tatiana looked at me with a smile that glowed nearly as bright as the nonsensical radioactive neon green in an old cartoon.

"Thank you! That really means a lot!" She said, her sincerity washing over me wonderfully.

We left the parlor when our treats were devoured, and walked east down Brady Street, which was now in full motion. People were everywhere, as she and I navigated the crowded sidewalks, hugged up, all smiles.

"You want to walk down to the lakefront?" I asked as we took lazy steps.

"Sounds fine to me." she said cheerfully. We conversed while passing a constant slew of shops selling everything from food to footwear, clothes to cameras, as well as other odd and interesting items.

Three blocks from the ice cream spot, Brady Street went from a road to a paved footpath that cut between the beautiful high rises overlooking the lakefront. That path became a bridge that went over Lake Drive, leading to the grass that lined the shoreline of beautiful Lake Michigan. Down on Lake Drive, Tatiana and I walked north, the water on our far right beyond the grassy field in that section of the lakefront. In other areas, a few metal retainer walls, an occasional concrete pier, and hundreds of feet of boulder-edged areas lined the waterfront. As we moved at a leisurely pace, our conversation was a pleasant mix of toying around and sincerity, which kept us both intrigued and expectant.

Near an intersection where cars entered and exited the parking lot for both the McKinley beach and marina, I asked Tatiana. "You don't work, schools on pause, how do you pay your bills?" I quickly stepped in front of her and looked deeply into her eyes, while she looked back into mine with an eyebrow arched in curiosity. "Tatiana, tell me...do YOU deal drugs?" Somehow, I managed to say that while keeping a straight face.

Tatiana squealed in laughter, dropping her head onto my chest as her arms encircled my neck. "Of course not!" She managed to get out as her laughing subsided.

I pulled her face to meet my eyes and stared into her eyes just as she did me, making her laugh again, before saying, "You are too much, you know that?" I shrugged and smiled, without any words.

"Actually", once I had stopped with my silly shenanigans, "my granny had insurance, which left me in really good place. I've always been frugal financially, so I am in okay shape."

"Oh." Was all I said, hoping I had not jumped on a sore spot by mistake, but she did not seem bothered.

"Have you done much traveling?" She asked as we continued down Lake Drive.

"Yep! Been to 14 states, lived in 3."

"That's a lot of states to have been to. I've been to...hold on, let me count." She mimed counting, looking into the air as if remembering, every now and then murmuring "And then there was" under her breath for a few seconds.

I studied her aptly like notes for a test. Then she answered, "Exactly what I thought! I have been to zero other states." She smiled.

"What??" I asked, laughing before I added, "Really?"

"It's true, I've never once set foot out of my lovely home state!" She said with a slight sound of regret.

We continued north, passing a small playground where kids ran around, emitting squeals of joy on the different slides and jungle gym stations. On Lake Drive to our left, candy-painted, bass-pounding vehicles cruised by. Joggers, bikers, skaters and other walkers passed us on the blacktop sidewalk in both directions. This part of the lakefront was more popular due to its proximity to Bradford beach.

"How can you not have even been to Six Flags?" I asked Tatiana as we walked, my right arm now wrapped around her slender waist.

"I've been to all portions of this state, but never beyond the borders." Tatiana explained. I did not know what to say for a few seconds, so I simply stayed silent.

The cars parked and in motion seemed to get flashier as we closed in on the parking lot for Bradford beach. Old school whips and newer models, all with fresh and unique paint jobs, as well as tall rims of varying heights and colors with music booming from trunks and backseats. Women wearing nearly nothing, teen boys and girls, men with dapper fits, as well as families and kids were all over the place, everybody either seeking someone or wanting someone to see them. The scene seemed like a block party without the free food and coming togetherness of one. Tatiana and I were focused on the path ahead of us solely for navigational purposes, ignoring the parade of things happening around us as we talked.

Still walking north, I asked, "How 'bout we do some traveling this summer? Just go everywhere, me and you? You wit' that?"

We passed a path leading to a pier with blue railings, which went 60 yards out onto the lake. "What about your job? And that takes money! We can't just up and go, can we?" she noted.

"Under normal circumstances I'd say no, but I believe I can arrange that. You game?" I asked with a smile.

Tatiana studied my face then said, "Alright!" with a bright smile. I liked how open she was to adventure.

Tatiana pointed out over the lake where jet skiers skimmed the water's surface, bouncing mildly. "That looks like so much fun!" she said, her face alive with excitement.

"It really does ma! Wanna try it one day?"

"Oh my god, you have no idea! I would absolutely love to! It looks like an all-out blast, shooting across the lake, going out as far as you want! That would be so awesome!"

"Let's see the prices on that." I said, and we walked down a path that led to a trio of sheds.

Two were brown and a smaller one was black. The black one had a counter set up with pictures and brochures all over. Behind the sheds you could see a metal launch area where the jet skis were put into the water. We looked at a sign showing rates and times of service, plus all other requirements related to renting the items.

Intrigued I said, "How about we wait for a blazin' hot day, rent a pair for the whole day and just explore? We can check out the coastline up and down, have a picnic...do whatever!"

By the look in her eyes, I could tell she was thrilled by the idea.

"Are you serious Chris?"

"Definitely ma!" I said.

She squealed in joy before throwing her arms around my neck.

After obtaining info on the jet skis, Tatiana and I walked back to the streetside path, and continued walking north. We reached the lakeside parking area for Bradford beach, the area where most people from the northern half of Milwaukee congregated when they wanted some lakefront fun during the summer. The lot and nearby area was like a party, with cars playing loud music, people mingling with beverages of varying alcoholic degrees, barbeque grills smoking and kids of different ages out there doing their thing too! Tatiana and I was hugged up laughing as we waited for cars to enter the lot at the behest of a green light. When we received the "walk" sign, and began to cross the entrance's opening, I noticed a pair of dark-skinned cats paying closer attention to Tatiana and I than was usual, but I pushed the immediate ideas of concern past my mind, deeming it simply paranoia from my earlier experience. The two of us were just another couple enjoying the weather at the beach on a summer day. One of the cats pointed his phone at us, but I just figured him to be checking something or just having glare issues.

"Hungry, thirsty?" I asked Tatiana as we passed a stand selling everything from food to suntan lotion.

"Nah, I'm fine." she answered.

"I knew you were 'fine'. I asked if you were hungry or thirsty." She swooned at that corny line, leaning on me tighter as we continued walking.

We decided to walk along the beach, barefoot with shoes in hand, while watching people enjoy themselves at the water's edge. "You wanna get in?" I asked Tatiana as we moved through the warm sand, hand in hand.

"Nope! I didn't intend to be anywhere near water today." she answered, shaking her head profusely.

"But ma, it's water. Nothin' major." I coaxed smiling down at her.

"Nuh-uh, I'm good!" she said, continuing to shake her head and adding a finger wag to the situation. Without warning, I dropped my shoes and scooped her thin-limbed body into my arm and started running towards the water! She screamed, then yelled, "Chris, nooooooo!" I ran until I reached the water's edge, where I slowed to a stop. She clung to my body like skinny jeans, squealing in mild protest.

"I'm joking' sweetheart, relax! Just wanted to mess wit' you." I said with a chuckle.

She punched me while she playfully pouted, saying, "Jerk! I should kick your ass for scaring me."

I laughed at her then asked, " You a cat?"

"What?" she asked, lost as I carried her back to where I had dropped my shoes.

"Are you a cat?" I replied slowly.

She looked at me a tad oddly, obviously trying to figure out my angle. "No, why?"

"Cats are afraid of water." I clarified, enticing a lovely laugh from her flawless face! She pushed me, and I fell backwards into the warm sand intentionally.

"I'm sorry." she said, reaching her hand out to help me up. I pulled her down atop me, eliciting a screech before I caught her. She laughed when she was secure, and I mirrored it. She quickly made herself comfortable in my arms.

"My bad cutie, don't know my own strength." I said, shooting a grin her way.

We sat in the sand, cuddled as we watched the beautiful scene around us of summertime in action.

"Saw a waterspout here once." I told her as we soaked in the brilliant sunshine.

"Really? A 'water tornado' waterspout?"

"Let me see if Google has another definition for that term." She gave me a look that was universal for, watch yourself so I said. "Yeah mama." I pointed south out over the water, adding, "It was over there, not far from the little island by the Maier Festival grounds. It was this exact week when I was 11, my first full year living here. The day was as clear as today.

"I didn't even know what I was lookin' at. The news said nothing about it that night but the next morning the radio station 860Am talked of it." I finished.

"That is weird." Tatiana said, eyes still focused where I had pointed.

"I know. A plane seemed to fly right through it, but it had no effect on the flight." I told her.

"Wow!"

"Yeah, that was my second reaction. My first was like 'Oh shit, I'm about to see a tragedy!'"

I pulled out my phone and googled the event. An article came up about the spout and I showed Tatiana.

"That is crazy!" was her reply after reading it.

"I'm thirsty. Let's grab some drinks." I said after about half an hour of us talking and laughing while hugged up in the sand.

"Let's just leave. I'm ready for some food." she said as we both stood, brushing away sand from our clothes and bodies.

"A'ight. What do you have a taste for?" I asked, as we walked towards a huge, multi-level concrete bathhouse, not far behind where we sat.

"You like Chinese?" she asked as we neared the concrete steps

"Yeah ma, love it!"

"Then the next part of this date will be dinner!" she said with a smile!

CHAPTER FIVE

Tatiana and I walked to the second floor of the bathhouse structure where a footbridge was located that crossed Lake Drive, holding hands. As we were on the bridge, with 4 lanes of traffic moving beneath us, I said, "Let's take a picture here."

Tatiana and I posed, my arm around her waist, our smiling faces cheek-to-cheek, her soft skin on mine. I snapped the photo. Lake Drive south was in the background, and I knew immediately that the picture was a masterpiece! I zoomed in to examine it. Tatiana noticed that just over our shoulders in the background were two guys pointing in our direction. "Are they pointing at us?" she questioned when I dialed in on the cats on my screen.

"I doubt it! I don't know 'em." I replied with a shrug.

The two of us turned to see the guys directly. A group of brothers were staring at us from the parking lot, a little over a half block away. As we watched, two of the men pulled guns out. Upon seeing the pistols, I grabbed Tatiana and pulled her, moving westward. We began to run over the bridge that now seemed too long. About two steps into our sprint, the pops began, sounding like firecrackers being set off.

Tatiana screamed in a way that scared me more than the surreal pings of bullets smacking the iron railings on both sides of the footbridge.

What was maybe 20 strides running seemed like 200 meters as we ran towards the cover of thick trees the path disappeared behind on the west side of the street. The shots seemed to end upon our reaching the tree-lined path, but I did not stop running.

Tatiana was no longer screaming but I heard a sob which ate at my heart like acid. "You, okay?" I asked, looking her over as we slowed a bit on the winding path.

She nodded as we stopped moving and I faced her, staring into her wide-eyed expression of fear. "Why are they shooting at us! Oh my god, they think I am still with Ricky!" she said in a panic.

"Just hold my hand and run!" I told her.

She nodded emphatically, and we took off, following the winding, blacktopped path south, at a mild incline. It came to an opening directly across from the parking lot where bullets sprang from. Thankfully, it was across 4 lanes of traffic and atop a huge hill too far for an accurate shot from anyone but a sharpshooter. Still, Tatiana and I ran the last 150 yards up to the street, spooked.

"Listen," I started, once we got to Lake Street and North Avenue, the intersection at the top of the hill, " I want you to get on that bus sitting there while it is on layover. Sit towards the middle and lean back so you won't be seen!"

Her eyes went wider, fear and panic evident in her distorted expression. She clung to my arm as we neared the bus stop where a bus was parked, preparing to restart its westbound route. "Chris, they are shooting at ME, trying to KILL ME and you want to get rid of me?" she said in a shriek.

At that exact moment I recognized two cars coming to a stop sign at the top of the road that wound up the hill separating the lakefront from the rest of the area. It was the cars parked near the men who shot at us. I snatched Tatiana's arm and said, "Run!" Both her and I bolted, running in front of a nursing home heading west. They gave chase, speeding swiftly behind us. Tatiana and I cut around the side of the nursing home, simply to be out of the sightline for the goons pursuing us. We darted across a street busy with traffic and disappeared into a parking garage connected to the back of a hospital. I saw the cars stuck at a red light and guided Tatiana into a stairway on the far end of the garage. We ran up the stairs, two at a time, passing the second floor and coming out on the third floor. Together we headed through the garage, towards the hospital entrance on that level.

Inside the hospital, I whispered to Tatiana, "Be cool ma." She nodded then wiped her eyes, obviously still afraid but finding a way to compose herself as we walked.

After we roamed the hospital hallways pointlessly for a few minutes, I stopped a nurse in a hall. "Hi," I began, smiling genuinely, "Can you point us in the direction of the cafeteria please?"

The plump, white woman smiled just as kindly saying, "Sure. Follow this hall straight until you see the elevators on the right side. Take them to the basement and you will see markers on the wall."

"Thanks!" Tatiana and I both said with smiles then walked the route given to us by the nurse, talking in hushed tones.

"Tatiana, I wasn't trying to leave you. I was getting you away from me." I explained as we neared the elevator.

"Excuse me?!?" she exclaimed in a heated whisper that came out like a fierce breath. Her eyes showed both anger and betrayal.

When I realized how that sounded, I chuckled at myself. "Relax ma, I mean I wanted you safe! They were shooting at ME, not you." We entered the elevator as I clarified things.

"What? Why you? Chris, what do you mean?" she responded, her eyes searching my face for information. The elevator doors opened on a lower level and a man in a white lab coat walked in.

"I'll enlighten you in the cafe, okay?" I stated, holding her close to me.

"Okay." she said simply. In my arms Tatiana felt so perfect, even while she trembled slightly.

In the cafeteria, I said, "Let's grab some snacks. I wanna chill here for a bit. Make 'em think we gave their asses the slip. Then we can figure out the next move."

"Explain everything and I will decide if I want anything more to do with you!" she stated with a fierceness showing that she meant business!

We bought cakes and milk, then sat at a table near an emergency exit, out of earshot of others, with an unobstructed view of the two other entrances. I told Tatiana everything from the start to the moment we met.

My eyes slipped in a constant triangle. Left entrance, right entrance, Tatiana's eyes. I could not help but stay watching for trouble. She didn't speak at all while I filled her in like a crossword puzzle. When I finished, she asked, "Is this for real?"

I chuckled unintentionally before responding. "Them bullets seemed real, but I don't carry a desire to test that hypothesis. Science was never my strong suit."

"What are your plans?" Tatiana asked as we sat. I was caught up in a wild situation, but she could walk away.

I paused in contemplation, sipping the last of my milk simply to buy time.

Our eyes connected and I said, "As of now, I hold no clue! I intend to just relax a bit. Now I'm wonderin' how they knew it was me and–"

"Chris, you said you left them at your place, and they took a picture of you. They may have tweeted that to all their friends saying do whatever on sight, or put it on Facebook or IG or Snapchat."

"That's true." I admitted, hating the implications of such a situation. "I really can't run because they could find me later down the road which would be really lame. I have to figure out a way to fix this whole situation while keepin' the gold." I added after a few ticks of silence found us.

Tatiana snorted a laugh, then said, "Usually I would say arrange to give the gold to them but that is a lot of money! My question is this...is the money worth your life?"

I shook my head, saying, "Nah, but isn't it idiotic of them to wanna x out the sole soul who holds the key to their loot."

"That is quite imbecilic!" Tatiana concurred, smiling.

We sat for another half-hour going over our immediate plan of actions before deciding it was safe to leave.

As we stood from the table, I looked Tatiana in her eyes and said, "You sure you wanna stay in my company? I'll do my best to keep you protected, but I can't promise you anything ma. I'd rather you not be in harm's way because you got a lot of promise, and I know you goin' places in life!"

"The only way for me to be sure you see the other side of this is if I am beside you. I sincerely like you, and I know you could definitely use another pair of eyes watching out for trouble."

I simply smiled, then reached out my hand. She smiled and took it. We left the cafeteria holding hands.

We took the elevator to the main floor, where I had her wait in the lobby while I went to check outside the hospital's main entrance for any issues. I saw no one who seemed out of place, and no vehicle of the suspicious sort. I surveyed the surrounding area for a bit, simply operating under an abundance of caution, wanting to be definite that things were completely kosher. Once satisfied with my thorough reconnaissance, I texted Tatiana and we took a cab that was waiting outside at the curb. It drove us out to the storage facility, a 20-minute drive west from the hospital. The whole time I kept an eye out for any car that stayed near us for too long.

When the cab reached the destination, I told him, "You can wait in the parkin' area or you can take us in, I'll pay you to keep the meter running either way!"

As with most times in this predicament, the cabbie was glad to make the added figures and decided to drive us up to the storage compartment. I opened the door to my itsy-bitsy storage unit, with Tatiana beside me.

"Wow, there are so many things in here! However, can you fit anything else?" She shared a chuckle, making me laugh too.

"You ever hear that it's about quality not quantity?" I told her as I lit the shipping crate sized space and picked up my bookbag.

She laughed softly as she stood beside me. I pulled out the bag of cash and handed it to her.

"This is a bank deposit bag Chris." Tatiana explained, as I pulled out the pair of work clothes that lived in my bookbag.

"I know ma. They are insured, I'm sure!" I said, as I laid the shirt on the floor, spreading it out. I placed the gold bars in 3 stacks to show them off.

"God Chris, those 3 little piles are worth nearly a million dollars?" She asked in unadulterated astonishment.

"Yep," I answered with a chuckle, "Shocked the hell out of me too ma!"

I asked Tatiana to take cash out of the deposit bag and place it in a compartment inside my bookbag. I put the bars into the plastic bag, then wrapped that into the work clothes. I put them in the corner, making it look like a haphazardly tossed pair of dirty clothing just in case the unit was looked into. Not that such a situation was likely to happen, but a little paranoia over nearly a million dollars was acceptable. As we left the unit, I told Tatiana about the guns that were also in the bookbag she was carrying as I locked up.

"You know how to work them?" She asked me as I held her door on the cab.

"Well, I've shot some before, so I know the general workings. I probably wouldn't win any sharpshooting contests, but I don't think that's too major an issue."

She was laughing as I rounded the vehicle and climbed the other side's backdoor.

"It will get their ass off of us in a jam. No one stands tall with bullets flyin' their way except for Superman, and we not dealin' wit' him!"

Tatiana was still laughing as the cab pulled away and out of the storage facility.

The cab driver dropped me and Tatiana off at a Chinese buffet in a strip mall on 65th and Greenfield Avenue, not but two miles east of the storage facility. Over a table with multiple Chinese cuisines, plus a few non-Chinese items (Chinese buffets carry pizza and French fries, why exactly?), we conversed about plans on handling this twisted predicament thrown at my feet.

"Immediately after staying away from oncoming bullets, finding out who the guy wanting the package is our priority." Tatiana said, with a fork of Egg Foo Yung headed towards her luscious lips.

"I know his face, and I think I can find out who he is from the cat that sent him to my place. But then what? I mean, how do we put him into a position where he's off our backs for good?" I posed, then scoped a huge helping of shrimp fried rice into my mouth.

Both Tatiana contemplated this in silence while chewing. Her phone chimed and she pulled it from her purse. Before answering, she said, "Excuse me." then answered. "Hey girl!" She said into the phone, as I focused on my plate. I don't overtly eavesdrop, but could hear everything on her end of the conversation, nevertheless. "Yes, we are still together...yes...yes..." Tatiana said, with a grin. She laughed before saying, "You do? Um, hold on, I'll check." Tatiana looked to me then asked, "Chris, my best friend would like to say 'Hi!'. Will you appease her for me?"

Tatiana had the sweetest smile shining forth as she posed the question, pointing her Samsung Galaxy my way. I wiped my mouth and hands with a napkin, then held out my hand. I considered playing with her friend by answering with a Cockney accent, but simply said, "Hello?"

"Hi, how are you?" a chipper, tiny voice asked.

"I'm in Heaven sweetness. How's life on your end?" I replied.

The voice on the other side of the phone chuckled, then answered, "I'm fine. Why are you in Heaven though?"

By the tone in her voice I could tell she was sincerely interested in my answer.

"You really don't know?" I asked with a grin, now toying with both Tatiana and her girl. I imagined the look of curiosity on Tatiana's face probably mimicked the one her friend had at that same instance.

"No, tell me!" The friend pressed. "Seems obvious to me. I mean, where else could I possibly meet an angel like Tatiana?" Both Tatiana and her friend cooed at that. I watched as Tatiana turned bashful, her hershey-toned cheeks going crimson cutely.

"Aw, that's both sweet and original! Double points awarded! You really like my girl?" The friend either asked or noted, though I missed the inflection as I stared into Tatiana's lovely, sparkle of a smile.

"Definitely! She's some kind of brilliance!"

"She's into you a bit too!" The friend said with a smile in her voice.

"How can you be sure?" I asked, simply extending the conversation because that was as obvious as Tatiana's eye color.

"Well...she blew me off to spend the afternoon with you. My calls all day have been bailout calls and she has ignored all but this one. Whatever you have done to her, she has not wanted to walk away from you! So tell me," The friend said, her tone changing to one I could not clearly decipher, "I expect the honest-to-god truth! Are you going to hurt my friend?"

I chuckled a bit before answering, "I will. I've been imagining it all day, but you can rest assured that she will love every second of it, promise!"

The friend squealed in laughter for a few seconds, while Tatiana tossed me a quizzical look. I smiled and she continued eating. "Nuh-uh, you are so bad! I meant, are you going to break her heart?"

"Not seein' that as a viable option at this point, but if things ever change, I'll call you and get you to talk me back to my senses, a'ight?" I said with a chuckle.

The friend laughed, then asked to speak with Tatiana again. I handed the phone over and the two women spoke for a bit, Tatiana laughing, then her eyes getting wide while looking at me, then she laughed again before ending the call with a smile on her face.

"Edie told me to steal you and run away!" Tatiana said, while she was putting her phone back into her purse.

I chuckled then asked, "Seriously?" after swallowing my food.

"Yep! Said if I don't then I am crazy and will always regret it!"

"All of that from a single conversation?" I asked, a skeptical grin on my face.

"Oh yeah, she is excellent at reading people. Told me to lose my last two from day one. Said that she knew from the second they first said hi to her that both were wrong for me."

I picked up my glass of Sprite and said, "Toast to good fortune!"

Tatiana smiled, picked up her glass of Coke, tapped mine, and said, "To good fortune, good fun, and exciting days ahead!" We drank to that.

CHAPTER SIX

After we ate, Tatiana and I went to a Walmart in a strip mall across the 4 laned Greenfield Avenue opposite the strip mall housing the buffet. It was about 6pm and rush hour, Friday night traffic was crazy! I told Tatiana the plan that came to me while we ate. "You think it will work?" she asked, as we entered the store.

I handed my book bag to a female attendant at the customer service desk. A ticket was handed to me, then Tatiana and I walked deeper into the store. "This will allow me to grab my important documents from my place. We'll have to come up with an idea on what to do after that " I said as we pushed a cart through aisles, getting the items we needed. "Can you drive?" I added.

"A car?"

"Nah, a horse." I replied sarcastically, before I could stop myself.

Tatiana laughed then pushed me as she said, " I was just asking, smartass!" I regained my footing while chuckling, then put an arm around her slender waist. Half a second later she said, "It was kind of a silly question."

I nuzzled her neck in response.

"We will buy a cheap car, just somethin' to use for now. I want you to drive ma, okay?" I told her as we walked through another aisle.

"Okay, but why don't you want to?" She asked as I grabbed something from a shelf and looked it over.

"I wanna be able to watch our back and who knows...if the police got on our ass, I would need to bail with the guns. You could just say you only met me a few minutes ago and give only my first name." I explained.

To that she nodded. We scooped up all the items we required, then headed to the counter to pay before walking out the store.

Tatiana and I stood at a bus stop on 63rd and Greenfield, just across the street from a Burger King, watching the heavy traffic slither east and west. After a few minutes, and nearly a half-dozen people walking up to the bus stop and standing with us, a bus heading eastbound squealed to a stop in front of us. Tatiana and I stood on the crowded bus for a bit as it moved down Greenfield, then turned onto National Avenue continuing east.

Tatiana and I stepped off the bus on 19th and National, across the street from a used car lot. We crossed over to the north side of the street as I explained, "We want a ride that is cheap but works and isn't too noisy!" We both looked over vehicles, until a 94 Ford Tempo caught my eye. The price painted on the windshield said $625. "What about this one?" Tatiana asked, pointing to a Toyota Corolla, late 90's model that was tagged at $1200.

"Let's see how they sound." I said, as I walked over to Tatiana.

A Hispanic guy came out of the dealership and greeted Tatiana and I with a heavy accent. "Hey-lo me amigos." he said, with a huge grin. I spoke to him in Spanish, causing him to first pause then smile wider. In Spanish I told him we liked the Tempo and Corolla. I had him grab the keys so we could see how both cars ran.

"Sure, sure!" The salesman said in Spanish, then shuffled off into the office.

Tatiana looked at me astonished, asking, "You speak Spanish fluently?"

"As good as I do English and Latin. I grew up in the Bronx. Spanish is mandatory in the South of it. Latin ain't that handy, but I went to a fancy ass school in Manhattan. They taught us all kinds of shit there!" I explained.

She walked to me and wrapped her arms around my neck, looking me into my eyes. "Later, I want you to speak to me in Spanish."

"Yo, you keep lookin' at me that damn sexily and later Imma have you speaking Spanish!"

She giggled, dropping her head on my chest. "Okay, let me try harder." She returned, with a seductive look in her beautiful brown eyes.

The salesman came out with both sets of keys, proudly saying in Spanish, "Come, come. We will look at the Toyota first?"

"That's fine!" I told him and the three of us walked up to the vehicle.

The attendant hit the ignition, and the car roared to life. It was a bit rumbly and I asked him to reverse it, then drive it back and forth, as Tatiana and I stood aside. The brakes protested loudly, so I asked him to do the same with the Tempo. When he did, the car was quieter, smooth, and did not squeal at all. We purchased the car right then and there.

Tatiana drove us right across the street to a Checker's Auto Center. "You wanna run in wit' me?" I asked as she parked and played with the radio.

"Not really, I hate car stuff!" She replied, wrinkling her face quite cutely.

I kissed her on the cheek then said, "You are crazy precious ma, truly!"

She beamed my way then said, "Thanks, I'll be right here!"

I ran into the store, grabbed a do-it-yourself window tinting kit, and was back to the car in a flash. "Now, let's gas up, and I'll put the tint in, okay?" I told Tatiana as I hopped in, and she pulled off.

We drove across National Avenue to a gas station half a block east. Tatiana parked and went into the station while I pumped the gas. Shortly she came out, a bag in her hand as I watched her sexy legs move my way.

"Figured you'd get thirsty, so I picked you up a Sprite." She said while coming my way.

"Thanks!" I said with a smile. She pecked me on the cheek in reply, then climbed into the car with a grin.

With the tank topped off, she pulled the whip over to a parking space on the side of the station, and we put the tint on all windows minus the windshield. It wasn't heavy tint, just dark enough to not be translucent at night. We looked over the end result and was very much satisfied with things.

"Now what?" Tatiana inquired as we both sat in the Tempo.

I took a long swig of Sprite, then answered, "To your place." With that she drove away.

Tatiana lived on the northwest side of Milwaukee on 62nd and Custer Street, in a low-income housing project best known as Westlawn. It was about 10 blocks, east to west, 6 blocks north to south. The apartments varied in bedrooms, but were connected two flats with walkways dividing them, with small porches. The front doors faced each other on the walkways dividing the place or on the streets that cut through the projects, the front doors faced the curb. All but two streets wound through the area, slicing it into maze-like quadrants.

Her apartment was a single bedroom, the corner unit in a set of 10 apartments. People were out in full force as we parked not far from her front door.

Kids, teens and adults were all outside, sitting and playing and standing around the area. Bikes were being ridden and laughs were regular background noise, along with joyous squeals.

Teen girls and boys mingled all around us. Older men stood by their cars or near each other simply talking while sipping beers and smoking with music blaring.

The sun was starting to lower in the western skies, but it was still bright out. Fireworks blasted all around the area as Tatiana and I exited the car. A few of the cats posted by their cars eyed me as we closed the car doors. I ignored it, knowing that it was basic protocol when new folks came through the hood.

I followed Tatiana in the direction to her place, talking. Seven kids ran up to her, with giggles and excited squeals as they said her name in chorus. The littlest ones wrapped their arms around her legs. They were all between 4 and 8 years old.

Tatiana was all smiles, saying, "Hey little people! How is everyone today?"

They all answered in unison, basically saying they were all good. I was beside her as we walked, the kids eyeing me curiously as some grabbed her hand.

An adorable little mocha-toned girl of maybe 6 who was sizing me up asked, "Is he your boyfriend Tatiana?"

I laughed to myself as all, but one kid seemed totally caught up in the situation.

Tatiana smiled marvelously as she said, "Yes nosy girl, this is my boyfriend, Chris."

"Hi!" I said to the kids, all the cutesy girls doing their best to dazzle me with their smiles as Tatiana introduced them.

"Chris, this is Tanya the nosy. This is Devin the terror. This is Kia the sweet. This is Vontae the bold. This is Leroy the sneaky. This is Angela the cute. And this little bugger is Mario the laugher." She patted each kid's head as she stated their name and title. Mario laughed hysterically when his head was touched.

"What up lil' ones?" I asked, waving to the little crew.

"Them doin' fiya kwakers!" Angela said, pointing down the path half a block away where a group of preteen boys stood.

"That is fine sweetie, you just stay far away if it scares you, okay cutie pie?" Tatiana said soothingly. The girl nodded, then smiled. "You all go have fun, okay?" She added, and without pause, the kids were all back to playing as they had been prior to greeting us

"Somebody's popular!" I said as we walked into her front door.

"Yep, I told you I loved kids!"

"I see! That is nice. Kids can usually judge people quite well. Mostly." I told her as she hit the lights in her living room.

"Yes, they can. We all get fooled sometimes though." She said while walking towards her couch and throwing me a look over her shoulder that I could not read.

I changed the subject as her purse and keys hit the wooden coffee table and she plopped onto her couch. I followed her lead, sitting the bags beside the door before I walked over and fell next to her.

I leaned closer to her and said, "You got a boyfriend, ha ha ha haaaa ha!" In a teasing, sing-song manner.

She chuckled then said, "Shut up! I told them that because it's About to be true!"

Her confidence caught me by surprise, making me snap my head back. She turned on her TV and began going through the icons. "Really? How oh how do you know this?" I asked, looking into her lively brown eyes.

"This is how I know," she began, pulling my hands into hers, "Will you be my boyfriend, Chris?" The look on her face carried such an innocence that I felt I had been returned to second grade and was staring into the eyes of the first girl I had ever felt any type of love for. I felt a tickle in my stomach as our eyes held each other.

"Uhmm, no!" I told her, causing her jaw to drop with her chin nearly bouncing off of her chest. I continued. "But, if it pleases you, I'd love to be your man!"

Her smile was pouty, then she blinked, and it blossomed brilliantly. "You scared me."

I chuckled softly, then said, "I noticed. Just had to throw you a bit. I've wanted to be yours from the second I saw you ma!"

"Well, now you are!" She said and we stared at each other, hands locked, sharing silence like it was the last bagel.

She broke the trance by asking, "You want a tour of my bite sized apartment?" She let an embarrassed chortle slip from her mouth.

"Believe me, this room is larger than my kitchen, dining room and living room combined. If your place has more space, it leaves mine looking like a wheelless hamster cage."

Tatiana laughed, then stood to begin her tour. Her place was small and boxlike downstairs. She had a tiny living and dining room, both only a few feet wide and long, but they were still huge in comparison to my own. Her kitchen, which was connected to her dining room by an elongated archway was also cozy, but it was nice, and I could see Tatiana cooking breakfast there with a smile and not much else on in that space. She led me up steep steps, where her bedroom was. Her bedroom was big, and quite girly, with teddy bears all over the place. Following a peek into her very clean and fantastically fragrant bathroom, we returned to her living room.

"See, very small, but it's just me so I am happy!" she said with a genuine smile. I sat beside her and wrapped my arms around her lean body. We talked and watched TV for a bit, happily!

CHAPTER SEVEN

At 9:30, Tatiana and I began getting ready for the night. I put gloves on and looked over the pistols, checking if there was anything I held unfamiliar with. Noticing they were basic in function, I returned them to my bookbag, and put everything else required for our plans into the bag too. At exactly 10pm, we were walking to the Tempo. Tatiana navigated us in the general direction of my apartment. The Friday night cruisers were in full force, with all kinds of candy-painted, fancy-rimmed whips on the street. Females on the sidewalks, in packs like hoards of sexiness, flagged down cats and cars with vibrating trunks from the subbing speakers all around us. The city was alive, and if I pushed beyond the danger, I sincerely liked the situation Tatiana and I were in long term.

For the first time I had no envy of the other cats who pushed fresh whips, catching cuties like bass during a fishing tournament. I now had every possibility to live as lavish as all the hustlers sans the hard work. We drove around my apartment and the blocks nearby 3 times, checking to see who was in the area, and if anyone seemed overly focused on my place. The kid who sold weed was posted on the intersection by the now closed store. That block ended in a triangle where the slanted Lisbon Street met 41st. Brown Street ended just to the right of the intersections of 41st and Lisbon. It was perfect for catching traffic, while offering multiple escape routes if police gave any static.

The kid seemed to be doing his normal thing, head on a swivel as his occupation required. I noticed no one else stationary, even though folks were roaming the area. Kids, teens and adults were outside enjoying the beautiful summer night. Simply observing, I couldn't help but smile as I watched the boys trying to holler at dames, reminiscent of what I was on years ago before graduating to clubs for my ponds to snag fish from.

I had Tatiana drop me off two blocks away, then park in a place where she could see both the front and back of my building. We kept our phones on, using them as two-way radios. I wore jogging pants and a hoodie, plus a baseball cap with shades on to complete the lowkey look I had going. I had my bookbag on under the hoodie, in the front so it made me look chubby. I kept my left hand in the front pocket of the hoodie where one gun was housed. I walked out of Washington Park with a slight limp, crossing the busy Lisbon Street at a relaxed pace.

Tatiana watched with binoculars, talking to me with a nervousness in her velvety smooth voice."A boy by the payphones is watching you. That is all I see." she said after I had gotten past the heavy traffic.

"Thanks ma!" I replied as I reached my building's front door.

Inside, I pulled out a bottle of WD-40, and sprayed the 8th step with the greasy substance. After a pool of the stuff was spread on the whole step, I knocked out the nearest hallway light, tossing the empty can aside, then grabbed my flashlight so I could find my apartment without issue. I first listened for sounds inside, then turned the knob, knowing the door would be unlocked.

It was, and with the flashlight fanning the space, I saw that the place was left destroyed. My tables were broken, kitchen trashed, entertainment center crushed, the 40" flat screen shattered, and I noticed my PlayStation was gone. But the bastards would never enjoy it without my ignition code, which was a moral victory! I gathered the photos of my parents and friends, then went to my bedroom.

I saw that all within the room was equally annihilated. I grabbed the items purchased earlier and stuffed it all into a duffle bag I had within my bookbag, then threw that by my bedroom window. I went right to my hiding spot, a false wall I had made behind my bathroom sink. I pulled out my fireproof lockbox with all my important documents inside. I walked that to my duffle bag and put it inside.

"Chris!" Tatiana said forcefully. "2 cars just pulled up, one in front and one in back. Guys are getting out both cars and walking towards the building. HIDE!" she finished.

"Relax Tati! Tell me when they are in the building." I said while moving towards the front door.

"Okay." she replied as I pulled out the 2nd and 3rd bottle of WD-40. I sprayed a ring around the interior of the front door, and then sprayed a huge half circle a few feet from the front door. A few heartbeats later Tatiana said, "Chris, two went into the front door, one in the back."

"A'ight, do what I told you right now!" I said, and heard her line go silent.

A moment later it picked back up in mid ring. I sprayed a trail of WD-40 from the area in front of the door all the way to my bedroom's window. I made sure the trail was thick, then sprayed the space under the window where the wall met carpet. I then did the same thing in my living room, making sure heavy amounts of the substance was all over.

I heard a few loud thumps in the hallway, then a man's laugh. I also heard as Tatiana spoke to a 911 dispatcher. "I just saw 4 men with guns go into my next-door neighbor's apartment on 4118 west Lisbon Street, apartment 2B. I hear commotion and—oh my god, they are shooting! Please hurry...I smell smoke!" The dispatcher tried to ask Tatiana a question, but Tatiana added, "Oh God, I hear more shots!" and hung up on the dispatcher.

I pulled out 2 strobe lights that I had purchased at Walmart and put one by the window, light bulb facing the door and turned it on. The other I placed on the sink in my kitchen space, facing the door. I turned that on also. Both of the lights were plugged into 2 separate extension cords that were then plugged into one that I had in hand. I went over to the doorway of my bedroom, where a socket was located, and waited, breathing fast, short breaths. I heard the doorknob jiggle, then whispers. A second later, a body slammed into the door, causing it to give off a slight creak but did nothing else in response.

After more whispers, the door was crashed into, giving way and allowing the goons entry into my apartment. At that instant, I plugged in the strobe lights. Both lights flickered brightly, disorienting the three men. One guy screamed out, and shots were sent in a wild frenzy. I used that as my cue, running towards my bedroom windows. I lit the WD-40 under the window then climbed up ready to jump over the six feet clearance between my building and the single story building next door.

I heard footsteps and jumped, barely landing on the roof. Immediately I rolled, which was a smart thing because shots rang out and bullets smacked off the lip I originally landed on. Behind me, over the rising I lay hiding behind, I heard someone yell, "Oh shit nigga, the whole place on fire!" I was moving at an army crawl, using the rising as cover while shot after shot seemed to chase me.

I sat for a moment, heart racing, until I heard the gunfire end. I raised a hand as a decoy to see if shots would greet it like a high-five. When nothing happened, I waved. Still nothing, so I poked my head up. The only thing hanging out my window was black smoke, so I ran to the western edge of the rooftop I was on.

"Tati, police here?" I said as I eyed the distance to the ground.

"Yes," she said in a near panic. "You okay Chris?"

"I'm good. Where the cops at?"

"2 in front, 2 in back."

"Outside?" I said, sitting on the edge, after tossing the bags I carried.

"Yes, but 2 more went inside through each entrance." she informed me.

I jumped from the building, landing in an unkept lot of grass and other litter between the one-story building and the corner store. I picked up the bags, lit a Newport and started walking nonchalantly toward the edge of the building. I saw that people were starting to crowd around, watching the action. I walked into the people, not looking back at the officers but focused on getting away. No one seemed concerned with me at all.

"Tati, I'm on the way." I said as I slipped through the crowd.

"I see you; I'll meet you." She replied sounding relieved.

I surveyed the people as a fire truck and more cops rolled up. No one cared about me. The fire wasn't huge, and the firemen moved swiftly. They had their hoses ready before I was in the car with Tatiana.

Driving away, Tatiana said, "The boy who stood by the store ran when the cops pulled up. He called someone, then the guy who was standing out in front of your building walked away. He disappeared around your building."

"I'll be mailing all the other tenants money orders so they can cop a new place with all new shit first thing after work tomorrow. They should be taken care of by the Red Cross tonight, I expect." I told her as we drove south on 40th Street. "Do you mind if I stay at your place tonight?" I asked Tatiana, not wanting to seem presumptuous nor thirsty.

"Yes, definitely!" She answered sharply, then caught herself and added, "I mean, yeah, your place is compromised and uninhabitable." She snorted a laugh, then tried looking at me with a straight face.

I smiled, then she started to really laugh.

"Someone's sounding mad excited!" I said, which made her squeal in laughter.

When she calmed somewhat, she said, "I did but you were NOT supposed to notice that."

"Notice what?" I asked with a blank look on my face.

"Exactly!" she returned with a smile.

I chuckled softly to myself, not really putting away my grin when I said, "I think I could mess around and marry a woman like you!"

Tatiana looked at me, her eyes burning a hole in the side of my face while I stared ahead of us, seeing her in my peripheral. She didn't speak, and I stayed silent trying to figure out the where's and why's behind such a bold proclamation. It was one of those things that just pops out, like a nip slip in public, and I decided against adding or subtracting from it. Tatiana smiled and went back to focusing on the road.

After a few minutes of driving, she said, "I was so scared!"

"I could tell, which is why I didn't say much. I wasn't sure if talking would've made you relax or not." I confessed as we found our way back onto Fond Du Lac Avenue at 43rd street and headed northwest.

"It would not have mattered. Especially when I heard the gunshots. I was just happy to hear you breathe. That kept me from going crazier than I already was."

"They destroyed all my stuff!" I said, switching subjects simply to push that from our minds.

She smiled brightly, saying, "That's fine. Gives you a fantastic reason to get all new stuff! Better stuff! All on them!"

I laughed and said, "True, true!"

She laughed then said, "You said you have to work tomorrow?"

"From 10 till 4 in the afternoon."

"Aw man, I wanted to do something fun!" she said in a mild pout.

"From 4 until, we can do whatever ma!"

"Okay, I'll figure out a plan. Do you work on Sunday?"

"Nope!"

"Great! We can pull an all nighter, okay?"

"I was planning on that tonight!" I said unabashedly, rocking a grin so wicked it should've been illegal on my face.

She blushed as she cut her eyes at me, saying, "You are bad! So, so bad!"

I chuckled suavely and said, "Honest and frank ma, always!" She bit her lip and put her eyes back on the road.

We parked half a block west of Tatiana's apartment and walked back to her place arm in arm. People were still outside enjoying the warmth. It was mainly older teens and adults mingling on porches or near cars. A few residents spoke to Tatiana as we passed them.

We entered her place and she said, "We both need showers. I'll take mine first."

Inside, I wrapped her in my arms, and she slipped her thin arms onto my shoulders. "Maybe we should share a shower. You know, save the Earth by saving water." I said, with a sly smile.

She bit her lip, laughing noiselessly as she dropped her forehead to my chest. She dragged the fingers from her left hand across my neck, then her hand down my shoulder and sighed. Then, a beat later, she said, "I want to, so bad, but let's show some patience! Remember, we just met not even 12 hours ago!" She lifted her face, connecting her eyes and mine. I kissed her on the lips, tenderly. No tongues touched, our lips remaining closed. It was a simple, yet soulful smooch.

When we separated and opened our eyes, Tatiana said, "That did not make things any easier!" We both chuckled as she pulled away from me. Backing away towards the stairs she added, "There are cookies and stuff in the kitchen. Just umm...I... I don't know, watch TV or listen to music...whatever! I need to go upstairs right now, or I will not make it. Bye!" With that, she ran up her stairs, leaving me with a smile.

I laughed, looking around Tatiana's living room. I stepped to her couch, sat, and pulled out my phone to check out the Milwaukee news websites. All had nothing new about the heist, simply regurgitated garbage. They did report on the Lakefront shooting, but said police had no one in custody, which was sad since sheriff and police were both within running distance of the shooters. Whatever, I thought, then checked my Facebook page, went over to Twitter, and finished my social media time with messaging and commenting on posts.

I stepped to the stairs and yelled up, "Tati can I smoke in here?"

"What?" she yelled back.

"Can I smoke in here?" I repeated, a bit louder.

"Go ahead. There is an ashtray in the kitchen."

I found it, then sat and lit a Newport while watching old Dave Chappell reruns on my phone. I spent half an hour laughing at the hilarious antics on display. I was laughing so hard that I didn't even notice Tatiana come down. I looked up in mid-chuckle and saw her posed at the bottom of the stairs. The laugh vanished with abracadabra flawlessness when I noticed her standing there.

She had on a peach-colored robe, her hair tied up and fuzzy peach slippers on her feet. For about 15 seconds I simply stared at her, unable to say a word. The contrast between her sable, smooth skin and the softness of the peach robe was ethereal. The robe was closed and went to her mid-thigh. I wondered what she had on underneath the thing. She turned left, then right, with her hands in the robe's pockets, showing off while she smiled.

"Did I get shot earlier?" I asked when I regained the ability to form words.

Tatiana tilted her head and wrinkled her brow as she asked, "What?"

"Was I killed earlier?" I clarified.

She took slow steps towards me then answered, "No! Why would you ask such a thing?" She was inches away from me and I could smell the scent of peaches floating from her skin. It was unbelievably intoxicating.

As she sat beside me, I answered, "Because I keep seeing this heavenly being and I have no other explanation as to why!"

Tatiana laughed, but it was a soft chuckle as she placed her right hand on my stomach, her left hand on my shoulder.

She kissed my cheek then whispered, "I'll be your angel! Take a shower and when you're done, I'll take you to Heaven!"

I slid my hand across her thigh while staring into her dark eyes, her skin like powdered sugar; smooth and soft.

"A'ight!" I said, before I gathered my boxers, muscle shirt, socks and shorts.

Tatiana led me up to her bathroom, giving me the other items needed for my shower. I pulled her close to me and saw her lips quiver.

"I'm goin' to devour you later!" I told her.

Tatiana whimpered at the thought, her pupils dilating right before my eyes. She seemed to nearly melt. She regained her composure, then gave me another closed-mouth kiss that sent tingles to every part of me. I was shocked by that effect because it was such a new experience for me.

"I'll be downstairs. Do take your time!"

Her smile ate at my stomach dynamically.

"I got ya bae!" I replied as she closed the door.

I showered thinking about her and sex and possibilities, trying to find patience that did not live within me. I didn't want to rush but I also really wanted to rush!

CHAPTER EIGHT

After an eternity of a few minutes, I was finished with my shower, and dried off. I dressed, then walked down to the living room. Tatiana was sitting on the couch, with candles lit all around the room. "This is nice!" I told her, smiling as the light flickered and danced around the room.

She stood, walked over to me, and wrapped her arms around my neck, saying, "I want this now!" while staring into my eyes with a hungry look.

Her lips touched mine—this time our tongues tapped, then danced together. I reached down, grabbed her left thigh, then lifted her and she wrapped both her legs around my waist. I slipped my hand up her thigh and hit lacy material. Our kisses grew deeper, like we were out to kiss our way into each other's being. She began kissing down my face to my chin, and hit my neck, my kryptonite.

"Tati you can't do that while we are standing'! We'll fall." I told her, almost pleading.

She giggled then asked, "Really?" while looking into my eyes.

"That drives me insane!" I explained, staring into her brilliant brown eyes.

"Okay. Get us to the couch so we can get started!"

"Your wish, my command!" I said, carrying her to the couch. I noticed the guns were now on her coffee table. "Plannin' on doin' some late-night target practice?" I questioned, nodding to the pistols.

"Nothing else stopped me from bursting in on you in the shower!" she answered, her breathing heavier.

I began kissing her, feeling the heat of her center boiling mine while our barely clothed bodies pressed into each other. Her moans were soft, enhancing my thirst for her. I kissed from her lips to her neck, then her shoulders, loving the taste and feel of her skin on my tongue and lips. Somehow, she tasted of peaches, and though I hated them normally, having that be her flavor only made me want more. I untied her robe and saw the upper half of her torso. Her bra matched everything else. I kissed between her peaks as her fingers played in my hair.

"Wait Chris, I want to be on top." Tatiana said in a voice so laced with sexual desire I felt it more than heard her.

We switched positions and as I sat, she took off my muscle shirt, saying, "Yummmm!" in a deep, throaty manner as she ran her fingers down my chest and stomach. I laid back, and she removed her robe, letting it fall beside us on the floor with a naughty smile. I ran my hand up her sides, so thankful to be in this position with a woman, a sister so gloriously beautiful. Tatiana smiled at me, leaning down to kiss me. I slid my hands up her back as our lips touched and ran my fingers through her bone-straight, raven colored hair.

As our kisses became deeper, the window behind the couch we laid on exploded with bullets, glass and plastic from the blinds flying into the living room. Instinctively, I rolled us, Tatiana landing on her robe with my arms underneath her as she screamed in terror, holding me tightly. "Tati, stay down! Stop screaming!" I said in her ear, while trying to figure out what to do.

The shots were rampant, cracks like that of an army movie sounded, causing the items on Tatiana's entertainment center to explode. I looked up and saw her blinds doing an eerie dance while bullets slipped through it like a brisk wind. I grabbed the guns with my right hand, sliding the coffee table over Tatiana.

"Chris, stay down!" She whined

I kissed her and said, "Don't move! They might keep shootin' or come closer if we don't give them a reason to back off!" Her eyes pleaded with me, so I added, "I'm not goin' anywhere, promise!"

Bullets still zipped and whizzed a few feet above our heads. I crawled to the side of the window opposite the street and through a corner I glanced out. 2 guys stood beside a car in the street, shooting rifle type weapons. I cocked both guns, pointed them from the slot I had looked through, and commenced to pull the triggers.

The booms were deafening in Tatiana's small living room. It was like being in the hull of a bell as it went off. I kept the pistols pointed in the general direction of the shooters. I waited a few seconds between each shot, simply to preserve bullets while hoping that the guys would believe I was taking careful aim. Seemingly, return fire must not have been in their expectations because they stopped shooting. As I shot back, I did not have the angle to see the men but I did see their car's window explode. I had hoped that I mimicked Eddie Murphy in HARLEM NIGHTS where he was outgunned but his three blind shots had quenched his adversaries. The squeal of car tires and witnessing the car pull away showed me shit like that only happened in movies.

With the goons out of the picture, I immediately asked Tatiana, "You, okay?" My ears still rang as I looked to her. She was trembling as I put the guns on the floor and went to her. She had her hands covering her ears and was curled up in the fetal position. She flinched at my touch."Mama, you, okay?" I repeated.

Tears in rivulets fell down both sides of her face. She opened her eyes and replied, "Yes. Did you shoot them?" in a voice nothing like her usual one. It was more of a child's voice.

"I doubt it, but they left and won't be back any time soon. I need you now ma, can you help?" She nodded slowly in response, so I continued saying, "Good! I have to get dressed and I need you to help me get all the shell casings that are in here."

She sat up, surveying her freshly destroyed living room in shock. I moved fast, snagging my bag from the corner and putting on the first outfit I pulled out. Tatiana moved as though she was in a gel world, slowly, robotically moving her luscious limbs. I hurried, grabbing the shells from her floor and couch. I double checked the whole area, seeing no more shells. Tatiana seemed lost, sitting on an armchair, scanning her eyes over the bullet-riddled walls, entertainment center and all it housed.

"Tatiana, listen mama, please sweetheart, I need you to call the police. Tell them your house was just shot up." She blinked, then blinked again, her expression blank. "Tati, baby, please. I need you to snap out of it or..." I didn't know what to say so I just held her. She trembled, then started to cry, her arms wrapping around me tightly.

I picked her up and carried her upstairs to her bed. "Tatiana, you are safe in here. I need to hide the guns and make sure I get things how they need to be when the police show up, okay?" She nodded, then I pulled the covers up over her body to her chest.

I ran downstairs, grabbing the guns and putting them in my bag. I put the shells in my bag and ran it all upstairs. I phoned the police. A female dispatcher answered the call. "My girlfriend's apartment was shot up. She is in shock or something, but we are both unhurt physically. I don't know her exact address but it's in Westlawn, just off the corner of 62nd and Custer, on the north side of the street. It's the one minus the glass in the front window. "Police should be there in seconds. You say your girlfriend is in shock?"

I was in Tatiana's bathroom swabbing my arms, hands and face with rubbing alcohol to get rid of any gunpowder left from my return fire. "Yeah, we were inches from the bullets as they flew in and ever since she has not been herself. I wanted to call sooner but I had to make sure she was fine."

I wiped my arms with a clean face towel, then sprayed a spritz of peachy smelling stuff on my arms to mask the pungent scent of rubbing alcohol. I ran downstairs, noticing most of the candles Tatiana had laid out were still lit. One was on the floor, no longer on fire. I blew them out as the dispatcher asked, "You sure she's alright? No wounds at all?"

"I looked her over twice and she had nothing visibly wrong. She talks but she just seems...shocked." I expressed, unsure of a better explanation.

"I have dispatched an ambulance just to evaluate her. Police are on scene."

"Great." I said, ending the call as I ran back up to Tatiana's room. "Baby, you, okay?" I asked her.

She was holding a teddy bear, laying on her side, while staring into her dresser's mirror. "Yes Chris. Police coming?" "Should be outside. I am just happy you are good!" I said, as I lay on the bed with her and held her. "You scared me girl!"

"I was...this is crazy Chris!"

"I know ma, I'm so sorry! I need you to tell the cops all that happened besides my shootin' back, a'ight?"

"Duh!" She said with an eye roll, then a slight smile.

I chuckled, then kissed her on the forehead, earning a grander smile for my efforts. "Put something on woman. Police can't see my future wife nearly nude."

She sat up as a bang on the door downstairs resounded through the house. "Pass that white robe there will you please?" I did, then ran downstairs.

I opened the door after seeing the officers through the missing pieces of Tatiana's tattered blinds. A black cop was on the porch, his gun in hand. "Thanks for comin' officer." I said as I let him in.

"No problem." he said as he looked around, gauging the scene. "Who's all here?" he added when he had taken it all in.

"My girl is upstairs. This is her place. She was a bit shaken up by this and I had her lay down!" I explained.

Another cop, a Hispanic dame stepped into the apartment. "So, what exactly happened here?"

"Well, me and my lady were on the couch—" I was saying when I noticed another candle in a corner still lit and flickering. I went over and blew it out sheepishly smiling at the two cops. "We were in the midst of quality time when bullets started pourin' through the window. We hit the floor and hid under the coffee table until they were done." I finished.

The female cop asked, "Did you see anything?"

"Besides the floor? Nah." I replied to the officer. As I finished, Tatiana came down in pj's and the white robe.

"This is my girlfriend, Tatiana." I announced while walking over to her. "You sure you, okay?" I asked her, clasping her hands in mine.

She looked me in the eyes and smiled weakly. "Yes baby, I'm fine."

I kissed her, then the lady cop introduced herself, took our names and all the other required info for their report. The officers plus a pair of detectives investigated the scene, thoroughly documenting the full damage. I sent Tatiana to pack so we would be ready to leave the instant we were given the all clear. She packed all her important documents plus some items she refused to leave behind, then talked with the officers while the window was boarded up.

It was two in the morning when we left, headed to a hotel. "Tati," I started while she drove, "Let's head to the outskirts of the town. I don't know how these fuckers found out I was at your place, but I wanna be in a place not likely to be on their radar! I don't want these bastards stumblin' on us again!"

Tatiana looked at me, smiling weakly as she said, "I think someone in the projects affiliated with him may have recognized you or me. I don't see any other way of them finding us."

I nodded, unsure of what else to say.

CHAPTER NINE

We drove an indirect route to a Sheraton Inn, outside of the city limits, in a western suburb named Brookfield. It was a big hotel, 7 stories high and half a block long. We found a spot in the packed parking lot, and grabbed our bags. We obtained a room in a fake name, pretending we were a big deal of some fashion. We rode the elevator up to our 5th floor room and keycarded the door open.

Tatiana hit the lights as we entered, "This is nice!" she said, dropping the sole bag she carried just beside the door.

"Yeah!" I said, dropping the multiple bags I carried next to hers, adding, "Damn place is bigger than my whole apartment." She laughed while I closed the room's door. "You chuckle but I am serious ma!" I said while she investigated the bathroom. I went to the panoramic windows which had their curtain open and looked out over the parking lot.

Seeing nothing out of place, I turned as Tatiana was walking towards me. I opened my arms and she slipped into them. Her arms wrapped around my neck. "I was goin' to wake all your neighbors once I got inside of you, you know that right?!?" I stated. She smiled sexily, the hunger back in her eyes. "You were?" She asked, a challenge in each consonant.

I kissed her, my tongue diving into her mouth and toying with hers. She moaned as I lifted her, her legs wrapping around me. I stepped to the bed carrying her svelte figure, laying her down softly. Immediately I began undoing the buttons on her pajama top. She was breathing heavily, her nose flaring adorably in her excitement. Her top now open, the exotic contrast of peach on ebony skin returned. Our lips disconnected as she pulled off my shirt, allowing me to get her completely free of her top as well.

Back together, our lips and tongues danced as she attacked my belt buckle, working it with her slender, nimble fingers, antsy to get my clothing gone. Buckle loose, they slid down and I slipped my hand between her thong and pajama bottoms just above her hips. I stood, sliding the bottoms down from her middle, exposing her slim thighs, and her pubic area still covered by peach panties. My boxers held an appendage aimed directly at her chocolate skin. I laid back atop her, feeling her now blazing middle as we began to kiss again.

I traced my fingers up her sides, then kissed over to her neck, as she slid her nails across my back. "Chris, this feels so good!" she whispered, as I nibbled on the muscle at the base of her neck. I moved to the other side, kissing and nibbling, before returning to her lips. I kissed down to the center of her chest, loving how her lacy bra held her plump breasts delicately. I unleashed them, the bra falling to her sides allowing her perfect globes to greet me.

Her nipples were hard as I wrapped my hands around her left breast, not squeezing but simply holding it. I kissed from the center of her breastbone to her right breast, licking as I closed in on her small buds. I sucked and licked, listening to her pleasured moans from my tonguing. I nibbled and she squeaked a gasp, her fingers playing in my hair. Then I reached her left breast giving it equal attention, exciting her to the point where her hips pressed urgently against my middle.

Finished with her chest, I kissed down to her belly button, tracing my fingers down her sides, positioning them between her skin and peach thong. I kissed down her indent then began to slide her panties free. Tatiana lifted her hips, helping me rid her of them and she laid there, her back flat on the bed. I paused to drink in her ebony nudeness, flawless in every way.

"You like what you see?" she asked with a devilish grin.

"I am lovin' what I see ma!" I admitted, causing her to giggle.

I lifted a leg, then kissed from her inner ankle down towards her swollen labia. I ran my tongue just beneath her dripping slit, above her ass, tasting her excited secretions, then kissed back to her other ankle. She rotated her hips in yearning as I placed my face above her hairless pussy. I let my tongue slide from the bottom of her hole upward to her clit. "Oh yes Chris! Oh yes!" she moaned, her hands again finding my hair. I wrapped my lips around her clit, sucking then flicking my tongue over and around it. Her moans elevated as her hip rotations became a bit sporadic. I eased 2 fingers into her tight, soaked pussy, and she let out a sexy whine. I went at her clit faster, pushing my fingers deeper, searching for her internal trigger points.

Tatiana seemed lost in her passion as I picked up the intensity. I felt her insides clutching and quaking on my fingers, then small eruptions of liquid exploded on my fingers. She was moaning my name and bucking uncontrollable as I licked all parts of her vaginal area. I felt her insides tensing, then Tatiana's thighs clamped closed on my head as she yelled, "Chris baby...I...I..love this!" Her pussy blasted cream all over my fingers in a way that caught me by surprise. She pushed my face away, and I removed my fingers, which dripped with her juices.

She laid there, her body glistening with a sheen of sweat as she panted and twitched. I took off my boxers and crawled over her. We kissed, and I felt Tatiana releasing herself to be totally into the moment, open to being taken where I wanted her to be.

"That was so...great!" She said, still working to regain some composure. "Do you want me to return the favor?" she asked with a sultry grin

"You are!" I said as I reached down to enter her. "Ready?" I added, as I placed myself at her pearly gates.

She bit her lip then nodded. I squeezed into her as she held me, her hands clenching my shoulders as I slowly pushed forward. Tatiana was heavenly tight and blazing as I glided into her wetness. Her face was pressed tightly against my right cheek, and I heard her moan in a sharp pitched manner as I dug deeper. She emitted a whine as I continued into her.

I reached her current capacity and went no further, deciding to wait. We began our motion, a relaxed rhythm that allowed us to become lost in the passion. "Chris!" Tatiana began to repeat after a dozen or so pumps, almost sobbing as her arms clenched me tightly. I added a circular motion to my strokes, hitting spots that caused her to go wild. "Oh God Chris, aaahhh!" she screeched as her inner walls vibrated. I pushed all off me into her, making Tatiana scream as I continued my motion, giving her more than she had bargained for. She squealed and yelped, exploding on my rod every few moments. She spoke in single-syllabled clips punctuated by extremely erotic sounds.

"This my pussy now mama, this amazing pussy is mine, right?" I said, then bit her neck.

"Yes! Yes...Chris...yes!" she yelled as we crashed into each other.

I slowed after a little longer, saying, " I wanna hit it from the back, okay?"

"Yes!" was all she said.

I pulled out of her, my manhood coated and dripping with her fluids. I kissed her then rolled off her body. She laid still for a few seconds, body twitching every now and again, a smile plastered on her flawless face. I chuckled and she opened her eyes, still smiling.

"What?" she asked, "I'm trying to...I don't know. Stop laughing at me!" she added, only making me laugh harder. "You are something boy, you truly are!" She said with a giggle then rolled over.

As I positioned myself behind her, Tatiana placed her face in a pillow, popping her little round ass into the air. The head of my lance was like a magnet, staying pointed at her entrance. Her lips were swollen, dripping with cream as I pushed into her slowly. I only went in halfway, then pulled out, before pushing back in deeper. Tatiana moaned into the pillow as I did this, getting myself into a good rhythm. She began letting go of muffled moans into the pillow.

"Damn Tati, your pussy is so tight and wet!" I told her while I worked her over! She looked at me over her right shoulder, while yelping and said, "Oh Chris, baby...you're hitting...my...my...my spot!" and I felt her pussy explode again. I reached under her body, cupping her breasts in my hands and lifting her body to where only our knees supported us, pulling her back to my chest. Tatiana screeched so sexily as we made love, her hands on my sides clawing at me.

I kissed her on the back of her neck, squeezing her breasts before saying, "I'm about to cum ma! You ready?"

"Yes Chris, oh yes!" she replies, and I felt her erupt, which pushed me over the edge.

I let loose all I had into her body, biting her neck from the intensity of orgasm. We both collapsed on the bed, gasping. I slid out, admiring the sweat-inducing sparkle on her skin, and the twitching of her body as she calmed down.

Neither of us spoke for a bit as we sought our composure and breath. She rolled to face me. Her eyes fluttered open while she smiled my way. I smiled back.

"You good ma?" I asked, basking in her beauty.

She inhaled deeply, then said, "Yes, yes, yes!" and giggled.

I laughed too, then pulled her body to mine.

I kissed her then said, "You got the best pussy ever girl!"

She laughed bashfully, then said, "You put it down like I never expected baby!"

With a chuckle I said, "Guess we handled each other properly, huh? Ready for round 2?"

"Hell no! Not for at least 6 hours! I am tired and I need to recoup from this." she said with wide eyes.

"I'm jokin' ma! After that, I need to rest too! You made my ears ring!"

Tatiana squealed in laughter, then said, "Yeah right boy!"

I raised my right hand saying, "I swear to the heavens you escaped from, you had my shit buzzing!"

She looked at me with a dazzling smile then asked "Seriously?"

"Yeah ma, I'm not jokin'! It was THAT intense mama!"

Staring at me in stunned silence, her eyes searched mine. After a few seconds she beamed with pride and said, "Guess I put it on you!"

"Let's see what you have to say about round 2, cocky ass lady!"

She laughed lavishly, saying, "You will kill me, but I can brag to my girls!"

I shook my head at her, then said, "Let's get some sleep! Some of us gotta slave for our pesos!"

"Whatever!" she said, nudging me as I eased out of bed. I killed the lights, set my cellphone for 830am and we talked ourselves to sleep.

CHAPTER TEN

The next morning I woke up to my phones incessant and irritating buzz. "Tati, you sleep in. I'll take a cab to work." I said as I killed the alarm.

Tatiana was stirring, but asked, "You sure? I don't mind!" Her voice was sleepy in a cute way.

"Yeah ma! You and your wild ass hair stay right there in bed!" I told her, a laugh in my tone.

"Leave me alone!" she pouted, then covered her head with the covers, adding, "Jerk!" I crawled back into bed and tickled her. She laughed, saying "Quit Chris!" I kissed her now covered forehead, then went to take a shower.

Dressed, I let Tatiana know that I was about to leave. "Come here for a second." she called out while I tied my shoes. We hugged and kissed deeply when I made my way to her. "Chris," she started as we finished kissing, a serious look in her dramatically rich brown eyes, "I'm falling in love with you!"

Her confession moved though me like a wave of something larger than life, and I was to be overtaken by surprise to reply. I smiled as I held her eyes. She pecked me on the lips, then said, "Work!" That snapped me out of my trance.

"Umm, yeah. I'll call you at lunch, text you on my breaks, cool?!?" I stated. She nodded in reply, and I was out the door.

I took a cab to my job, stopping at a McDonald's for breakfast. I watched the news on my phone while eating. My fire had made the news, mainly because police caught 3 armed men who they believed to be arsonists. The fire was contained to my place, but I still intended to send the other residents funds for a better place. Why not? They all deserved better, and it didn't hurt my pockets. I could give them all 2% and not even miss it!

I got to work 20 minutes early, exactly as planned. I posted up outside the building, smoking a Newport while checking things on the web. Why I had yet to tweet about this, I did not know, but I knew it would make an exciting story, so I decided to start. "Met my future wife yesterday. Goddess given flesh heaven must be losing its appeal 2 angels letting them cum 2 earth. N beauty was her name!" I typed, smiling at the line from an old Dru Hill song. I added the pic of Tatiana and I on the bridge by Bradford Beach.

I composed a second tweet for my 73 followers; "Shot @ 4 times, crib destroyed, sexed an angel, stumbled upon sum $$$, all n 12 hrs. When did my life bcum an action movie?"

Laughing at my tweets, I dropped my phone into my pocket, glancing around. I was in a great mood and decided today would be the day I spazzed out on my lame ass boss for all the bullshit he had pulled over the years of my employment. I had just tossed my cigarette butt when I noticed a cat in a hoodie lean out the passenger side window of an older model, lemon-toned Cadillac holding some kind of compact submachine gun. I spun off, running along the sidewalk between cars and the factory's parking-lot-facing wall, as the ratta-tat-tatatatat started. Bullets pinged off the wall where my shadow was as I kept my head low moving as fast as I could, trying to use the cars as cover.

I ran deeper into the parking lot, the cars I used as covers barely doing the trick, their alarms sounding as bullets chased me but only caught the vehicles. I saw the wrought-iron fence which separated the alley from the factory's property and cursed. The goon was out the whip at the other end of the lot. I had no gun and was stuck minus an exit strategy while crouched behind a car. I pulled out my phone and took videos of the car and the cat himself, using the car windows as cover.

Surveying the scene, I saw a way out. Quickly, while still crouched, I took off running past 3 cars lined against the wrought-iron fence, bullets crackling behind me. I jumped on one cars' hood, then roof in stride, using it as a trampoline to hop the 7-foot fence. I landed unsteadily, bullets still cutting through the air in my vicinity. Scraped hands helped keep me in motion as I darted across the alley, not daring a glance behind me as I stayed in a crouched run. I slipped between two garages into a backyard. I kept going, exploding out of someone's gangway onto a one-way street. I did not see the car until I hit its side at full speed, rolling over the hood in a weird kind of flip, reminiscent of those done by Power Rangers when they had things explode at their feet.

The driver screeched to a halt. I was in pain both before and after landing on the pavement, my back hitting first, allowing me to catch myself before my skull kissed the concrete. I popped up like a jack-in-the-box, unsure if the gun toter had kept after me or not. The driver, a black, teenaged girl was out of her car, apologetic and teary-eyed, two seconds from a panic attack. She was about to phone for help when I said, "Listen, I'm good! I'll give you 50 dollars and forget this happened if you drive me away from here now! Right now!"

    The girl was shook up and confused, but when I pulled the cash out, she said, "Okay, let's go!" I hopped into her backseat and laid down, my body sore. She pulled off, continuing westward. "I am so sorry about this! I didn't-" she began.

    I cut her off saying, "Sweetheart, no worries! I was inattentive. I'll be good after a blunt and some Tylenol! Just drive please." I glanced periodically in out the windows checking for the yellow Cadillac.

    "Where am I taking you?" she asked, giving off a look of confusion at my paranoid scanning of the area.

    "Um, just drive 5 blocks from here in any direction you wish to go, and I'll be good. Thanks truly sweetheart! I know how crazy this seems. It is even wilder than you know, but you may have just saved my life!" I explained, my back now aching more than before.

    The girl dropped me off at a gas station on 75th and Appleton Avenue. I handed her the 50 dollars, but she declined. I insisted, and she accepted.

I phoned Tatiana as I walked into the gas station. She answered on the second ring. "Hey! You almost made it a whole hour without contact." she said with a sleepy chuckle.

"Actually, that's only half true. They were at my job, chased me wit' bullets." I explained, looking at things in an aisle.

"Oh god Chris, you, okay?" she gasped, now sounding alert.

"Yep! Got hit by a car too! Thank God because that was how I got away! Right now, I'm at a gas station on 75th and Appleton. I need you!"

"I'll be there soon baby! Please be safe!" she said, and I could hear her moving around.

"I will. Call me when you are close."

"Okay, bye."

"Bye ma." I said, then ended the call.

I bought a coffee, bag of powdered doughnuts, bottle of aspirins, then walked to a do-it-yourself carwash connected to the gas station, ducking behind it to sit on a bank of car vacuums. Two cars were in the place, both in stalls, being sprayed with a hose. I ate wondering what to do. I was tired of being chased, shot at, and scared all day. I decided it was time to flip tactics and be the one proactively working to put an end to this. I looked at the pictures on my phone of the attackers, happy to see them be so clear. One had the shooters face, the other was of the car he had gotten out of. The driver's face was hidden so that was a bust. I sat in consideration, wondering what to do with the pictures.

Tatiana called me when she was a few blocks away. I jumped in the car when she rolled up and she wrapped her arms around me immediately, kissing me profusely. "You sure you're okay Chris?" she asked with a frightened look on her face as she examined me with her eyes for any visible wounds.

"Yeah bae, I'm good!" I assured her. As we drove away, I said, "I need some time to figure things out. What I'm thinkin' of doin' isn't exactly legal, but it will get us answers."

As we headed in the direction of our hotel, she looked at me asking, "Are you going to shoot anyone?"

"Doubt it!" I said, watching all the cars that were behind us.

When we got back to our hotel, both of us laid back in bed and slept for a few hours. I needed the rest, and I turned my phone off, so we'd have no interruptions.

CHAPTER ELEVEN

Housekeeping woke us at noon. Tatiana showered, dressed, and we left. The sunny morning had turned overcast. We went to a Wendy's and had lunch in a booth by a far corner. I explained the plan I had come up with.

"You think that'll work?" Tatiana asked, before chomping on her chicken sandwich.

"It should for a few reasons, but it isn't foolproof!" I told her then bit into my bacon-double cheeseburger.

She studied me then said, "Okay. I am ready for this to end!"

I smiled, then said, "Me too! Being shot at 5 times in 24 hours is crazy! I think you are a good luck charm."

She chuckled softly, then said, "Not really because if I was, you would not be getting shot at in the first place!"

"Maybe," I began, smiling, "But I could've been shot anyway yet I've gone unscathed. Plus, you keep me attentive because I'm hopin' to see what tomorrows wit' you'll be like! "Her smile shined brightly, and her joy danced between us. It was a great feeling!

From there, Tatiana and I went to Brookfield Square Mall, located on the southern edge of Waukesha's city of Brookfield. It was the first city outside of Milwaukee county's western border. In the mall we shopped for all the items we needed for the plan I had come up with, and a few extra things for us. After shopping, we went to our hotel, and got ready for what was next.

Prepared, we left, heading towards my roasted apartment. I saw the kid who sold weed standing outside the store as usual. I had Tatiana drop me off in the same place as the night before. I walked at a casual pace, wearing a white spring jacket, with white shorts, a short-sleeved button up, with matching shoes and a hat. I ended the look with a pair of bug-eyed shades. I had a gun in my waistband. Tatiana was on my Bluetooth as I walked towards a pair of payphones beside the store, head down, hood up.

I picked up a receiver, pretended to put some change into the slot, then pressed buttons as though I was dialing. I began talking to the computer-generated voice that politely asked me to please hang up and try my call again. I let Tatiana know I was in place. She drove from where she had parked and pulled up 10 feet from where I stood. She climbed out, walked around the hood, then turned the corner into the store's parking lot.

"Be flirty!" I reminded her.

Tatiana was dressed in a pink miniskirt that had little white hearts all over, barely hiding her lady part's, a form fitting pink and white baby-Tee, and platinum stilettos. Her hair was done up with crinkles, and she had makeup on that absolutely accentuated her gorgeous face. She looked like a walking video vixen. She was shy about wearing the outfit, a bit too modest to dress so provocatively. At the mall I had to beg her and reinforce her sexiness at the hotel. I looked forward to peeling her out of it later that night! People walked past me: kids, teens, and adults, but they paid me no mind. I listened to Tatiana talk.

"You do?" I heard her say as she was walking towards the store. She was going to purchase a box of blunts, some apple juice, and anything else that caught her attention.

"Well, I would have to get money for that from my car. When I come out, you can walk me to my car, okay handsome?" She said in a sexy tone.

The kid must have said something more because Tatiana chuckled and added, "Okay."

"Chris, I am in the store now. I will let you know when I am nearing the car, okay?" Tatiana said over the Bluetooth.

"A'ight, I'll be here!" I replied, then we went silent.

Seconds later, I heard Tatiana laugh then say, "Thanks sexy! I'm glad you like it!" She giggled at another remark he made just as I heard the two of them behind me. As they neared the car, Tatiana said, "Hop in!" Then, as she rounded the front fender, said, "Wait! I do not want any guns in my car!"

I heard the passenger door open, as the boy said, "We good Shawty, I ain't holdin' no gun!"

"You sure? Lift up your shirt!" Tatiana directed, and the boy did just that. Tatiana then said, "Okay, you good!"

The boy climbed in saying, "Shit Shawty, you fine ass fuck! Where ya nigga at?" I was already moving towards the car in long, smooth paces.

"I am single, why? You like what you see cutie?" Tatiana answered coyly. I could hear the smile she had on her face.

"Hell, yeah sexy!" the kid replied.

"Well, can I have a hug?" Tatiana asked as I neared the car. The boy obliged and just after his arms engulfed Tatiana, I slipped into the backseat.

I put the gun's barrel to his left side as he looked my way in complete confusion, and said, "Be stupid and you'll be wit' God, yo!"

The kid froze like an ice statue.

Tatiana pushed him off of her and said, "Silly boy, you are NOT my type!" Quickly, she pulled the car away from the curb.

"Hey nigga, what's this about?" The kid stammered as Tatiana drove through the busy traffic.

"Seatbelt, now!" Tatiana directed as she drove.

The kid complied as the car continued northwest. I made the kid recline the passenger seat all the way back, then I put a pillowcase over his face. "Yo, answer all my questions and you'll make it home tonight wit'out any issues, got me?" I asked him as Tatiana turned west onto Lloyd Street.

"Yeah man, just don't hurt me." the kid said, obviously spooked, even though I had no intent of doing him any harm at all.

After three blocks, Tatiana made a left onto 47th street, and pulled onto the expressway heading south. Tatiana focused on driving, obviously and understandably shaky behind the whole situation. She knew I wasn't going to do a thing to the kid, but it was still a highly illegal act we were doing.

"You kno' who I am, right?" I asked.

"Nope!" he lied swiftly.

"We gone play games? You feelin' suicidal or somethin' kid?" I asked, pushing the pistol into his shoulder.

"Okay man, okay. You the nigga who picked up my cousin bag yesterday when I was supposed to!"

"Exactly! Now, who the fuck is ya cousin?"

"His name Drama. He run this part of the hood." the kid said, now happy to volunteer info.

"How he find me in Westlawn?"

"He said his nigga Vince saw y'all and hit him up wit' the address." I mulled this over as Tatiana turned onto an eastbound section of the freeway.

"Give me ya phone!" I commanded, and the boy pulled it from his pocket. I snatched it from him.

"Man, Drama just want the gold. He told me to keep an eye on your place and let him know when you came back." The kid spoke rapid fire like the bullets that had chased me earlier that morning.

"Shut up." I said calmly. "What's your pin? "He gave it to me, and I pulled up his phonebook. I found Drama's name and called him.

"What up lil' cousin?" a familiar voice said on the second ring.

"Ya lil' cousin can't talk right now. He a bit tied up at the moment, but why don't we converse." I said, cocky and cool.

"What? Who the fuck is this? Where my fuckin' cousin? If you did somethin' to him, you and ya whole family is dead!" The heated goon shouted, obviously not used to being on the losing end of any situation.

I chuckled, finding his nose-flaring fury over the phone comedic. I was a tad spooked but having his cousin lent me a modicum of confidence. I controlled the fate of his beloved cousin, so I was good.

"He breathin' but fuck him for now! What's important is the fact that I now kno' who you are! I kno' that you and ya cronies shot a cop, robbed an armored car, shot at me and my wifey multiple times, and that is just the beginnin'. You want these gold bars, so I suggest we trade." I said, then went silent so he could talk.

"What you wanna trade?" he asked emotionless.

"How 'bout ya cousin comes home safely an' you back off us?" Drama snorted comically, then truly laughed. I told the weed-peddling teenager, "He just laughed, ya big cousin care more about 90 bands in gold bars than he does you! How twisted is that?"

"Aye nigga, don't tell him that!" Drama spat in anger

"Why not? I say I'll return him, and you laugh. That gold is only worth 90 thou and change. I did the math." I spoke.

I could hear Drama smile when he said, "A'ight check this out homie. I'll throw you 100 G's and you just gimme my lil' cousin plus the gold. I'll let you two be also, on my nation bruh!"

I paused as if contemplation of the offer, then said, "That sounds smooth if I only had one thing for you. But I got ya gold and ya cousin. How 'bout you throw 2 pounds of weed, and a key of white onto that, and we got a deal!"

"You testin' my patience, nigga!" Drama said in a demonic time. I put the kids' phone on my lap, hit speakerphone, and cocked the pistol right above the mouthpiece.

"Hey, chill nigga! I didn't say no. Okay, I'll give you that. Where do you wanna make the trade?" Drama asked in a softer voice.

"I'll call you back!" I said, then hung up on the cat.

"Sounds like ya cousin loves you after all!" I told the hostage.

"Yeah, he like my big brother, he always takes care of me." The cat explained

Tatiana still had us on the freeway, driving the loop that Milwaukee's freeway system was set up in. We started in the northern middle then went east into Downtown. From there we went due south, until Layton Avenue, near the airport, where the highway went west, into the suburbs of Greendale, Greenfield and West Allis or gave the option of continuing south, in the general direction of Chicago. From just about 100th street, the highway curved north again. It continued in that direction for a few miles, with an East-West split near the northside/southside border. We took the eastbound split, heading towards Downtown again. We figured driving around like that was a safe way to go with a kidnap victim in our vehicle.

After we had turned south, and had driven for a few miles, I told Tatiana to turn left near the Plainfield curve, continuing south towards Chicago. We didn't have a plan beyond that, so I wanted to put one in play. We drove beyond the city for about 20 minutes until we spotted a rest stop with a McDonald's. Tatiana pulled off the freeway and into the parking lot, driving us to an area nowhere near any other vehicles.

"You hungry boy?" Tatiana asked, adding, "We are at a McDonald's."

"Uh, yeah. Can I get a 20-piece nugget meal with a chocolate shake please, with lots of sweet and sour sauce plus ketchup, please?" the kid requested.

"I'll take 2 apple pies and a vanilla shake." I said to Tatiana with a smile.

She smiled back, simply replying with an "Okay."

With Tatiana gone, I told the kid, "If you do anything stupid when I take this hood off you, you will be dead, and by the time anyone finds your body, her and I will be long gone! We'll take the gold, move to Paris and have a great life, you got me?"

"Uh-huh. I'll be chill!" the boy said, and I pulled the hood from his head. The gun was in my opposite hand, pointed his way. He squinted then looked around.

Tatiana returned a few moments later with the food. We ate, then Tatiana and I stepped out of the car to talk. I had the radio turned up, with the boy back under the pillowcase, his hands tied, and him seat-belted in place.

"Ma, I have a detective I can call, and we can set up Drama to take the fall for at least the dope and cash, which should get him off our asses." I told Tatiana as we stood facing the car's interior, holding hands.

"You trust Drama?" She asked, her face showing all her concern.

"Nah, not at all. But I kno' we can set things up so we will be safe and get him collared by the cops." I explained.

From that, we put the next part of our plan together.

CHAPTER TWELVE

Tatiana drove back to the city, pulling into the parking lot of a Target on south 27th Street, positioning us far away from the other cars. Minutes later, she returned with all the items I sent her to purchase. Then, we rode to the storage facility. I went into the unit to prepare the bars. I was back in the car and headed towards Downtown when I called Drama.

"Yo, this the deal." I said when he answered. "We gone meet at the Museum Downtown on Wells, behind the library. Be right by the IMAX theater in one hour. My pickup person will be there waitin'. The second they are out and safe after givin' you the bag of gold bars, and takin' the shit you got fo' me, ya cousin will walk in. I'm showin' him the gold bars now! Hold on!"

I pulled the bookbag I had placed the gold bars into from the floor and handed it to the kid. "I'm puttin' you on speaker. Be stupid and you'll find ya cousin in a ditch!" I said with as much menace as I could come with.

"A'ight, we hear you!" Drama said. I put the phone on speaker.

"Lalo, you good lil' cousin?" Drama asked, his voice now extremely humane.

"Yeah, big cousin, they been real straight to me. You doin' what they say 'cause they kno' what they doin'!"

"I kno' my nigga, and this paper ain't shit to me! I'll have you back on the block ASAP, feel me?"

"A'ight bruh, thanks! The gold is valid. I see it all and I'm touchin' it." Lalo said, excitement in his voice.

"Okay." I said, ending their conversation, cutting off speakerphone and pulling the bookbag holding the bars away from the kid. "You see Drama, he good! Now, one hour at the IMAX. You be there wit' what I want and he'll be let go, cool?"

"Yeah." Drama said, and I ended the call

Tatiana took us to a gas station on the edge of Wauwatosa, where she gassed up the car and I made a call on the kid's phone while Lalo was tied up and still reclined inside the Tempo.

"Detective O'Malley, I wanted you to kno' that the guys who robbed that armored truck and shot ya officers over by Washington Park will be at the IMAX in the museum within 45 minutes. They will have the gold bars, guns in a bag they carryin'."

"Wait, the IMAX in the Public Museum?" the detective asked.

"Yeah, in less than 45 minutes." I repeated.

"Who is this?" The detective asked.

"Be there in less than 45 minutes. You take more time than that and they won't be there. You will never see the perps or the bars again!" I said swiftly, then hung up and got into the car.

We drove around for a bit, then Tatiana pulled into a parking garage a few blocks from the museum 10 minutes before the exchange. I sent Tatiana inside of the Milwaukee Public Museum, but she was not the pickup person. There wasn't one. I told her to sit at a table where she could see the area outside of the IMAX theater and watch who showed up. She had her Bluetooth on, and we talked while she did this. I stood outside the car, just out of earshot of the kid, who had his hands tied inside the vehicle.

"Bae, 2 guys with a duffle bag are here. Both are tall and dark." She told me, sending a picture of them men. Neither of them was Drama.

I walked to the passenger's side window and showed the kid the picture and asked, "Which is Drama?"

The boy studied the photo, then pointed to the guy with nothing in his hands, saying, "Him!"

"You sure?" I asked.

"Yeah!" the boy said shakily. I walked away from the window to the hood of the car. To verify, I called Drama from the kid's phone.

As the phone rang, I asked Tatiana, "Bae, any of them reachin' fo' a phone?"

"No." she stated.

"Shit!" I said, realizing that Drama wasn't there.

"Oh wow! Chris, the police just ran up on those guys, weapons drawn, and are arresting them as we speak!" Tatiana informed me with a bit of glee in her tone.

"Good! Meet me where I said! I'm on my way, a'ight?"

"Yep!" Tatiana replied.

"Get out!" I told the kid. I opened the door, and I handed him the bag after untying his hands. I pulled away, leaving the parking garage.

I called Drama as I went for Tatiana. "I see you into playin' games!" I spoke.

"Where my lil' cousin at bitch nigga? You set my boys up, and if you hurt my boy, you dead!" Drama spat out like a volcano spewing lava.

"Relax ma'fucka, Lalo on his way to the museum wit' all ya gold. Now, let me and my girl be, a'ight? I set them up figurin' you'd not be there, and to show you I wasn't a rookie! You got ya gold and ya cousin, so, move on!" I said then hung up as I pulled into Saturday night traffic downtown.

I drove to the meeting place I gave to Tatiana. It was a park just west of the museum, and a block north. Tatiana was there waiting. She climbed in and kissed me, smiling. I hopped onto the freeway heading to our hotel.

"Why you so giddy, Tati?" I asked as we drove west.

"Just had a very exciting 36 hours! This was the craziest thing to ever happen to me! I can't believe I was able to hold my poise!" she explained, grinning.

I chuckled, saying, "You're mad precious ma! I'm shocked you ain't separate ya'self from me when they tossed shots at us when we were on the footbridge."

She leaned over my way, rubbing my arm while saying, "And risk the chance to not have my apartment shot up? I'd never dream of it!" We both laughed, then she added, "Actually, I couldn't leave you. I was yours from the second you said Tatiana and Chris sounded great together!"

I glanced at her as we passed the baseball stadium where the Milwaukee Brewers played, continuing west. Her smile was huge and sincere!

"I wonder how he'll feel when he finds out all he has are gold-painted metal paperweights?" I said, which made both of us laugh.

At the Target store, we stopped to pick up a dozen small paperweights, some gold spray paint, and 2 identical bookbags. When we were at the storage unit, with the boy tied up, I sprayed the weights. The paint dried fast, and stuck. I bagged them and when in the parking garage I showed the kid the bag with the real gold in it. I knew he would sell the ruse exactly as I planned. I hoped Drama would be at the exchange, but I didn't believe he would be. Still, 2 of his goons were boxed in, plus we cost him cash and drugs, so we did the community a service. Added payback for the 2 cribs he had destroyed! We reached our hotel, parked and headed straight to our room.

"Tati, let's order room service, then I wanna do a bit of role playin' while you got that outfit on." I said as we entered the room. I dropped our bags, carrying all the things we had taken with us.

She kicked off her heels and flopped backwards onto the bed, then said, "Am I your call girl tonight?"

I chuckled as I sat beside, lifting one of her teeny beautiful feet and began massaging it. "Sounds like fun, but you'd be more of a slave, doin' as I please!" I told her, studying the delicate foot I held in my hand.

She smiled, then lifted her leg all the way over my head, resting it on my shoulder as she asked, "What would you like me to do for you, Master?" Her voice was so sultry, smokey and sexy that it made blood rush to all the right places. I ducked under her leg, crawled up her body until I was face-to-face with her. She stared at me with a pert, daring smile.

I kissed her softly, then said, "Get me some damn food woman!"

Tatiana squealed in laughter, her head tossing back into the pillow. I kissed her exposed neck, as she rubbed my lower back, her hands under my shirt as she finished her laugh.

"You are too funny Chris!"

"Yet another reason I'm yours, yes?!" I asked staring into her eyes.

"Yes, definitely yes!" she answered, then kissed me. When we parted, she said, "Let's go out, celebrate!"

I smiled, remembering how I too wanted and planned on going out that night. "Great idea ma! I also wanna snag some money orders for the fire victims. Food first though."

"Okay, we should eat downstairs at the restaurant!"

"Let's go." I said, then pecked her on the lips before rolling off of her. She sat up, fixed her hair, put her heels back on, and we left.

We took the elevator located in the center of the floor in an alcove down to the main floor. Rounding the corner from the dead end that held the elevator bank, we turned left, and walked a couple dozen yards to the lobby area. A restaurant was just across from the front desk, with a bar. We walked into the dim, moody room which had a bar in an L-shape that stretched across two walls, and tables spread intimately in the remaining space. 2 TVs were on above the bar at different ends, one playing ESPN, the other FOX NEWS CHANNEL. About 40 people were in the place, it being nearly 6 in the evening.

Tatiana and I found a table away from others and as we sat, a waitress approached with menus. "May I get you 2 drinks while you look over the menu?" she asked in a bubbly, friendly tone.

"I'd like an iced tea, please." Tatiana said

"I'll take a Coke, thank you." I said.

"Okay, that'll be up in a few breaths." the lady said, then left us with the menus.

"I like how this steak and baked potato is lookin'. What about you mami?"

Tatiana studied the menu then said, "Oh, this veal looks exquisite!" her voice was haughty, which made me chuckle. She looked at me, huffed, then said in faux exasperation, "Well, I never!" I laughed harder which made her crack a smile, then start laughing too.

"Know what sounds even better, ma?" I quizzed in an excited voice.

"What?" Tatiana asked, looking at me as I pointed at my menu.

"You plus whipped cream!" I answered with a mischievous grin.

"Shush Chris!" she hissed, blushing while my smirk stayed true.

I shrugged saying, "Jus' sayin' ma...if they had that on the menu, I'd be they number one custy!"

Tatiana bit her lip, shaking her head as I smiled. "You will be my number one customer as soon as we get back from the club tonight, watch!"

"Yey!" I replied childishly earning a smile from both Tatiana and the waitress who returned with our drinks and some fried, breaded cheese curds with different sauces to dip them in as appetizers. We ordered our food then ate the cheese curds while talking.

"Why exactly did you go to work this morning Chris?" Tatiana asked with an odd smirk. "Surely you weren't out to end on good footing."

"Actually, I was goin' to put in my 2 weeks, so I could use them as a reference in the future." I said, then popped another cheese curd dipped in a ranch sauce into my mouth.

Tatiana was suspicious and stared at me with a penetrating gaze until I broke character and started laughing. "Why are you toying with me?" she asked with a grin.

"New toy, why not play wit' it?" I said then felt her foot tap the side of my shin as she made a face.

"So, why did you go there?"

"To make an ass outta my sadistic shyster of a boss! Jerk wad docked my pay this week and I was prepped to have a massive spaz-attack in his honor!" I told Tatiana. She smiled while shaking her head. I switched subjects, asking, "Where do you wanna move to?"

She shrugged as she washed down a cheese curd with her iced tea, then answered, "I don't know. What are you thinking?"

"Figurin' that out now." I answered her, earning an eyeroll. I added, "I mean, are we gettin' separate places or what?"

"Uhm, how about this. We pick a nice place and rent it as roommates, then go from there " Tatiana offered, thoughtfully.

Our dishes were delivered, and as the waitress vanished, I said, "I was actually talkin' along the lines of location."

"Oh...um..." she stammered, then bought herself time to think by taking a forkful of her dinner into her mouth. I thought about bailing her out but let her flounder to see how she would finish. "Well, I didn't want to move too fast."

"Oh." I said simply to toy with her.

She continued, adding, " I'd be okay with either."

"So, roommates it is then?" I said.

"You think we'd be okay as JUST roommates?" she asked, with an expression I could not read across her flawless face.

"Never said 'just'. We'd be a couple. What I mean is we would get to kno' each other, but still have our own personal space."

"Okay, but when I want sex," she started, making me nearly choke in laughter, "You better be ready because I have no issue at all with taking what I want boy!"

When I was able to stop laughing, I said, "Tatiana, I am not serious! I want us to live together, sharing a bed, bathroom and beyond bae! You're incredible, and I have never known a dame so down and devoted as you are. I only wanna explore what is to come for us! Plus, we had sex without protection so movin' too fast for us is somethin' we can't pause now." I told her.

"I so love that!" she said in a heartfelt manner, then leaned over the table to kiss me!

CHAPTER THIRTEEN

We had just about finished our meals when my jacket pocket began to vibrate, and an odd ring tone went off. "What the hell?" I said, knowing my phone would never kick out such a lame sounding sound like that which played. I reached into my pocket and pulled out the weed peddler's phone.

"Oh yeah, I never gave the kid back his phone." I said with a single-syllabled laugh, as I looked at the screen.

"Who's calling?" Tatiana asked with a whimsical grin.

"Drama." I told her, then decided to answer. I unlocked it and said, "Yep?"

"Figured you fooled me, huh pussy?" Drama said in a seething tone which sounded like he would love to murder me at that exact moment.

I gave Tatiana a 'busted' type smile. She mouthed, "The jig is up?" I nodded and we both shared soundless snickers.

"Whatever do you mean Drama? You got exactly what you deserved." I said in an airy, playful tone.

"Bitch ass nigga, this shit a joke to you. You think I'm stupid? You dead, you and that black ass bitch is dead!" he growled at me, his anger rising like a helium filled balloon

I chuckled then said, "Why so disrespectful? That is so rude!" I took a bit of food and noticed Tatiana raptly watching me talk.

"Eat lady, all is proper!" I told her, covering the mouthpiece while doing so. Tatiana shook her head, smirked, then continued eating.

"Oh, this a game to you huh? Check this out!" Drama said, and a text alert tone came up on my phone. I pulled my phone out, then opened the text. I saw a picture of the Tempo, then the hotel, then a third picture of the car being set on fire by masked characters.

"Got that nigga? Found you!" Drama said with a cackle, which I found a bit alarming because I had never actually heard an evil cackle in real life prior to that!

I hung up and said, "Shit Tati, they found us!" I looked over my shoulder and beyond the entrance to the eatery.

Tatiana was wide-eyed, asking, "Seriously Chris, don't play!"

I stood from the table and said, "Wait here, I gotta check somethin'!"

"Chris." Tatiana called but I held my hand up to quiet her as I walked away from the table. I poked my head into the lobby, looking in the direction of the main exit. A commotion was happening, with people just beyond the glass doors of the hotel entrance. I cursed under my breath before turning and walking back to our table.

Tatiana had paid the bill and having read the panic on my face was ready to go when I got there. "Chris, talk to me." she said in a fearful tone, grabbing her purse and my hand as I led her towards the exit of the restaurant.

"Mami, they found us. They got my number. They set the Tempo on fire. We need to vanish fast!" I explained, then poked my head out the exit. I saw the crowd of people, all seeming to be focused on the situation transpiring in the parking lot.

Sirens wailed in the distance as we hung a left into the corridor, then rounded a corner moving fast towards the elevator bank. Down the hall I saw a cat standing just inside the doors at the far end of the building. He saw us, but he did not move in our direction as we rounded the corner into the dead-end area housing the elevators. An elevator opened immediately upon my pushing the call button.

I smashed the close door button once we were inside the car, Tatiana already having punched our floor number. With a ding, the doors closed, and the cart moved upward. "Chris, do you think they have the whole building surrounded?" Tatiana asked as we glided up.

"Seems like it but I can't be 100%."

"Then what are we going to do?" she asked with a quiver in her voice.

"I don't know, I need some time to think. That's why we headed to our room." I said as the elevators doors opened, and I looked out into the enclave to see if anyone was waiting.

Seeing no one, I moved with Tatiana by my side, hurrying towards our room. Inside, I grabbed a towel, put it under the door and started saying, "Tati, change into shorts gym shoes-" but I saw she was doing it already and smiled.

"How'd they find us?" she asked, fear perverting her normally ready voice.

"GPS on the kid's phone, I imagine. They coulda gotten my number while at my place but they can't GPS my phone wit'out my password." I answered, then grabbed the binoculars Tatiana had used the night before. Tatiana was dressed, so I killed the lights and said, "Ma, use the flashlight on your phone from now on. Be as quiet as you can. I'm goin' to see how deep they are outside." I walked to the window, peeled back a corner of the curtain, and saw that the Tempo was fully ablaze, with the car on its left and right being on fire too. The fire department sprayed the inferno.

I scanned the crowd by the main exit and noticed two cats focused on the people in the crowd, something rather odd when everyone else faced the fire. I could only see one more exit, on the far left of the building, and there I saw two more guys amongst the smaller gathering of people. I looked over the entirety of the parking lot but noticed no cars that stood out from the rest, nor any that seemed familiar.

Lalo's phone rang in my pocket. I snatched it out swiftly and answered, "Yeah?"

"Your bitch ass still think this a game? My boy saw y'all! He kno' what floor you on. We comin' fo' you!" Drama said, then hung up on me.

"Kill the sound on your phone and whisper if you have to speak. He said they kno' what floor we on." I said, facing her.

In the illumination of the flashlight, I could see her fear glowing like neon. "How Chris?" she inquired in a hushed tone.

My heart and mind were both on overdrive, but I wanted to calm her, so I sat on the bed with her beside me. I wrapped my arms around her. "Tati, I don't kno'. Maybe the cat in the hallway saw the numbers above the elevator." I said, while racking my brain for exit strategies.

"Chris, can't we call the cops?" Tatiana asked.

"Yeah, but they may not get here fast enough. We need help immediately." I explained. I turned on my phones' flashlight feature and searched the bedroom walls.

"What are you looking for?"

"Was there a fire alarm in here?" I asked Tatiana.

"I only saw a smoke detector, why?" she replied. "If too many people are in the halls, they may not shoot us, plus we could get downstairs in the crowds." I told her.

I went into my bag and pulled out 2 hoodies, handing one to Tatiana. "Put this on ma, I have an idea."

She did, then asked, "Okay, now what."

"You call 2 cabs on your phone. I will call 2 as well. Use two different companies. I'm going to call the lobby and tell 'em that there are cats wit' guns on our floor. I will also call the cops and say the same thing. Then I'm callin' the lobby, actin' drunk and sayin' I accidentally set a fire on the sixth floor. That'll hopefully get the alarm fire alarm sounding. If not, we'll figure somethin' else out." I told her.

We did that, then waited for a few minutes. Nothing happened. After a few more excruciatingly long minutes where Tatiana and I sat huddled while whispering silently, we gave up on that idea and I laid out the second one. "Tati, I'm going to check things out. I am filling my bookbag with clothes, so it is rounder. You can wear it in front, actin' like you pregnant. If I see no one, I want to go hit—" I was saying when a knock came on our room's door.

I put a finger to my lips, grabbed a gun from my bookbag and walked the floor silently. I checked the peephole but saw darkness as if something was covering the viewer. The second knock was harder, more determined. I wondered if just shooting through the door would work but realized that if I didn't hit whoever stood on the other side, Tatiana and I would be dead. I knew that they had me outgunned and no matter what I'd be committing suicide and killing Tatiana in the process.

The third knock was more of a pounding. I ran noiselessly to the window, peering out with the hopes that the cops had come to our rescue. I saw a trio of police cruisers roll up and park near a cop car already on scene. I ran back to the door and looked out the peephole. There were 2 guys at the door across the hall from ours, one with a chrome pistol in his hands, the other standing to his right, with a black gun behind his back.

"We hotel security and we are searching for two crooks who hidin' on yo floor." I heard one of the cats say to an elderly white man who opened the room door. The goon added, "They dangerous so stay in yo room till we let you kno' you safe, a'ight?" The elderly man nodded in a wide-eyed fashion, then closed his door.

I looked behind me and saw Tatiana on the bed, trembling in fear. I walked to her and did my best to comfort her. I heard a phone sing and ran to the door. Checking the peephole, I saw one of the goons answer the phone, say something to the caller, then end it. "We got to bounce. Police is here." One goon said to the other and they jogged off.

I went to Tatiana and said, "We good but we need to leave now! Police are here!" We grabbed our things, making sure Tatiana's belly bulged properly, tossed on baseball caps on us both, then went to the door. I cracked the door, then poked my head out. The hallway was clear.

"Tati, breathe like you're in labor. 'Kay?" I said, earning a nervous head nod from her. She began immediately, and we walked out the room carrying our bags.

After we had gotten about 15 steps, 4 cops turned the corner from where the elevators are, both with their weapons in hand. "Breathe baby, the hospital isn't far away. Just breathe!" I said, seeing the cops. Tatiana did, even clinching her eyes like she was experiencing pain.

Two officers walked in our direction, with the other two headed away from Tatiana and me. The two coming towards us, eyeballed her and I with suspicion as we neared, so I said, "You're doin' great mami! Keep your breathin' even! We will be there soon!" I kept a worried, but still pride-filled look on my face while I ushered her towards the elevator bank.

"Okay, but hurry baby! I can't hold her in, she is ready!" Tatiana said in a way that would've spooked me had I not known she was acting. I put all my focus into her as she waddled towards the two officers.

"Do you two need help?" A blond-haired cop asked when we had reached them. His gun was pointed aside, his partner, a black-haired guy with green eyes scanned the hallway for trouble still.

"She's in labor wit' our first baby and—" I started but Tatiana cut me off with a loud moan, causing me to say, "Sorry officers, but we have to reach our car." With that we pushed past the cops and to the elevators. I hit the call button and we both waited, Tatiana still breathing heavily.

Seconds later, the door opened, and an empty car faced us. Inside, I hit 2 causing Tatiana to ask, "What are you doing?" obviously perplexed by us not going directly to the lobby.

"This is better ma, watch!" I told her. I felt a phone vibrate in my pocket and pulled out the kid's phone.

"Think your good cause the boys in blue came through? Nah, they gon' leave and with my niggas watchin' every door, you not escapin'!" I hung up on him.

When the doors dinged open, I said, "Tati, come on." We exited on the second floor, took a left out of the elevator nook, seeing 2 exterior exits and a halfway down the left corridor were stairs that led down to the lobby, near the main entrance. Beside the vending machines and ice machine, I saw a fire alarm.

With Tatiana beside me, I pulled the lever. A loud squeal sounded, and strobe lights begin to blink. "Tati, walk slow like you're preggers, to give people a chance to get out they rooms." I said to her as we moved down the hall.

Not being sure of how many people were in the hotel, I hoped it numbered in the hundreds since there were about 50 rooms per floor and it was the weekend before Independence Day in a busy city's outskirts. People first popped their heads out of their doors like whack-a-moles before exiting their rooms around us. Families, couples, and single folks of all ages moved past us as I guided Tatiana toward the main stairs, walking along the wall slowly. Walking down the stairs slowly allowed the crowd in the lobby to grow and by the time we reached the doorway, it was like moving through Time's Square on New Year's Eve!

Outside, under the dusk skies and mob of folks talking and completely unsure of what was transpiring, plus the cops and firefighters, we saw the 4 cabs idling and climbed into the second one queued. "To the bus station in downtown Milwaukee." I said when Tatiana and I were situated.

"You got it!" the driver replied as he pulled away from the drop off area. I was crouched down some, watching people as we crawled through the mob of folks outside of the hotel. "What happened back there?" The driver asked.

"Fire or somethin'. We were in the lobby checkin' out when the alarm went off. There was a fire in the parkin' lot too!" I shared.

"Woah that's crazy." The driver replied, looking towards the pandemonium. "You two headed out for the holiday?" He added as we exited the hotel property.

"Yep! She has convinced me to spend the week in Kenosha to meet and spend time with her parents." I said, then playfully nudged Tatiana.

"It's been 2 years, and you are the father of their only child's belly baby, and her fiancé! If not now, then when?" Tatiana said, then kissed me on my cheek.

"Yeah, sounds like it's a bit overdo, but don't fret son. Some in-laws are great! Mine are a dream. And loaded!" The driver said with a large grin in the rearview mirror. Tatiana put her head on my shoulder as we pulled onto the highway, headed east.

"Yes, and my parents will adore you! You've been the bestest everything to me, so relax honey!" Tatiana said in the sweetest tone.

I kept an eye out for any vehicles that seemed to be trailing us.

None showed to be behind us, as I continued the conversation, saying in a whiny way, "I guess, but I really wanted to do Summerfest tomorrow! The fireworks show and all!"

"We will see the ones in Kenosha." Tatiana said to me, adding, "Stop pouting already!" The cabbie laughed at us, as did I. Tatiana whispered into my ear, "We get away?"

"So far." I answered.

"Turn that phone off!" she said in a forceful whisper.

I pulled out Lalo's phone and sent one last text before turning to off. It read; "Find us yet, bitch?"

We reached the Greyhound and Amtrak station on 5th and St. Paul Street about 20 minutes later, paid the cabdriver with a nice tip, then went into the bus/train depot. "I'm going to the restroom." Tatiana told me as we walked by a row of seats.

"Okay ma, you want somethin' to drink?" I asked as she removed the bookbag she wore as a belly by taking her arms out of the sleeves.

"No, I'm fine, thank you." She replied, handing me the bookbag.

"A'ight, I'll meet you by the vending area." I told her.

The station was a wide-open space, with about one hundred seats split up in a few different areas, glass and brick walls with glass doors separating the boarding area from everywhere else. The space had high ceilings with steel beam rafters that allowed sounds to bounce around with ease. The ticket counter was L-shaped and on the eastern end of the building, with roped off lines to the left of the main entrance. A video arcade, vending machines, and a small diner were all situated across from the walls to the boarding areas, side-by-side. There were 2 sets of restrooms on opposite ends of the building.

I felt my phone vibrate and swiped absentmindedly. "Yea?" I said when it was up to my ear.

"Think you good cause you pulled that stunt? Nah nigga, we goin' to stay here waitin' for the smoke to clear, then we right back on y'all asses! Y'all dead, you two just don't know it yet!" Drama spat in my ear.

I chuckled, more out of relief then comedic value. "Yo, I feel you and everything, but I don't BELIEVE you! Still, I feel you! Regardless, my question for you is this: What happens to ya 900 thou in gold bars? I mean, I ain't worried 'bout you, but we the only people who kno' where its stashed. How will you ever get ya hands on it?" I replied.

As he paused in contemplation, the intercom above me boomed, "The local bus to Minneapolis/St. Paul is now boarding at gate 9. I repeat, the local bus to Minneapolis/St. Paul is now boarding at gate 9." I didn't have the time to cover the receiver.

Drama actually laughed in a way that made me smile. "Ah, you and that bitch slick as hell! Y'all got away, huh?! Cool! You did that! Fuck that money! You 2 at the train station downtown. Y'all dead nigga!" he said with a scary kind of glee in his tone, then ended the call.

Having already obtained everything I wanted from vending machines, I walked swiftly towards the restrooms on the western end of the depot. I stood there somewhat nervously. Tatiana came out seconds later. "Bae, we need to bounce, now!" Her eyes grew wide as she expressed on her face the fear, I had within me.

"How'd he find us?" "Called me and heard the shit from the PA system." I explained as we moved to a side exit.

Tatiana's fear was palpable, her voice and tenseness conforming it as we walked. I felt so very sorry for dragging an innocent, heartfelt, genuinely good dame into this dangerous situation. I wanted to figure out a way to get her to a safe place while I ended this too wild game of hide-

and-seek that I was trapped in. I didn't want her shot or raped or killed because Chris decided he'd be a damn dummy. I, myself, held no intention of ending up a memory. That was not on my To-Do list for at least another half century plus a couple decades. I understood how hopes, plans, and reality rarely merged in our lives.

Still, Tatiana stumbled upon me, and I had to keep her protected. If I held any sincere feelings towards her, it was my responsibility to put her in a safe, secure place. "Where are we going now Chris?" she asked, almost in a sob.

We were exiting through a set of doors on the north side of the building. I walked us to the nearest cab waiting for passengers. I helped her into the cab, then climbed in behind her and told the driver, "The Days Inn by the airport on Howell. Take the Bridge." The driver didn't hesitate, pulling into the one-way traffic headed east on St. Paul Street.

Returning my focus back to Tatiana, I held her hands and said, "Ma, just relax! I'm goin' to figure out how to end this. For now, I just wanna lay low, get it completely together, and we will be good!" I told her as we neared the eastern edge of downtown, nearing the art museum that was used as the rich ex-boyfriend's office in the movie, 'Transformer's 3'.

Tatiana's phone sang, and I saw panic wash over her face immediately, as if a dark cloud blocked out the sun in front of her. She only relaxed when she had her phone out and saw the caller ID. She smiled. "Hey Dana! What's up girl?" she said, her voice quite chipper.

At the end of St. Paul, the driver hung a right onto the Hoyne bridges, which was the southern cessation of Lake Drive. The Hoyne bridge rose above the Maier festival grounds, which held all the summertime ethnic festivals as well as the epic SummerFest. Also, under the bridge was shipping docks, warehouses and the mouth of the Milwaukee River, where it drained into Lake Michigan, which was just beyond the east side of the bridge. There was a water treatment facility, a junkyard and a few other things underneath the bridge, before it ended and became a highway that stopped at Layton Street, 4 miles south at the northern edge of the airport fencing.

Tatiana talked with her girl while I looked up things on my phone, trying to figure up our next move. I found nothing worth my time, then checked Facebook just to be busy. When I prepared to put my phone away, it bleeped letting me know that the battery was low. My charger was in my apartment, so I had to buy a new one. "Driver, can you stop at the nearest Walmart? I'll pay you to keep the meter running!" I asked as we rode south.

"No problem. Which one are you talking about?" He asked.

"Closest one, I guess. How about the one on 27th and Cold Spring Road." I told him, and he got us there in a matter of minutes. Tatiana stayed in the cab while I ran directly into the electronics department, picked up a Samsung kit and iPhone kit for Tatiana, then returned to the cab, heading to the hotel.

CHAPTER FOURTEEN

The hotel was a squat, two level, amber colored building across from the airports entrance. Next to the Days Inn was a Holiday Inn, and a ritzier Marriott. I paid the fair and we exited the cab, walking a few steps to the glass-doored main entrance. We walked through the small lobby to the receptionist's desk. On a long table sat a coffeemaker, a case housing what were probably now stale doughnuts, plus a few other insignificant items constituting a bootleg continental breakfast.

Behind the counter, a bored-looking white woman tossed Tatiana and I a weak smile yet greeted us with a voice much brighter than she seemed. We rented a room for the night on the second floor. The hotel had no elevator, so we took the stairs beside the entrance up to the second floor. The second level was 2 halls that made a wide 'V', with rooms on both walls, and stairs at the ends. We found our room, opened the door, and walked in. Tatiana dropped her bags and walked directly to the bed and plopped into it. The room was plain: small bathroom, table by the window with 2 chairs, a bed, a dresser that doubled as the TV stand, and 2 nightstands with lamps atop ended the decor.

I closed the door, dropped my bags, and walked to the bed. I climbed onto Tatiana who was on her back, spread eagle. Her eyes were closed and, didn't open when I mounted her. I caressed her cheek as I moved to her side, loving the texture of her skin.

"Tati, I want you to take the gold bars and go somewhere safe, out of the state! I don't want you in this shit no more." I said calmly.

She smiled but her eyes didn't open, as if the situation had sapped from her the miniscule energy required for such an act. "Chris," she began softly after a sigh. "I don't want to abandon you. You are my man, and I don't see that as being acceptable. I'd be calling you every 10 minutes, so stressed by you being who knows where." Her eyelids fluttered but didn't open.

I kissed her, then said, "Bae, I've been your man for not even 24 hours, and I'm not enjoyin' the fact that you have been near me when bullets were chasin' me one too many times." I told her, hoping she would understand my intent.

"Chris, we will beat him at this. We are smarter and more creative. We only have to use our heads." she said, opening her eyes and looking at me. In them I saw just how definite she was about this.

I then became sure about it too. My sole question was do we stoop to their level, stay on higher ground, or just play it by ear, doing whatever the situation required? I posed that query to Tatiana, adding, "They are animals, and live criminally every day. We are not that way ma, but do we singe our souls by fallin' to they level of morality?"

Tatiana stared at me with a look that was beyond my immediate scope of comprehension for a few moments. When she spoke next, I had greater respect for her. "We are not and can NEVER be like them. We will be us!" With that she closed her eyes and said nothing.

I laid beside her, wrapped in her arms. My phone buzzed then bleeped, reminding me of its battery situation. I answered it while getting out my charger and plugging both into the unit and wall socket. "Yeah?" I said, answering it

"Think you got away?" Drama asked as if he was just beyond the door magically, or by the window watching us lay in bed.

"Actually, we are about halfway to Chicago and from there we may go back east, south or west. We gone with the gold, so have a great life. Thanks!" I said with a chuckle.

"You sure 'cause the Chicago bus just left and you weren't in that line." Drama said smoothly.

Tatiana watched me as I spoke. I laughed at that and said, "Yeah, you got me. Not the Chi. Maybe we went west, Minnesota, Iowa. Or we could be headed to Green Bay—trainin' camp starts next week. Shit, we could be in a suite at the Hilton 2 blocks away from you on Wisconsin Avenue or the Blue Diamond on 70th and Appleton. Fuck, we could be at the Howard Johnson in West Allis or the one on 6th and Michigan, 2 blocks from you again. Oh, and don't forget the Holiday Inn or Motel 8 in Oak Creek, the Sheraton in Glendale, or the Embassy Suites connected to the Grand Avenue Mall, a block away from you. All you know is that we ain't where you are! You lost kid, let it go!"

Drama seemed to contemplate my words, but his sense of superiority overran the logic of the situation. "Fuck that nigga! You and that bitch can't run! I'll find you!" He said with a scary kind of determination.

"Stubborn huh?! Fuck yo, you can be as pissed as a urinal in a bar, but when we hit Madison, Appleton, Janesville or wherever, me and my gorgeous girl will be goin' out to have a great time, then sexin' till we can't no mo'e and spendin' a lot of that cash yo' dumbass stole and tossed at my feet!

"Stop callin' me! I got ya number, and if I wanna speak wit' a bitch made cat, you'll hear from me! I'm out!" I said with a smile, then ended the call.

"Think he can find us again?" Tatiana asked

I shook my head to her question. "Bae, he is mad that we removed all control from his hands. That is what this has been about for a while now. I'm ready to fuck wit' him in return!" I said.

Tatiana's brow furrowed, as she asked, "What exactly are you saying Chris?"

I rolled atop her. "Maybe it's time we be proactive, fuck wit' him. Maybe we have fun at his expense!" I said with a grin while she caressed the back of my neck.

Tatiana chuckled, a look of pity or something similar washing over her face as she shook her head. "Is that smart?" she asked me.

With a cocky smile I said, "Yeah, I came up wit' it and we both know how epically brilliant my ideas have been so far."

She chuckled, shaking her head slightly as she said, "I am crazy about you baby, but how about we bring the narcissism down a few notches, okay cutie? You have it on 'sickening' and maybe you should be shooting for 'adorably obnoxious'." I laughed at her. She continued, adding, "You may be confident, but do keep in mind that he has guns, guys and experience."

I nodded, recognizing the facts in her words. "You're dead-on, but he can't outthink us, nor think beyond the confines of his own squareness. And he doesn't have you by his side either ma!"

She grinned wide, her fingers dancing in the tracks between my braids as she said, "Playing to my vanity huh, lover boy?"

I gave her a Cheshire cat smile, all teeth and said, "Can't argue wit' facts ma! I'm jus' pointin' out what's evident."

Tatiana rolled her eyes in reply, then laughed silently.

"Can you see ya brain when you do that?" I asked her.

"Do what?" She asked, lost.

"When you roll ya eyes. I wondered if you did it to see what was on ya mind!"

Tatiana laughed aloud, her head on the pillow. When she regained her composure, she said, "Shut up, that was extremely unfunny!"

I scoffed at her return, saying, " 'She says, while wiping tears from her eyes, smile unmoving.' "

She stared at me blankly, determined not to smile, then cracked saying, "Get off me, I'm not your friend!" I chuckled, rolling off of her. I stood and walked to the room door, then left. "Chris, Chris!" she yelled, but I didn't stop as I closed the door.

Seconds later she opened it saying, "Where are you going? I was just playing!"

I turned to face her while walking backwards. "To the vendin' machines. I want some chocolate before my next servin' of ya chocolate delights. You want somethin'?"

"Yes, jerk! I will be hurting you after you bring me back 2 Reese cups and a Milky Way!" she said with a smile.

"Okay but promise to be naked when you do!" I threw back at her then spun back around to watch where I was walking.

Tatiana laughed, then whispered-shouted, "Shut up!" disappearing her head back into the room.

I walked to the vending machines with a grin. The area, just beside the central stairway in the apex of the "V" had a trio of machines—one with candy and chips, one with juices and sodas, one with cakes and sandwiches. I put three $5's into the change machine, then commenced to buying ⅛ of the contents available.

A pair of white girls looking like the next set of strippers prepared to go on stage passed me. "Hey cutie!" a blond with emerald eyes said to me as they came up on my left.

"Hey ladies! May I go wherever you two are headed?" I said, before I could even catch myself.

"Why? You lonely?" the blond asked, stopping on the top step headed to the lower level. A brunette also paused by her side, looking my way.

Shocked by her pause as well as the other girls stopping too, I stammered, saying, "Uh...nah, my um...I'm just bein' stupid ma, ignore me!" I told her, trying to rip my gaze from her emerald-margarita toned irises.

"You sure because we will stay for you, sexy!" she said as I struggled to move away from her overheating gaze.

"Yeah, my girl..." I said, and the girl pulled out a card from a place it should not have been able to hide.

She handed it to me saying, "We can have fun with her too!" She threw me a naughty wink.

"Yeah, nah, we good but thanks though!" I told the two ladies.

The blond shrugged, then the pair walked off. I stood wordless as I watched their firm bodies bounce in all the right places as they moved down the stairs.

I returned to the room door with an icebag full of goodies, plus the card of one escort. I knocked and was asked, "Who's there?"

"Really Tati?"

"What's the password, sir?" she asked, then giggled.

"Oh yeah, that's what we on huh? Okay, what about...Orgasm!" I said quite loudly.

Tatiana laughed, then said "Eeeeennnttt!" mimicking a buzzer on a game show.

"A'ight. How 'bout this...'two-escorts-just-approached-me-sayin'-come-to-our-room-for-fun.' That work?"

The door opened, and she snatched me inside. I chuckled as she smiled. Tatiana asked, "Is that true?"

I handed her the card then unloaded the goods in the bed.

While ripping the card into little pieces, she said, "You will not be needing this!"

Tatiana and I sat on the bed, eating chocolates with the TV on, talking over a plan. I told her the things I had in my head, and she told me which seemed feasible, which were not, then her and I looked for ways to perfect the ones we liked.

"First, we need to figure out who he is and where he lives. That will let us be the predators, not the prey." I explained to Tatiana in the middle of my second Snickers bar.

She was on her second Reese Cup.

"Ooh, I can do that! My friend is a super nerd and had a cheating boyfriend. She caught him at another girl's house. She found an app for that. You put the cell number in, and it gives you ways to GPS it. You can also get the owners info if it is not a prepay deal without company ties." Tatiana shared, continuing with her candy.

"Wow!" I said, a bit shocked by the news. I added, "Maybe she should'a been givin' him more sex and spendin' less time on the computer."

Tatiana shot me a look, then punched my left thigh, saying, "Leave my friend alone! She was great to him! He was just a jerk!"

"What's it called?" I asked after shrugging to the boyfriend's character bashing.

"Asshole syndrome!" Tatiana said with an evil grin. I threw her a look that meant to convey "Really?!?" and she laughed. She continued. "Oh, you meant the app, huh? It's called 'Where now!"

I snorted then said, "Creative!" while I grabbed my phone and went to the App store. It popped right up. "$200, seriously?" I said while buying it.

"Stop being a penny pincher and download it!" Tatiana admonished, nudging me.

"Leave me be woman, I did!" I replied, nudging her back. "Give me the kid's phone. It's in the bookbag." I added while I looked at the app on my phone. "Because the phone—wait, let me see that." I said before Tatiana turned in the phone. I took it and turned the phone over in my hand. "Damn!" I said, disappointedly.

"What?" Tatiana asked.

"I hoped this phone was one with a sim card that I could take out and then they'd not be able to track it. Now we will jus' have to chance bein' traced in the few moments it'll be on." I told her.

Tatiana stared at me with a look of sincere concern. "You sure Chris? I don't enjoy being chased. it's too scary and I don't want to continually deal with that." The softness in her eyes made me want to run away to a different continent with her. Tatiana's vulnerability was so present and knowing something could happen to her made me want her a million miles away from this mess.

"Tati, I have a better idea. We'll wait till we have the plan properly diagramed, then turn on the phone in traffic. That'll give us the upper hand since he won't be able to hit a movin' target." I explained, placing the phone over on a nightstand.

Her face lit up and she said, "Great! What's the plan?"

At eleven that night, I left our hotel dressed in a black hoodie, shorts, a baseball cap, gloves and shades. I had a wire coathanger in hand as I walked around the back of our hotel, then behind the Marriott's also. Beyond the hotel were 2 rental car agencies, a Hertz and a Transport, Inc. . Their vehicles were lines up in two side-by-side lots, with a covered walkway between the two long rows of vehicles, the design like rudimentary tree branches.

I figured the office to be closed and empty by this time of night and stayed low, so I'd not be seen. I hopped the 4-foot chain link fence that separated the Marriott's lot, from the Transport Inc.'s property. I jogged at a crouch through their lot, staying in the shadows as best I could until I reached the Hertz fence, and climbed it quickly. I went to the key drop box, and made a hook from the wire hanger, then reached it into the drop box's slot, which wasn't big enough for a hand or anything else. I pushed the wire all the way to the bottom, using a trick my boy Rio back in New York told me he and some cats would do to snag new whips for chop shops. I'd never done it, but I figured that if Rio could, I'd be able to do it as well!

I dragged the hanger across the bottom a few times, keeping an eye out for anyone seeming to spot me with the traffic passing by on the busy, 4 lane Howell Avenue, I was about 30 yards west of. I was on the opposite side of the glass-windowed office, but from a distance, cars could catch me in their headlights. After 5 minutes and no luck, I returned to the Transport Inc.'s lot. I stayed low as I ran between the parked vehicles, then to the fence, stalking like a big cat. I climbed the fence fast and ran to the other branches of cars. Watching for any detection, I kneeled near the rear bumper of a car. Just across the street was the Airport's main entrance to their parking structure. It had TSA guards on duty, 24/7 and I did not desire them enlightening the sheriff of my presence, nor the Milwaukee police. Thankfully, no one seemed to be paying attention to me.

I moved to the drop box in a crouch. Hanger in hand, I fished it into the slot, and felt metal hit metal. I heard the unmistakable tingle of keys! I scraped the bottom, heard the keys again. I kept at it, feeling the keys shift around. I pulled the wire up but had no extra weight on it and dug around the bottom again. After 3 empty lifts of the wire, I felt something. A set was on the line. I pulled up slowly, and just as it reached the opening, the keys fell back into the pit. I cursed, then went back to digging. After ten minutes that felt like an hour later, I had more failures than I will dare admit here. In that eleventh minute, I finally had a set of keys securely on my hook. I was elated when the keys fell onto the concrete beneath me.

I picked the keychain up and looked at the logo. BMW—how lucky! I hit the door button on the key fob, watching the cars on the left and right of the path. Headlights winked on a 4-door Beamer, 6 rows down the south facing path. I jogged to the Mist blue sedan and climbed in. I hit the ignition button, once situated and after preparing the mirrors, and the car roared to life.

I checked the area, then pulled out of the parking spot. I drove out of the lot and turned south on Howell Avenue. Tatiana was in our room, waiting for me. I hit the horn 4 times, the signal I told her to listen for, and in seconds she was walking to the passenger side, hoodie on with a cap and shades on too. I hopped out and grabbed her door for her.

"Hey Batman!" she exclaimed, kissing me on my cheek.

I chuckled, replying, "Hey Catwoman! Is ya phone off?"

"Yep!" She said then sat in the car. I closed her door, rounded the car, then jumped back into the car, driving away.

I took the highway north to Downtown, then drove west up to 35th street, where I pulled off the freeway. We parked in a 24-hour Walgreen's parking lot, located on 35th and Wisconsin Avenue. First, Tatiana stepped out of the car with my phone, as I turned on the kid's phone, pulling up Drama's number after punching in the pin. Tatiana turned my phone on far away enough from the car that it would not connect it to the Beamer's Bluetooth System. I told her Drama's number and she typed it into the locator app, then walked into the all-purpose store to purchase the things we needed for our plans. With the kid's phone, I connected to the car's Bluetooth system, then called Drama.

"You still in Milwaukee, stupid?" he said with venom.

"Ouch! 'Stupid'?! Couldn't come harder than that? Just wanted you to kno' we wasn't 'bout to run from ya lame ass, got me? You be cool now, a'ight?" I said then hung up and turned the phone off again. A few minutes later, Tatiana walked out of the store with a few bags. I then ran into the store to snag the remaining requirements. I jogged out, and Tatiana drove away.

"I have his info, and all we have to do is pull it up when your phone is back on, then we can track him in real time, block-by-block, house-by-house if desired!" she explained.

"Damn bae, that's deep!" I said with an astonished chuckle. I added, "Please know that if you ever worry 'bout me bein' untrue, simply ask! This GPS shit is way too wild ma!"

She looked at me as she drove south on 35th, tossing me a skeptical grin, then asked, "You'd tell me if you cheated on me?"

I snorted then said, " Nah, cause I wouldn't have to! I would end us before I did that to you. If I'm not happy then stayin' wit' you and just cheatin' will not fix that! People are retarded for believin' that."

She chuckled softly then asked, "So, if we were married and had kids, you'd just leave me?"

"Woa! Wait, wait, wait! Who said I'd dare marry you 'cause it ain't happenin'!" I exclaimed swiftly.

"What?" she quizzed, her face a mask of all out shock.

I laughed and she punched me when she realized I was only joking.

"Asshole!" she said, then laughed.

CHAPTER FIFTEEN

We were southbound on 35th street, just hitting the bridge that connected the north and south sides of Milwaukee, talking. Our plan was to park along the banks of the Menominee River's western leg, under the 35th street viaduct, putting together the major actions regarding Drama.

"I'm just jokin' gorgeous. I'd never just leave you wit' our kids. Our kids sound kind of awesome!" I pointed out, caught up in the notion. I continued, saying, "I'd not leave a lady who mothered my babies unless it was just unfixable. Even then, it would be after tryin' everything! If I'm just unhappy, I'd sit down wit' you, go over my issues, see what yours might be, and we'd do what was needed to find accord again."

Tatiana digested what I explained in silence for a bit. "You'd never cheat though?" She asked as we were a block onto the bridge.

"What would be the point?" I asked her, pulling out a pack of Mamba fruit chews, and opening them.

"You eat a lot of candy!" she pointed out as we neared the halfway point on the bridge.

"Yep! Great oral hygiene habits, regular dentist appointments, so I'm good! Plus, you should be glad that I love the taste of chocolate 'cause I'll never get enough of tastin' you!" I said nonchalantly, then popped another piece of the fruity candy into my mouth. She threw a sexy smile my way.

"The point could be as simple as a desire to have sex with a woman other than me. You could be bored. You could simply be curious." she said, returning to the question I had asked prior to her candy comment.

"Hang a left at the lights in the middle of the bridge, okay ma?" I told her.

"Yeah."

"Those are valid points—stupid reasons but valid all the same. If I wanted sex wit' another dame or I'm bored, why not come to you? You can then—"

"Not having threesomes Chris, I'm not that way!" Tatiana said, slashing my sentence in two. We rolled down the eastbound lane of a ramp leading us to the Menominee River Valley, the unofficial dividing line of the north and south sides of Milwaukee. Tatiana followed the road through its curve and hung a right on Canal Street, heading east.

"Never said that. What I was gettin' at prior to bein' rudely interrupted was that we could look into ways to add sparks to our bedroom behaviors. We don't gotta add new ladies to our bed ma!" I explained to her.

Driving east on Canal Street, the Menominee river on our left, with its steel wall that rose about 3 feet above ground level. Ahead of us and to our left a few miles, we could see the lights of downtown against the blueback backdrop of the night sky.

"You sure because I've been cheated on before and I do not like how that feels." she admitted, staring at me with a hint of pain in her dark eyes, the ghost of boyfriends past haunting her precious heart.

"I kno' both sides of that situation myself which is why I carry this philosophy on it." I confessed, pointing her to a single row of parking slots beside the riverbank. She pulled into one and we began preparing ourselves for the actions we planned.

The Menominee River Valley was once a major industrial area, a huge part of Milwaukee's economy, carrying a high percentage of the city's factories, breweries, slaughterhouses plus many other key pieces to the the city's prosperity, historically. Now it was a tad rundown, with empty factories and warehouses, carrying only a minuscule number of those who once called the area home. The developers were doing their best to revitalize the area. The older places were being modernized, and new businesses had been introduced into the area.

The Milwaukee Brewers had an updated home there, and the Pottawatomie tribe of Native Americans had built a hotel/casino there as well. There were companies like Harley-Davidson trying to make residence in the valley, as well as other smaller organizations. I stepped out of the car when we had set everything up and walked a nice distance away from the vehicle. I pulled my phone from my pocket, pulled up the app and saw Drama's info on my screen:

Name: Cameron R. Bolden,

Address: 2017 North 41st street Milwaukee, WI 53208.

Underneath was a street map indicating his current location. It was a blinking icon, showing him currently located on 35th street, about four blocks from where Tatiana and I had been 10 minutes prior. I copied his personal info into my phone then turned both phones off and walked back to the car.

"What are you eatin'?" I asked Tatiana when I was in the car, and she was turning the Beamer on.

"Nothing." she said, her breath coming out as a fruity blast of yumminess.

"You liar! You stole my candy!" I said, making her giggle.

Her mouth barely opened as she again denied the accusation, saying, "Nuh-uh!"

"Jerk!" I said with a grin.

She laughed and as she swallowed the candy said, "I'm sorry, but they smelled so good!"

I chuckled then said, "Candy pilferer!" earning another laugh as she pulled the car out and drove us back west on Canal Street. I had Tatiana drive us by my old apartment, telling her that Drama's place was literally around the corner.

As she drove, we talked. "Chris, when this is all over, I expect a nice vacation, preferably on an island in the tropics!" she told me as we drove north on 35th street.

I snorted a chuckle, then said, "Don't stress that ma. I plan on us goin' to a few spots where we can just lounge. We gone need it! I've never been this stressed in my life!"

"You?! The only reason I ever even heard gunshots was because I resided in the projects. To have them flying in my direction intentionally has had me nearly peeing on myself!" Tatiana confessed with a nervous titter.

"Believe me ma, I've lived in hoods my whole life. It's a totally twisted predicament when guns are actually aimed your way. I swear to God Tati, I'm still—STILL— shocked and grateful that I don't have any new holes in my body, and that you are free of 'em too! I worry 'bout you more cause...I do silly shit regularly. Always been that way! But if you're hurt 'cause I refused to give his gold back..."

"Chris, stop that!" She said as we hit the lights on 35th and Highland Boulevard. "We will get this over with. Our plans will work! Okay?" She added, and I smiled, her faith in us heavier than my own, lending me confidence. "Okay Chris?" She pressed, her optimism adding bars to my own like improving signal strength.

"Yeah ma, it will! You right!" I replied with a sincere grin.

We drove to Lisbon Avenue, about 9 blocks north of Highland and hung a left, heading west to 41st street, passing my old place in the process. It was a half-hour past midnight and things were quiet on the block, but it was not bare of people as we drove north on the one-way street. We drove down Drama's block slowly. His place was a single-family home, 2 storied with a porch that went the full length of the houses face. It was dark colors, maybe brown with a covered porch. It sat atop a hill as did all homes on that side of the street. 2 candy painted cars were parked in front of the address his phone was registered to. The porch was empty.

"I should call him, see if he home 'cause I don't kno' which whip is his, ma!" I told her as we rolled past to a stop at the intersection of Lloyd and 41st street, 45 feet from his place.

"None of them look familiar?" She asked as she pulled away from the intersection.

"Nah ma, I don't recall seein' any except when I was out and about. None were in the lot at the hotel. Keep drivin' till you hit North Ave, then hang a right. There's a gas station on 37th. I'll get gas and we can see where he is usin' my phone, cool?" I explained, no other options coming to mind at that time.

"Okay but keep the gun in your pocket or something just in case he has people nearby who know your face." Tatiana said as we passed Garfield Street.

Minutes later we pulled into a Citgo, the first black owned and operated gas station in the area. Tatiana pulled the Beamer beside the outer pumps, and I climbed out, then headed to the station's interior.

A tar-toned brother asked me, "You need some of that good bag bruh? I got that proper greenery fam!"

"I'm smooth on that yo, but good lookin' anyway." I returned as I walked by him. I pulled up the app on my phone and as I entered the store, and told the fly black dame behind the glass panelled counter, "$25 on the B-M."

"Nice car, is it yours?" she asked.

"Nah, the wife's." I told her passing the cash with my focus on the phone

"She white?" The dame asked, and I pulled my nose out of my phone to meet her eyes. She was maybe 30, with a nice shape and pretty hazel eyes.

"You think so?"

"Most fine Black men go with white women." She said with a sad look in her eyes.

Tatiana happened to step from the car right then, and I pointed her direction. "There is my beautiful, strong, brilliant Black queen!" I said with conviction and pride in every adjective.

The lady smiled and said, "Happy to see that some of you appreciate us!"

"There is more than you kno'! And I'm very happy too!" I replied then walked out the store.

I stood by the pumps talking with Tatiana. "He's back home! I have a way to figure out which whip is his." I told her.

She squeezed my hand then asked, "How?" staring into my shaded eyes with her own.

"I'll tell you when we back in the car."

Tatiana climbed into the BMW as I watched the final pumping, paying attention to anyone who seemed to stare excessively. People came and went, but none seed to do more than admire the car, see me and keep moving. I replaced the nozzle and hopped back into the car.

Tatiana drove us away as I told her my plan. She took us back in front of my apartment, parking on the park side of Lisbon, right by the bus stop on 41st street.

"You sure this will work?" She asked as we sat there, looking over in the direction of a bar across the street that was in full swing, with people entering and leaving. The music leaked out onto the street with each opening of the door.

"Yeah. He'll come out whenever the kid's phone is turned on. He should hop into his car and bam, we good to go, a'ight?"

"Be quick then Chris, I am not trying to be in a high-speed chase!" Tatiana expressed, worry in her tone.

"Relax bae!" I started, smiling with all the confidence I could muster, finishing with, "He won't even kno' we here watchin' him!"

I called up Drama on the kid's phone. When he picked up, I said, "Hey lil' fella, you still woke?" Tatiana and I watched Drama's house attentively, waiting for him to emerge.

"Yeah bitch, I've been havin' my connects check around fo' you and that hoe you wit'." He spat venomously.

I chuckled then said, "Ah yeah, you see her up close yet? She gorgeous, yo!"

"Fuck, guess she'll be pretty in a casket too then!" He spoke.

No one had left his place yet.

I continued talking. "Morticians make most people look good. It's how they operate. You kno' what, I just wanted to see if you'd be cool wit' simply takin' ya gold and forgettin' 'bout us? Is that an option?"

Three guys stepped out Drama's front door. Tatiana nudged me but I waited to see what car Drama got into. "You 2 dead nigga!" he cackled.

"You sure 'cause I'm gettin' it right now. I'm in my apartment." I said in a friendly tone.

"Y'all dead!" he repeated.

I hit end call and killed the power to the phone as we watched Drama and a taller guy get into one car, while another guy hopped into a second car all alone. The cars pulled away from the curb headed in the opposite direction of our position. Tatiana drove away from where we had parked, heading east until she turned south on 40th street. We rode along the eastern edge of Washington Park.

"Relax ma, they not followin' us! They have no clue we in this car!" I shared with Tatiana when I noticed her eyes were nearly glued to the rearview mirror. I smiled as she glanced at me. "Now, my dear, we kno' both of them cars belong to him and his minions. Drive to Wisconsin Ave. Let's grab somethin' to eat. That'll give 'em time to get back home, and we can get some payback in motion, right ma?!"

"Right!" she replied with a girlish giggle.

We pulled into a Taco Bell's drive-thru on 22nd and Wisconsin Avenue. We scooped some tacos, burritos, drinks and cinnamon crisps, then parked on the busy Wisconsin Avenue to eat.

"What isle you wanna vacay at first?" I asked Tatiana between bites of my beef and bean burrito.

She crunched into a hard-shell taco then said with a sound nearly mimicking something emitted during lovemaking, "Goddd, I love Taco Bell!" I laughed at the look of sheer joy on her face. "This will be my pregnant food, watch Chris! This is soooo good!" Another pair of crunches later she answered my question. "I don't care! I just want to lay in the sand on a beautiful beach, play in some water, and enjoy every minute of every day!"

I smiled at that, picturing her in white bikini in white sands, her sable skin all kinda of sexy in the juxtaposition. "Sounds like perfection to me, no lie!" I told her, then continued to destroy my own food.

After we finished the late-night meal, Tatiana drove us over to the block Drama lived on, and absolutely no one was outside. It was just after 1:15am. She parked around the corner in an alley.

"Bae, I'm goin' to do this very fast, okay? I want you to stay right here. I'll be back in a couple minutes." I told her.

Tatiana leaned over and gave me a deep kiss. When we parted lips, she said, "Be careful Chris!"

I smiled, hoping to calm some of the anxiety she was feeling. I was nervous too, but I was doing this no matter what! "I will!" I told her

"I can keep an eye out for you. If I beep the horn, meet me at the gas station we used to gas up at earlier, okay." She said. I nodded, grabbed the bag of things we had prepared, and stepped out of the Beamer.

CHAPTER SIXTEEN

I walked nonchalantly from the Beamer parked at the lip of the alley on Lloyd Street, between 41st and 42nd streets, to Drama's block. I went to the first car, a red and black, brand-new Lexus, with crazy huge rims and dark tinted windows. I pulled out two bottles of lighter fluid, usually used to start up charcoal barbeque grills, and commenced to squirting streams of the clear liquid all over the car. Then I got down and sat the first set of six bottles of rubbing alcohol duct taped together under the gas tank spraying another line of the lighter fluid over the bottles.

I quickly went to the second car, a black and gray old school Impala from somewhere in the 60's, and did the exact same thing, staying attentive to any movements around me. When it was all set-in place, and I had drained every bottle of liquid flammables, I took a picture of both cars. I set the Impala ablaze first, then the Lexus. I took pictures of the cars on fire, then Drama's house, and jogged back to the B-M where Tatiana was waiting, sending the pics from my phone to the kid's.

I climbed in and called Drama on speakerphone as Tatiana reversed out of the alleyway, heading east on Lloyd. "Drama, I got a surprise for you!" I said, then sent him the pics without hearing him speak. "You see the flicks nigga? Ya cars are on fire, bruh!" I said with all out glee!

"What the—my Lex is—my Impala too?!?" Drama began as Tatiana, and I laughed. Drama screamed things at whomever was there with him and cursed into the phone. "You fucked up nigga! On my momma, I won't quit until I get my hands on you two! I swear to God pussy! I'm killin' every single person that you two love, jus' wait!"

Again, Tatiana and I laughed.

"This only the fuckin' beginning, Cameron! You kicked this off bitch! Now we play my game, and I promise you won't like the rules 'cause they a bit one-sided. Next ya crib goes, then the people close to you." I told him. I could hear sirens as we drove along the eastern edge of Washington park on 40th street headed south again.

"Imma catch you and you dead nigga, you dead!" He stated with a menace that probably could have caused someone in his presence to cower completely.

Again, Tatiana and I laughed, then I said, "Catch is if you can! Be careful though, I heard your cars were hot!"

Tatiana tossed in after laughing, "Those were nice cars too! Too bad they had to burn, but paybacks a bitch!"

"Shut the fuck up you stupid, black ass bitch! Imma rape you before I kill you, jus' watch!" Drama spat with more venom than a hungry cobra.

Tatiana's face turned dark instantly. "You bitch ass, worthless, small-dicked, Napoleon-complex-having, frail bodied pussy! Don't you ever disrespect me like that again or I will personally set fire to every aspect of your life!"

"Damn!" I said, then laughed. "We out Cameron! You stay cool now!" I added then hung up. Tatiana was still breathing fumes as we rounded Highland Boulevard, headed south. She was taking slow, deep breaths.

"You okay gorgeous?" I asked as she turned left, following Highland's eastern curve, driving alongside the Miller Brewery grounds.

She was quiet for a few minutes, saying nothing as we reached the lights on 35th street.

We turned south and after a few moments, she said, "Yes, I'm okay now. I hate when men talk to me disrespectfully, and I abhor them calling me 'black ass'!"

I reached over and rubbed her arm, saying "Tati, you are so beautiful! Yes, you are of a chocolate tone, but that is part of your appeal ma! Everything from your face to your figure, your hair to your hips, your lips to your legs, your smile to your soft skin, your darlin' persona to your dynamic mind all equate to perfection! I've never met a chocolate-toned dame half...shit, I've never met ANY woman in my life of any skin tone that carried beauty like you! Fuck how lowlifes view you Bae, because I see you as the goddess who left heaven for my heart and I thank you!"

Tatiana pulled over on 35th, but a few blocks north of the viaduct. She was in tears. I wasn't sure why, but she smiled as she leaned my way. The smile was as pure as Floridian spring waters. She placed her lips against mine, and as we kissed, I felt every drop of her adoration flow into my soul, as our tongues waltzed together. When she pulled her lips from mine, the world seemed to be one thousand times richer in color.

She stared at me with an epic smile for a few moments before saying, "I'm yours for as long as you want me! I promise!"

"Just cause I told the truth? What if I add, 'I adore your sexy little feet!?"She laughed loudly while shaking her head, in response.

We took the highway back to our hotel. I dropped Tatiana off, then took the car a few blocks north of the hotel, where I wiped every surface completely clean. I left hoping it would be reported stolen, and they would check the Bluetooth system, seeing the kid's phone number in its logs. I figured that would add a little more payback to the max. Walking under the starry skies. I smoked a Newport while thinking about the future. Howell Avenue was all but dead at this hour of the morning. I smiled carrying the bookbag we had taken with us, feeling fantastic. Every day of our life from there on had the potential to be all kinds of perfect, and I was excited to see what each moment would hold.

When I entered the room, Tatiana was in the shower. Her clothes were in a small pile in a corner of the room, folded neatly. I sat in the armchair, reclined, and relaxed. I heard the shower stop as I played on my phone, and not long after the bathroom door opened. Tatiana stepped out in nothing but a towel.

"Do I get to take that off you?" I asked as she walked my way.

She sat on my lap and said, "Do as you wish!" I carried her to the bed without a drop of hesitation.

I undid the towel and stared at her naked body. She pulled my face to hers and we began to kiss, her arms wrapping around my neck. I ran my left hand between her legs, rubbing her fiery middle, feeling its moisture. She released my neck, stood, and went to unbuckling and unzipping my shorts. I stood also, kissing on her and rubbing her wet pussy. My shorts fell and she made my boxers follow suit. I felt her grab my steel and our lips parted.

I removed my shirt as she held my rod in both hands, running her fingers up the underside, causing me to twitch. Then she began kissing me, slowly until her mouth engulfed the head of my piece completely. Staring at me, her brown eyes glowed like embers of passion blazing on my behalf. She went about her motions with a ferocity that had me lost in the feeling.

"Damn Tati...this...damn ma!" I managed to say, almost falling as I felt my knees go weak. "Shit ma, I love this ma!" I was able to finally get out during a point where she slowed, watching my reactions.

She returned to a hectic pace that led me to the edge, then paused asking, "You like this daddy?"

"God ma, you are amazing!" I replied, causing her to smile widely! She went back to it, pushing me back to an explosion which she let go into the towel she'd worn. I sat on the edge of the bed with a ringing in my ear.

"Enjoy that?" she asked with a smile.

"The best ma! Will you marry me?" I heard myself ask her.

She laughed then said, "Yes, but make love to me first!" I pushed her on her back and kissed her deep, loving how it felt to be this close to her again. I began kissing down her neck to her chest, playing with her nipples in my mouth. I nibbled, hearing her gasp and moan. When I began kissing down her torso, she stopped me. "What?" I questioned, confused.

"I need you inside of me, now!" she said, her eyes relaying an urgency I wouldn't dream of denying.

"Your wish..." I said then prepared the invasion if her equatorial area. I slid the crown over her swollen, soaked labia, feeling it glide between the lips.

"Oh yes!" Tatiana moaned, once I was squeezing into her.

I paused, though she rotated her hips wanting more. I pulled her hands above her head, entwining our fingers.

I stared into her eyes and asked, "You ready?"

Her lips quivered and she nodded emphatically. I slid slowly into her, watching her face contort from pleasure to a degree of pain as I pushed completely into her. She let out a sexy whine as I filled her with me, her hands squeezing mine tightly. I began a slow pace, nearly pulling completely out before filling her to the hilt. Her insides were like a human furnace, grabbing and wringing with every rotation of her slim hips and tight tummy.

I watched her slip through faces, her sounds beyond exciting. "I love you!" she gasped after her gyrations led her to an inner explosion. Her juices felt unbelievably grand on me.

"I love you too, Tati!" I said, picking up the pace. I let her hands go and she wrapped them around me, while I plunged into her, pushing her through another orgasm.

"Hold up, let me get at you in a deeper way, ma!" I said, pausing. I lifted her right leg up, her knee now near her breasts and asked, "You ready?"

"Oh god baby, this is going to drive me crazy!" she said, her eyes wide. I smiled and squeezed back into her. We started slow and her moans quickly shifted to yelps and squeals as I dug deep within her. She was squeezing me, bucking, and twitching as I felt her muscles contract and then she exploded, screaming out.

I went harder, now a slave to the pleasure granted by her tightness and warmth, until we were clapping into each other like a sexy applause. As she clutched me all over, I was sucking on her neck, feeling the vibrations of her vocals on my lips.

After a few more moments of our excursions into bliss, I pulled out of her asking, "You wanna ride me?" Her body was still in the midst of an extended orgasm, arching beneath me. She let out a whimper, her eyes rolling back in her head. I just watched until she was calm enough to react!

She took a breath where her lips quivered, then said, "You are killing me!"

"You wanna stop bae?"

"No!" she nearly yelled in response. I laughed then rolled onto my back. She climbed atop me and began kissing me. Her kisses held a sexy hunger that I was enjoying. I guided my stiffness into her, causing Tatiana to moan and squeeze my chest. I slid completely into her. She rotated her hip, then her lips slipped from mine, and her face slid to the left of mine. "I love how you make me feel Chris!" she moaned into my ear. "I'm lovin' every aspect of you ma!" I said as we began a slow pace, my hands cupping her perfect ass.

"Chris," she began, gasping softly, adding, "I want to have all of your babies!"

"You will!" I said as she began to pick up speed, her body sliding atop mine marvelously.

She was whining in my ear, saying, "I love you, I love you!" driving me insane.

She lifted her upper body up and started to bounce on my dick. Her face was in a sexual ecstasy and agony equally as she pounded me. I was really digging her in every manner. She felt exactly as a lady should and my hands held her precisely atop of me. I pushed my dick into her cream-soaked pussy as she grounded down onto me. She was yelling as I saw the white ring coating the lips of her chocolate pussy.

We both went faster, the bedsprings squeaking while the headboard made raucous love to the wall behind us, her and I lost in our pleasure. Then I felt my own climax on the verge of happening. "Ma, I'm 'bout to bust!" I told her.

She screamed out, "Oh Chris, do it, please!"

Together we both exploded, me holding her still as I shot into her. She thrashed and spasmed so sexily it only added to my enjoyment. We both seemed lost in orgasms that went on way longer than usual. I laid there with my eyes closed, both our bodies soaked and still lost in post-climax contentment. I was watching white explosions on my closed eyelids.

"Tati." I said when we both seemed to catch our breaths.

"Huh?" she answered.

"You make me see stars!" I told her.

She giggled then asked in a sugary tone, "Really?"

"Seriously ma! I've never met a dame who could do that!" I confessed.

She giggled again, planted a few kisses on my chest, then said, "You give me orgasms that seem to last forever! I feel like they just keep going!"

"Whatever!" I said playfully, hoping to goad her into more compliments.

"I'm for real!" she said in a whiney kind of tone.

"You got that good, good!" I said and she squealed in laughter.

"I love you boy!"

"I love you girl!"

We both laid in bed, talking until we drifted off into a peaceful slumber.

CHAPTER SEVENTEEN

I woke the next morning to my phone ringing. I stretched, searching for Tatiana who wasn't in bed with me. I grabbed my phone, noticing that it was just past 10am and Tatiana was the one calling me. "Hey love!" I said when I answered.

"Chris, get dressed! We have to leave, NOW!" Tatiana spat swiftly, panic in her voice.

I bolted up, quite concerned as I put my feet on the carpet. "What? Where are you?"

"Baby, get dressed! They saw me, they have found us!"

I scrambled, grabbing my boxers, then shorts while repeating slowly, "Where are you?"

"On my way into the lobby! Please get everything ready—we have to leave!" she said, then her phone went silent.

I was lost and confused like an Alzheimer's patient as I jumped into the rest of my clothes with the urgency of a fireman after an alarm was sounded. I was fully dressed, tossing things into bags when the door opened, and Tatiana entered the room looking like she had seen a goblin.

"What happened?" I asked, seeking clarity.

She dropped the white bag she had in her hand and grabbed her bag as she said in a whisper, "I'm so sorry Chris!" Tatiana was in the verge of tears as she headed for the bathroom.

I stopped her and said, "Explain what is goin' on bae!"

She trembled in my arms and dropped her face on my chest, sobbing as she spoke. "It was an accident! I woke up and checked what time it was! I grabbed that boy's phone and turned it on without paying any mind to what I was doing. When I recognized what I had done, a few minutes had passed, and I cut it off!"

She broke down when her words ended, falling into me as she cried. I caught her and sat with Tatiana on the bed. She added, "I went to get us some food from the hotel next door. When I left their restaurant, he was at the front desk with some other nigga. They noticed me but a lot of people were around, and I ran out the back exit, through the parking lot, to this hotel."

I didn't want her to imagine I was mad as she started tearful apologies. "Bae, relax! We have to stay clearheaded so we can get out of this. It was an accident, so forget it. This won't be like last night. Come on!" I said.

We got our bags ready near the door and I told her, "Mama, call the lobby. Ask the desk attendant if they saw your boyfriend. Describe what he had on and see what is said."

"Okay!" Tatiana said, trying to gather herself.

I grabbed the guns from my bookbag, sitting them on the bed then throwing the bag over my shoulder. I went to the room window and peeked through the curtain. I looked from one corner eastward then from the opposite corner westward. I saw no one as I heard Tatiana speak. I grabbed a plastic cup on my way to the door, where I put the cup to our room's door and my ear to the back of the cup.

Tatiana stopped talking, then ran to me, snatching me away from the door. She was noticeably spooked as she said in a scared whisper, "The desk attendant said him and his friend were headed up the stairs as we spoke."

I put on a hoodie, then had her do the same. "Listen," I began in a whisper, "I'm goin' to need you to stay close no matter what, a'ight?"

Tatiana nodded, her eyes still drenched in terror. "I love you, Chris!" She whispered.

"Love you too, duh!" I said smiling.

Tatiana returned a weak smile. I grabbed a gun, put it in my hoodie pocket, then picked up the other gun, keeping it in my hand. I went near the room's door, Tatiana right beside me. I saw no one through the peephole. I put the cup back to the door and heard talking that I could not decipher. I told her that. I was thinking about opening the door when my phone chimed. I moved faster than my thoughts, dropping the cup and snatching my phone out. I hit ignore. I switched it to vibrate immediately, seeing that the call showed "unknown caller" on the screen. Another call came through, showing "unknown caller", which I knew to be Drama. I ran to the room's phone, picked it up, and dialed the room across the hall, 4 rooms to our right. It rang as I allowed my phone to vibrate. I let my phone ring then hit ignore just as I ended the call to the other room.

"Tati, go see if they are nearby!" I whispered to her as she stood near the coat rack, to the right of the door.

She came back and told me, "He's to the right of us a few rooms."

My phone rang again, still only vibrating in my hand, and I dialed the other room's phone on the hotel phone. I let both ring a bit, then I hung up the hotel phone as I answered my cell.

"Drama, what's up?" I whispered with faux joy

"Found you! Saw that bitch! I'm here!" he said with an evil glee in his voice. I ended the call.

I waited for him to call again. "Tati," I said, "See if he still down the hall. " She checked, then looked my way nodding. My phone again began to vibrate, and I dialed the other room's phone again. I let both ring three times then hung up the hotel phone while answering mine. "What nigga? Damn!" I said.

"You and that bitch ready to die?" He asked in a cocky way that actually bothered me.

I chuckled nervously then said, "Really? I doubt it! Outta all these rooms here nigga? Axe that garbage!" I hung up on him again. "Tati, check the peephole again. If he still down the hall, unlock the door but do not open it. Jus' keep an eye on him and anyone wit' him."

"You sure?" she asked, face full of worry.

"Yeah ma, trust me!" I said as she bit her lip, holding back a sob.

My phone vibrated again, and I called the other room. After letting both ring a few times, I answered my cell with an irritated "What?!"

"You in room 225! I'm 'bout to come in!" he said excitedly.

"Oh shit!" I said under my breath just loud enough for him to hear me.

"Yeah, bitch nigga, we here!" he said with a sick cackle.

I play whispered, "Bae, get in the tub!" Tatiana looked at me, but I waved for her to stay where she was by the door.

"So, you opening the door? If I break down the door, I'm rapin' that bitch in your face before I kill you two!"

"Stop talkin' pussy! Run in here if you got nuts! I got somethin' fo' that ass, yo!" I said, then walked to the door. I checked the peephole, seeing Drama and another cat standing beside the other room's door. I saw Drama whisper into his goon's ear.

The henchman backed to the side of the hall our room's door was on."Time's up!" Drama said, and I saw the goon crash into the door

It didn't budge. Both Drama and his lackey, pistol in hand, rammed into the door, vanishing into the room as the door gave way. That was when Tatiana and I moved, dashing out of our room, heading in the opposite direction down the hall! Her duffle bag was on my shoulder, as she carried a bookbag. They were still inside the room as I looked over my shoulder just as we reached the stairs that headed to the rear doors at the apex of the "V".

We flew down the stairs dangerously fast, me with guns in both hands as we blew past the reception desk and out of the glass doors into the rear parking lot. We turned right, onto a pathway that led us east, looking to reach Howell Avenue. Suddenly something stopped Tatiana, who was in front of me. A dark-toned cat sat on an all-too-familiar yellow Cadillac. He saw us and reached towards his hip. I threw a shot in his direction from the gun in my right hand, as Tatiana began to run in the opposite direction.

The kid relocated as I chased after Tatiana who sprinted towards the back of the hotel, both of our heads low, trying to use the few cars lined along the pathway as bullet stoppers. The now familiar ratat-tat-tat-tat of automatic gunfire informed me that the kid had regained his composure. The ping-whiz of bullets ricocheting off of the concrete wall let us know he was not friendly. Car and hotel room windows exploded around us. I threw another shot at the guy, looking over my shoulder to get the shot near the gunman. He paused his firing just as Tatiana and I bent a corner of the hotel.

We ran to the front of the hotel, continuing past it's front parking lot, and connecting area with the Marriott, just as Drama and his original goon came out of the lobby doors of the place we had spent the night.

They both shot at us from about 60 yards away. We ducked between two dumpsters right beside the Marriott. All the bullets missed as we continued running. We rounded the front of the Marriott and I stuffed both pistols into the stomach pocket of the hoodie I wore, as we stayed moving eastward to Howell Avenue.

"There!" I heard someone yell and glanced over my shoulder just in time to see Drama and his goon raise their pistol even though we were about 50 yards from where he stood, moving quickly into 3 lanes of southbound traffic on Howell. Cars rolled past as we flew across the median, shots cracking off behind us while we moved at a slight slant through the northbound side of traffic. We didn't stop when the shots did but kept moving towards the nearby parking garages for the airport.

A pair of armed TSA guards watched as we ran past the glass windows of their office structure but didn't move. The roar of planes landing and taking off compounded with the traffic on the street must have drowned out all the gunshots. Tatiana and I probably looked like an everyday couple running late for a flight—the TSA guards did not even pay us a second glance. We reached the far northern end of the three-story parking structure and entered a small stairwell. Drama and his boys did not pursue. No one at all trailed us on foot but we moved up the stairs without pausing. I hoped they would have tried coming into the parking structure because that would have gotten TSA involved, seeing how they search all vehicles that enter the structure like Border Patrol at our country's border with Mexico.

On the second floor, Tatiana and I stepped out of the stairwell, walking south as we caught our breath, heading for the enclosed skywalk bridge to the terminals of the airport. "You a'ight Tati?" I asked as she sucked in deep breaths.

"Yes!" she replied, sounding seconds away from tears.

I stopped walking, and said, "Bae, block me from view."

She stopped, looked around, then stood in front of me. I used her body plus a car to shade me. I dropped the guns into my bookbag, then took off my hoodie. The sun was behind clouds, and the pavement was damp from predawn sprinkles, but I was sweating like I had been in a sauna. I put the hoodie away. Tatiana took hers off and put it in the bookbag as well.

"We gotta sit tight for a bit ma. They won't fuck wit' us here 'cause of the police presence, and I wanna be sure we all clear before we bounce!" I explained as we began walking again.

"Check the GPS." she reminded me as we crossed the bridge above the drop-off, pick-up point for passengers.

I chuckled at my own idiocy, palming my forehead, saying, "Duh! Good thinkin'!"

"At least I did something right this morning." she said in the saddest tone I had ever heard.

I stopped and pulled her into my arms. She had a pitiful look on her face, and her eyes could not meet mine. I lifted her face with a curled index finger under her chin. "Tati mami, it was an accident!"

"Yeah, one that almost turned us into Swiss cheese!" She said. I saw the yellow Cadillac drive below us as she spoke, but I decided to ignore it! There were words she needed to hear.

"You are good! I love you, and without you, I'd pro'ly be dead! I need you so buck up ma!" I said. She smiled, putting her hands on my face. She kissed me. Though I didn't want to, I cut our smooch short.

"Thank you!" she said. We walked the last few yards of the bridge, then into the sliding glass doors which let us into the airport terminal's main space.

"They jus' drove underneath us, so let's find a seat, relax for a bit until they are gone." I said as we stood in the terminal, surveying the scene.

The terminal was huge, with ticket counters on the opposite wall from the entrance we used, stretching about a hundred feet. There were signs with directions, roped lines, and many scanners for luggage being checked. Hanging from the ceiling were 2 antique planes, 1 from World War 2, the other from the Korean War. There were kiosks, chairs, TVs, small spaces partitioned for office-like privacy, and phone booths. The airport was somewhat busy, but not as much as I had imagined. People were all around us.

Tatiana pointed out a sign showing the direction to the food court, and we walked hand-in-hand towards that area. It was in the west end of the main terminal. The far west wall was all glass windows that lent us a panoramic view of the west end of the airport runways. We stepped into a line for a McDonald's and ordered. Standing in line, Tatiana picked lint from my face.

She smiled when I made a face, saying, "You have stuff there. Stop!" We grabbed our large meal and left the counter.

"Know what I had gotten us for breakfast?" Tatiana asked as we walked towards a far set of tables.

"Whip cream?" I answered as we sat by the windows in a corner where we could see all the people who came to the area. There were armed sheriffs walking around in pairs, talking and surveying the airport, giving Tatiana and I some comfort.

She laughed at my silly remark, then said, "No naughty hornball! Panny cakes—"

"Whatty what's?" I cut her off asking.

"Pancakes." she corrected, rolling her eyes as I smiled. She continued, "Eggs, hashbrowns, toast and sausages."

I snorted, chewing a sausage patty. "Ah, basically, exactly what I ordered then." I noted.

"Yep!" she said with a smile adding, "But I picked scrambled AND fried eggs. I did not know which you would prefer."

"I'm good wit' either, as long as they are fully cooked. Runny eggs gross me out!"

"I know right? I almost vomit on sight when people are eating that! It's like, 'Eww!'." she exclaimed, making an adorable disgust-face.

I smiled at how animated she had become over eggs. I couldn't help but chuckle.

"You are laughing at me, aren't you?" she asked as she pouted playfully.

I nodded, chewing on a hashbrown. She wrinkled her nose, then laughed. "You're serious 'bout ya eggs!" I said and she tossed her head back in laughter.

"Shut up!" she admonished, lightly whacking me on my forearm.

"You're some type of heaven, I swear!" I told her, and she blushed, dropping her face shyly as she smiled.

She looked at me with her head low, then said, "Thank you!" sweetly. We ate and conversed for a while.

I pulled out my phone as did Tatiana. I saw that I had a few messages and texts I had missed during the melee. I saw a voicemail from Drama and listened to him spew some threats that he could not make good on at that exact moment. I checked his location using the app and saw that he was on the expressway now heading towards Downtown.

"Bae, we can go. He on his way home. Guess he decided all the law in the area cramped his plans." I said, then watched Tatiana's eyes close in a sorrowful way. "Let it go Tati!" I told her, in a calm tone while rubbing her hand.

"Huh? How can you read me already?" She asked, her head cocked to the side with a curious smirk on her face.

"Jus' saw it, sensed it." I answered. When she smiled at me, I felt her love flow into me like the air I breathed.

We put away our tray, then headed to the ground level of the airport.

CHAPTER EIGHTEEN

While walking through the main terminal, a female voice called my name. I slowed, looking around for the face it came from but saw no one I recognized. "You hear that too?" I asked Tatiana as she too surveyed the area.

"Yeah, it was a woman's voice." She replied. I heard the yell of my name a second time, just to our right.

I looked to see a tall, brown sugar toned sister with a sexy figure waving at me as she neared Tatiana and I. "You know Tasha?" Tatiana asked as the lady got closer.

"Shit, the better question is 'YOU kno' Tasha?'" I replied, staring at Tatiana with the exact same inquisitive look she was handing me.

Tasha was thin, but had long legs, with a face that was easily expressive, but always a work of pure beauty. She was tall, with wavy black hair that hung just below her shoulders, and brown eyes that reminded me of coffee with that perfect blend of milk. She happened to be one of my greatest loves from those late-teen years when you are really starting to understand the dynamics of romance.

"Hey Chris, hey Tatiana! What are you two doing here?" She asked, adding, "Nice to see you two. Odd, but nice!" She leaned into hug Tatiana, then me.

"What's up Tash, how ya been?" I asked while embracing her.

"Great! I've been great!" she replied with a sincere smile. "How have you been doing Tatiana?"

"Good, girl. Really good!" Tatiana answered happily.

"How do you ladies kno' one another?" I asked, extremely curious about this new revelation.

"We are longtime friends! SOMEONE was too good for a university in Southern Wisconsin. Ran off to Michigan. And that is why my Golden Eagles CRUSHED your puny Wolverines in the Sweet 16!" Tatiana said, then stuck her tongue out at Tasha.

Tasha feigned hurt by gasping and holding her chest. Then she rebounded, saying, "So! That's why we have a football team, and you don't!" She stuck her tongue out in return. All of us laughed.

"Tati, Tasha and I dated a couple years back." I said, when our laughs subsided.

"Really?" Tatiana started, glancing at me and Tasha with a shocked grin. "Tash, you never mentioned a 'Chris'." she added.

"I spoke of him by the nickname my mom gave him. 'Cee-Kay'." Tasha explained, then a mask of sadness flashed across her face as she continued: "Chris is a sore spot."

"YOU are 'Cee-Kay'?" Tatiana asked. Then she pushed me, saying, "You had better not have done my girl wrong, cause—"

Tasha smiled, cutting her off saying, "Relax Tata, he never cheated or did me improperly at all! He followed his heart to me, and... circumstances pulled us apart. He's a good one!" After saying that, Tasha seemed fade from the moment, seemingly lost in a yesterday. Quickly she was back, and said, "Well, what are you two doing here? My flight from my boyfriend's parents place in Atlanta just landed. You two coming from somewhere?"

I spoke up to keep Tatiana from lying to her friend. "We jus' got in from O'Hare. I took Tati to see my mommy. We've been datin' for a few months and came back to do SummerFest today."

"Oh." Tasha said, then asked, "You still living in Westlawn?"

Tatiana shook her head, saying, "Nope, moved out. I saw your mom move and I was so sad. But moving out of the projects is always a great thing!"

"Yes, it is, yes, it is! Where do you live now?"

"We," I started, still not wanting Tatiana to lie, "have an apartment on the South side near Forest Home and Morgan, in the Jackson Park neighborhood, right by Alverno College."

Tasha's eyebrows raised then fell, "Wow! You two are serious! Living together, meeting parents. We were together for over a year, and I never had his home phone number." She said.

"Tash, you kno' it wasn't like that. You had my cell number, and I was never at home!" I said, defending a situation that at the time, was way more complicated than it should've been for a love so laced in promise.

"I know, I know. I'm just being envious! Ignore me!" she said and flashed a smile to Tatiana and I. She continued, saying, "Tata, give me your number so we can gossip about Chris behind his back." They laughed then exchanged numbers. Tasha gave us both hugs, then we went our separate ways. Tatiana and I hopped into a cab.

"Running into me with you was bittersweet for Tash." Tatiana said as we rode northward on the freeway headed to the Pfister hotel downtown, one of the most storied and ritzier hotels in the city.

"I kno', but what was I to do? Be honest? We have been livin' together since we met. You WILL meet my mom. The past I cannot change, and would you want me to if I could?" I asked.

"No." Tatiana answered.

"I surely wasn't 'bout to explain our real reason for bumpin' into her."

"Yeah, I know. I just felt bad seeing her hurt. She was my best friend before she left, and we drifted apart."

"Well, she has a boyfriend so..." I put out there.

"Yeah, I know."

"Oh," I began, changing the subject. "I wanna go to SummerFest today." I said as I stared out the window, watching the scenery go by beside us.

"What? Are you insane?" She exclaimed, her eyes wide with disbelief.

"Naaahhhh. We can bae." I said calmly.

"We CAN do a billion things. We CAN jump from buildings without parachutes to see how flying feels. We CAN shoot ourselves in the genital area to see what that is like. We can play in an alligator's nest to see how the animal will react, but I'm not suicidal! Going to SummerFest today, a day where most people will be there, a small fraction of them actively looking for us is suicidal!" She said, still looking at me as though I had lost my mind.

I chuckled, then said, "And the Oscar for Most Dramatic Actress in the back of a Cab goes to...wait for it...TATIANA!!!"

She gasped, saying, "Thank you, thank you! I'd like to thank my jerk—" she punched my left thigh "—hubby for not—" another emphasizing thigh punch "—taking—" punch "—me—" punch "—seriously!"

"Ouch! A'ight, okay, okay!" I said, partially laughing as I tried to catch her small fist while the cabbie eyed from the rearview mirror with a look that said he deemed us the epitome of dysfunction.

"Listen ma, it'd not be dangerous for a few reasons." I said, and she gave me a gaze full of skepticism.

"Really? Name one!" She challenged.

"Metal detectors, hundreds of police. No way they try movin' on us wit' that many witnesses! Plus, I doubt anybody'll be havin' an eye out for us like that! Friday was an anomaly. 2 days...folks ain't got that kind of attention span to maintain interest like that." I explained

"I do not like it, Chris! It feels like an unnecessary risk." She said, concern in her eyes.

In the whiniest 3-year old's voice I could muster, I said with my arms folded and a pout, "But it's the best day to go because of the fireworks, and I don't wanna be stuck in a telly all day! Also," I added, my voice and demeanor back to normal, "Friday I had on the same clothes from when they took my picture. They ain't holding' a clue as to what we rockin', where we at or nothin' ma! Even if they snapped a pic of us at the Lakefront, we don't stick out like that in a crowd of hundreds of couples. That's a low estimate for SummerFest ma, you kno' that! We will be safe bae, believe that!" I said.

Tatiana looked away from me in contemplation, facing west as we reached the Hoyne Bridge, just moments from Downtown. I pulled out my phone, the pulled up the calendar page for SummerFest to check the artists slated to perform for that day. Seeing who was doing shows that afternoon and night, I went to my music cache. I played a sing by Melanee Fiona named "Wrong side of a love song".

Tatiana spun my way, smiling as she said, "I love that song!"

"Really? She'll be there! Along with Corinne Bailey Rae, Jon Legend, and T.I. Those are jus' the ones I like!" I informed her, hoping this attempt at manipulation was what would win her over.

I saw her internal struggle for a few moments. Finally, she said, "Okay, but if I say I want to leave, we leave!" She made sure I knew she meant business by the intensity of her look.

"I don't doubt ya intuition slightly! Say the word and we out!" That earned me a smile as we pulled up in front of the Pfister.

A doorman opened the cab door for us, as I paid the fair. I handed the doorman a $10 after he walked us to the door and opened it for Tatiana and me. We entered the lobby and went up to the concierge desk.

The Pfister's antique, turn of the century design, kicked off a vibe from a bygone time. The lobby was spacious with a refined elegance from an era well removed from today's ideals in that regard. It was crystal chandeliers, Oriental rugs, wrought-iron handrails, marble, and beautiful, old-fashioned drapes. Walking in, you saw people in modern dress, but it wouldn't have raised an eyebrow if a lady in a bell-shaped dress, all ruffles, wires, and lace with elbow-length gloves and an itty-bitty umbrella passed you in the place. As a matter of fact, there were many rumors of their being ghosts clad in such garments floating around certain areas of the building. It was a prestigious place, classy with its time-capsule type of nostalgia. The hotel held a relaxed environment, and wasn't the place many dope-dealing, hotheaded hustlers came to on the regular.

    The front desk was on the left, a couple yards from the Wisconsin Avenue entrance. A small hallway led us under stairs until it opened up to the spacious lobby. Glass floor-to-ceiling windows composed the east facing wall for the whole lobby. The space between the counter and windows were full of leather couches and chairs, with plants, coffee tables and beautiful rugs. People sat sporadically, in small numbers, conversing, reading papers, and enjoying the ambiance. The people were mainly white and a tad closer to senior citizen age then twenty to thirty, which I was happy about.

    We were greeted by a 30-ish lady at the desk, who smiled brilliantly, which matched the shade of blue her eyes emitted. "Hi! How may I help you 2 today?" She asked as pleasantly as I had ever heard anyone address me before.

"We would like a room for tonight please." Tatiana said, with an equally vibrant smile.

"And tomorrow." I added. Tatiana looked at me, so I said, "It's the 4th ma. We'll need a place then too."

She nodded, then said to the receptionist, "Yes, then next 2 days please."

"Sure." The lady started, then began typing into a keyboard I could not see. "Now, will that be one bed or two?"

"I don't kno' if I wanna share a bed wit' this one. She might try 'touching' me again." I said to the concierge in a conspiratorial tone while leaning closer to the desk.

Tatiana and the concierge lady laughed. After a few seconds Tatiana said, "Shush! Just for that, you need not EVER worry about being 'touched' by me again!"

I chuckled, then kissed Tatiana on the cheek. The lady behind the desk smiled saying, "You two are adorable! May I have a credit card?"

Tatiana looked at me and I made a face while shaking my head. She pulled her purse from the bookbag she carried and handed over a Visa. "Can we pay in cash though? I only use that in times of absolute emergency, and we have the cash."

"Really Tati?" I said, throwing her 'the look'.

"Second thought, bill the card." Tatiana said, chuckling to herself.

"Oh, and may we have a room as high up as possible in the southeast edge of the buildin' please! I love the lake and skyline views in that direction." I said as Tatiana handed over her credit card.

"That is doable!" the lady said. Seconds later, she handed back Tatiana's card and a keycard for the room.

With that, we walked over to the elevators on the opposite end of the Wisconsin Avenue entrance. Together we stepped into a very modern (Thank God!) elevator car, riding up to the 7th floor. It was literally in the corner of the square-shaped building. We opened the room's door and was greeted with an amazing view of the Lakefront, 4 blocks east of where we stood, all at a downhill angle.

"Tati!" I exclaimed, standing in front of the windows. "You can see the art museum, most of the SummerFest grounds, the water...it's beautiful!"

Tatiana wrapped her arms around me from behind, chuckling slightly at my excitement as she looked around my right shoulder. "Yeah, it is a beautiful sight! We can watch the fireworks from here if things get sketchy." She said.

"That's acceptable!" I said, turning to face her, then wrapping her in my arms and lips.

The room was spacious and exquisite. The bathroom was in the wall behind the bed, which was in a position allowing you to lay in bed and see out the windows on both the south and east walls. The flat screen TV sat on an area where the windows were spaced wide apart, a love seat and armchair facing it, with end tables and a coffee table finishing up that area. The wall beside the door had a minibar with a teeny refrigerator, plus a small table with two chairs. On an end table and on a nightstand beside the bed sat a pair of cordless phones. The bathroom only perpetuated the ritzy feel of the hotel. It had a nice, Jack and Jill sink, claw footed tub, and an all-gold finish.

Tatiana shared a bath in the oversized tub. It was different, and a tad difficult at first, especially since being naked in each other's presence turned us on light like switches. We figured out a solution though. Tatiana crawled on top of me, and we made love, slowly, the warm water enhancing our pleasure. My hands caressed every part of her upper and middle body as her moans, whines and the water sounds made an awesome symphony of our passion. I sent her through countless orgasms before I let loose a torrent into her tight body. We kissed for a while until we returned from our heavenly venture, and then we were able to bathe minus issue.

"I can rebraid your hair if you want." Tatiana offered after we were out of the tub and dressing.

"Would it take long 'cause we got a few things to handle before we go to SummerFest and its already one." I told her while putting on my socks, then one Air Jordan shoe.

"Like what?" she asked, adding, "It would take no more than 30 minutes. I'm not taking them down and doing it all from the start. Just rebranding them as they are. Get them back crisp."

"Yeah, 'cause somebody made me sweat out my perm!" I said, accusatorially.

She laughed, saying, "Whatever!"

"Jokes aside, that'll work. I want to go get some money orders and a new car."

Tatiana poked her head out the bathroom, where she was still curling the edges of her hair as she asked, "A car? Why?"

"Well, they really help you get from one place to another." I said, earning an eyeroll from Tatiana, which made me smile. "Nah, for the final plans regarding Drama! I wanna end this shit tonight, bae!"

"Noooo!" Tatiana said, pouting and whiney. She put the curling iron down in the bathroom, then stomped to the bed and plopped down heavily beside me. "Chris, I want to spend the rest of today and all of tomorrow simply enjoying ourselves. I am tired of being shot at, chased and scared!"

Tatiana was in tears, and I felt my heart begin to shred. I pulled her into my arms, then said, "Tati, I hear you ma. Listen," I began, and she looked into my eyes. "Today, we do SummerFest. Tomorrow we will do somethin' special. Tuesday you can stay here while I put in action whatever plan I come up wit' regradin' that nigga, a'ight?"

She smiled while still sniffling, then said, "Yes and no! You are NOT doing it by yourself! I am going to help! We just have to put together a plan that does more than piss him off!"

I chuckled slightly, then said, "Definitely ma, this shit is NOT fun! I've earned 25 years' worth anxiety from this, and I'm ready to lean back wit' you and see what we can do together. But we do need a car to drive for now ma."

"I see how that will help!" She said, now all smiles. I kissed her. When our lips disconnected, she asked, "What 'something special' will we do tomorrow?"

I chuckled slightly, then answered, "You'll see!"

She pouted, then pried, saying, "Tell me, puh-leeeesseee!"

"Nope! You'll love it tho', promise!" I said with a grin.

She stood, pushed me to a reclining position, saying, "Meanie!" She laughed, then walked back into the bathroom, tossing over her shoulder, "Evil one!"

While Tatiana rebraided my hair, I counted out 20 thousand in loose bills, and we left as soon as she had my hair crisp.

CHAPTER NINETEEN

We took a cab west up Wisconsin Avenue, driving through rather relaxed Downtown traffic. On 27th street, we took a left heading south and crossed the 27th street viaduct. On the south end of the bridge, we passed the Mitchell Park Domes, a trio of huge botanical gardens in glass, Fabergé egg looking domes which seemingly grew from the grass about 75 feet high. We continued south for about 20 minutes until we reached a used car place located on the northeast corner of 27th and Layton Drive. The cab let is out in from of the glass-windowed dealership. The lot was like a garden of cars, the sun reflecting off hoods and windows brightly. I paid the fair as we exited the vehicle, surveying the rows of not-so-late model rides in great condition.

"Are we seeking a long or short-term car?" Tatiana asked as we walked down one of the lanes between parked vehicles.

"Hadn't even considered that, but we can spend a decent amount of cash, so we can cop a decent whip, ma." I told her as I checked out a grey Monte Carlo, newer model.

"So, what do you like in cars?" she asked, walking up to a black Chrysler Sebring.

"Fast cars!" I answered

She chuckled, looking over her shoulder as she laughed. "I figured that. What I meant was type or model."

"Oh," I responded with a grin, adding, "Older model Mustangs are my fave ma!" "We have a '67 Shelby back here." a man's voice with a southern twang said from behind us. Tatiana and I turned facing him. He had a schiester smile with slicked back hair, as he rocked the suit of a Southern Protestant Deacon. Tatiana and I met eyes, cracked grins, then looked back at him.

"Uh, you do?" Tatiana inquired, forcing back a chuckle.

"Yeah," he began, extending a hand to Tatiana, continuing, "we surely do ma'am. I'm Roger and it's a true pleasure!"

She shook his hand reluctantly, saying, "I'm Tatiana and this is Chris."

He reached my way, and I too shook the clammy appendage. "Nice to meet you, Roger." I said, doing my best to ignore the look Tatiana was throwing me from over his shoulder.

"Def'nitely, the pleasure is all mine!" He said, releasing my hand, adding, "Overheard yew sayin' how yew fancy Mustangs. We have a '67 Shelby plus a few others more recent if you'll follow me."

We did, with me wiping my hand the moment he turned away from me. Tatiana then clasped my hand, snickering into my shoulder as we walked, and Roger talked. We reached a whole family of Mustangs, ranging from newer models to the '67.

"These are all quite lovely, as you can see. The Shelby is in great condition, runs well, has all its original equipment. Some things need to be updates due to normal wear and tear, but all we are seeking is a very respectable $5,700. She has no major problems, could use a paint job, maybe some new tires, but that's what young folk do with older cars today anyway, right?" Roger said.

I circled the green Shelby to the driver's side, checking the interior as Tatiana walked to the passenger's side investigating the car. "How many miles?" I heard Tatiana ask and I looked over at her, surprised that she'd know to make such an inquiry.

"About 50 thousand, but don't quote me there." Roger answered.

It was my time to speak. "Any accidents leading to body work? Can we get the Carfax?"

"Not a one!" Roger answered, then said, "How about I run, grab the keys, so we can check it out closer?"

"Sounds great to us." Tatiana said as I looked at the tailpipe and back end, noticing a few tiny rust spots.

"Is he for real ma?" I asked her, popping up from behind the car, a chuckle in my tone, when the salesman was out of earshot.

She laughed as I walked towards her. When I reached her, she put her forehead on my chin, then said, "I know! He is a walking, talking stereotype!"

We both laughed aloud. After a few seconds, I asked, "Do we trust him?"

Tatiana emitted a scoff of a laugh, then answered, "Um, let's trust us and do what best suits us!" I smiled, planted a kiss on her lips, then we both watched as Roger walked back towards us.

"Alright then, let's open her up!" Roger, the slicked back hair, (probable) shyster with the southern ascent said. He opened the driver's side door and climbed I'm, then opened the passenger's side door. Keys in the ignition, the car made a chug-chug sound, trying, but not managing to turn over. He turned the keys a second time and the engine chug-a-chug-chugged itself to life. "She's been sittin' for a while, which accounts for that bit of hesitation." Roger explained.

"Hit the gas." I said, walking to the rear of the passenger's side and standing there. The engine roared again, causing the car to shake slightly. A pair of dark clouds exited the exhaust. I walked up to the driver's side when the clouds vanished and asked Roger, "Yo, the black clouds aren't a regular thing, are they?"

"Just a product of infrequent use. Those are just clogs from it sittin'. She's a beauty, truly!" He replied, a wide crocodile smile on his face.

"Tati, close that door please. Roger, drive it a lap around the lot." I said, straight faced.

"Oh, well alright." He said, then closed the driver's side door.

I backed up, watching the vehicle while idling. With a slight chug, then a clunk, the car pulled away and slowly drove the square path around the lot.

"Sounds fine baby, what do you think?" Tatiana asked as we both stood, my right arm around her waist, listening and watching the car. "Yeah. I wanna ride in it too, see what it's like inside as well." I told her

When Roger returned, I told him, "Can we ride a lap wit' you?" "Sure, hop in!" he replied excitedly. Tatiana and I climbed in, me sitting in the backseat.

"Such a gentleman!" Tatiana chimed in, using an adorable southern accent as she fluttered her eyes preciously. Robert and I chuckled at her.

"You only have an AM-FM radio, but the heat and AC are in workin' order. The mileage is at just under 63 thousand, which isn't bad. All the dials work."

Roger spoke with a passion as he navigated the small lot. The vibration felt normal, and all the sounds seemed regular. Tatiana asked a few questions then I tossed him a few as we drove a 2nd, then 3rd circuit.

After the 3rd lap, he pulled up in front of the sales office and asked, "What ya think?"

"Give us a moment." I said and gave Tatiana a head motion to step out of the car. She opened her door and climbed out, with me following behind her. Roger cut the engine as Tatiana, and I walked away from the car. I stopped and said, "Tati, we gotta check the engine and trunk bae." We both retraced the few steps back to the car as Roger climbed out. He looked expectant but my face stayed relaxed. "I'm sorry but we need to take a look at the engine wit' the car on."

Roger's face went a twitch down at the word 'Sorry' but lit back up when I posed the question. "Sure, sure, hold on." He said, slipping right back into the car with exuberance. It came to life in the first try. He popped the hood and I stood there watching the movements. Tatiana stood a bit to my left, looking at the motor, then glancing at me.

"Can you kill it, then start her up again?" I asked Roger.

"Surely!" he said as Tatiana walked up beside me.

"What are you looking for?" Tatiana asked, curiously examining the moving gaskets and doohickeys. The engine died, then a few seconds later was restarted.

"No clue, but let's pretend, a'ight?" I said, smiling at her. She laughed, hip bumping me lovingly.

"You are too silly!" she told me

"I'll need you to be the bad cop, okay?" I said, watching things I knew nothing about as they hopefully did exactly what they were supposed to do.

"You like it, I don't, right?" she asked, and I nodded.

"Roger, give it some gas!" I yelled, leaning around the hood to catch his eyes.

"Alright, I'm fine with that!" Tatiana confirmed as the engine roared.

"We good Rodger. Can you pop the trunk?" I asked, closing the hood with a slam.

"Sure can." He said. Roger exited the car and used the key to open the trunk. It was clean and had a spare inside. Tatiana looked it over with me. We looked at each other, shrugged, then I closed the trunk.

"Roger, give us a few ticks to talk things over!" I told the salesman.

"Go ahead, take your time." Rodger said after he climbed out the car.

Tatiana and I walked to a nearby bus shelter along the curb of the northbound side of 27th street traffic. The salesman leaned against the car, watching us.

"Don't smile Tati." I said as we stood about 10 feet from the curb.

"I won't." she said straight faced, one eyebrow raised in a challenging manner.

"Like it?" I asked her.

"I do, but that hesitation scares me. What if it is a real issue?" she asked, a mild attitude in her words.

"I don't kno' ma, but I would love gettin' that rebuilt. We do have the paper for that!" I told her with a smile.

"Stop!" She exclaimed angrily, catching me completely off guard with her display. Quieter she added, "You can't smile, or I will break character!" Her admonishment was complete with a pissed look on her face.

Animatedly I said, "We'll get it, but I'll tell him 4 thou, and haggle to somewhere just under 5, okay?"

"Why? I liked the used Lexus from the dealership in West Allis. It looked nic-er, was cheap-er, ran bet-ter AND came with a war-ran-ty!" She yelled at me, using her hands to accentuate her points.

I gently wrapped her hands in mine, and held them in my own as if pleading, then said, "As soon as I finish talkin' storm away, and when I approach you again, wave me off." She winked at me, flung my hands down off of hers, then stomped away to a spot 5 yards away.

I looked to the sky, now sunny and clear, rubbed my face, eyed Roger and gave him the 'one second' show with my hand, then walked over to Tatiana, whose back had been to me. "You's a good ass actress lady!" I said, wrapping my arms around her from behind.

She laughed, motion and noiselessly, then asked, "I know! Ready for your costly victory?"

"Almost! Make me work for it a tad harder." I answered.

"Go for it!" she said, and I slid around her until we were face-to-face.

I put my hands in a clasped position as if begging, my face matching my pleading look. Arms folded, her right heel tapping. She stared off over my right shoulder. "Mama please. Please Tati!" I said. She did not say a word. For a few seconds, the only sounds were of the passing cars and the click of the ball of her heel hitting the sidewalk.

Finally, with a grin only for my eyes, she clicked her tongue and said, "You owe me big time!"

"Yes!" I exclaimed, hugging her.

Tatiana waited a second then said loudly, "Get off me! Let's do this so we can leave!" with more venom than a Coral snake.

We walked to where Roger stood. He shot us a grin while asking, "Everything okay?"

Tatiana still had her arms crossed and gave neither the salesman nor myself anything but attitude. "Um..." I began shakily, adding, "Pro'ly not gettin' any fo' a while, and Imma be workin' plenty overtime shifts to get the funds for makeup gifts, but we will take the car!"

Roger put on a solemn expression and led us into the building then into his cubicle office in a sea of half a dozen other indistinct ones. 2 glass offices sat to the left of the entrance. We sat in a pair of chairs directly across the desk from the salesman. "Here's the Carfax " Roger said, handing us a printout history of the car. It said nothing concerning about the car.

"A'ight Roger, we are lovin' the car—"

"No, YOU are loving this car!" Tatiana said, slashing my sentence with the ferocity of those fancy knives they are always advertising on TV.

"Recalibratin' that statement. I am lovin' the car. The sole issue is this...the figure you puttin' out there is top heavy. Its beyond our budget by way too much. Can we chop that down to about 4?" I explained with a semi-hopeful gleam in my eyes.

He leaned back in his chair and looked to the ceiling. He exhaled noisily and slow. "I cannot go so low. How about we do 5200? That too far above your range?" Roger asked.

"It really is. Look, I get that you gotta make money, and ya bosses gotta make money, but work wit' me man. My lady isn't at all enthused about gettin' this car and—" I began, with Tatiana jumping in unexpectedly.

"Baby, the car is too much, and the Lexus from the other place is so much better! This car has none of the features and is not worth the money!" Tatiana said, showing an obvious lack of desire for the Shelby.

I exhaled, and was about to respond, when Roger decided to jump in. Seemingly, he saw a potential sale seeping through his fingers. "Listen, what I can do is drop it to $4,900. How does that feel?" I looked to Tatiana expectantly. She lent me a pissed gaze, rolled her eyes, and turned her face away from me.

I took a deep breath, looked at Roger and said, "Sounds proper to me."

The instant the words left my mouth, Tatiana stood, turned from us and walked out of the cubicle, saying only, "I'll be outside."

I reached for her, but she pushed my hand away. "Bae? Tati! Tatiana!" I exclaimed as she stormed off. When she was out of the building, I focused on the salesman again. I took a deep breath, then exhaled, putting my face in my hands.

"Yew want to go check on her?" Roger asked me sympathetically.

"Nah, she'll be fine wit' space and time." I said into my lap. Lifting my head, I added, "Yo, let's do this!" I pulled out $5,000 I had separated and took $100 from the pile. I put the money on the desk for Roger.

Roger counted the bills, then paused, smiled, and said, "How about we do $4,700 and you go and buy your woman somethin' to calm her down and warm her up tonight, okay?"

"Wow, thanks man! That's...that's great!" I said with an astonished smile.

"No worries. Keep me in mind when it's time for the family-sized vehicle." He said, while grabbing the paperwork.

Minutes later I was out the building, keys and paperwork in hand. I helped Tatiana into the passenger seat, then drove away. "How much did my storming away save us?" She asked with a wicked grin on her so angelic face.

"$200. That was fabulous! Shocked the hell outta me." I admitted, causing her to laugh. She leaned over and kissed me as we drove north on 27th street.

"Brilliant huh?!?" she asked while we cruised through the somewhat heavy traffic.

"Yes, yes, yes lady! You were marvelous! Caught me so off-guard that I almost ran after you. It had a very real feel to it."

"Duh, that was the point!" she said playfully.

"Good job ma! I love how you so easily surprise me!"

We drove to a Currency Exchange on the southwest corner of 16th and National Avenue, and together we purchased 5 money orders for $2,700 each. We decided to wait until later that evening before trying to get the money orders to those affected by the fire at my apartment. I didn't know if anyone would be there, nor the extent of which my fire had affected their lives, but I figured $2,700 would help get them to a better place and I planned on handing them more in cash if they needed it.

CHAPTER TWENTY

From the Currency Exchange, I drove us east on National Avenue until 1st street, turning north for a trio of blocks, then northeast on Water Street. We hung a right on Chicago Street, one of those that led to the Henry Maier Festival Grounds where SummerFest was held, driving east towards the lakefront. We parked 2 blocks away, having to search heavily for a spot, since the area was alive with people and cars.

Tatiana in glittery, grey and pink short-shorts, a white, pink and grey Baby-Tee, with matching heels and purse looked star-like beautiful. I had on grey khaki shorts, a grey polo with matching Jordan's and fitted cap. Hand-in-hand we walked with a crowd of people, all headed towards the festival grounds, talking about everything and nothing. The huge, smiley faced SummerFest logo over the southernmost entrance greeted her and I as we stood in front of a ticket booth. I got our tickets and we stood in a line to go through metal detectors, the music from the nearest stages was heard loud and clear outside of the fenced in grounds for at least a block in every direction beyond the barriers.

SummerFest being one of the largest musical festivals in the world, held on the beautiful shores of Lake Michigan during early July, drew crowds in the tens of thousands daily. It was 11 days long, usually from the last Thursday in June, skipping Independence Day and wrapping up on the first Sunday following the 4th. Every year hundreds of bands, singers, rappers and other musicians did their thing on nearly 2 dozen stages set up on the grounds.

Not simply rinky-dink, small, Indie performers, but everyone from Aerosmith to Trey Songz, Twista to Saving Abel, Rihanna to The Eagles, Fabolous to Pink, Katie Perry to Lady Gaga, Usher to Jesse McCarthy, Train to Dave Matthews Band, plus so many more from every imaginable genre have graced one stage or another at the "Big Gig", as the festival is so often called.

It had all the music you could stomach, plus the other awesome things you'd find at small carnivals like games, foods, rides, people and smiles! For the price of admission, every concert held that day could be viewed for free except the one held in the Amphitheater that night. Many big ticket artist touring during the summer had a stop at SummerFest. It was always an amazing experience for everyone involved.

After making it through the metal detectors, Tatiana and I took a left, following the inner walkway, festival structures on our right, the " Big Gig" stage on our far left. Foot traffic was heavier than Time's Square at 7pm on a Friday in early July. On stage, a group whose music didn't ring a bell, rocked out to a crowd of over a thousand. There were picnic tables set up near the path, where teens bounced around or just mingled while younger and older adults with translucent cups holding beer-looking substance and plates of food watched the musicians. Beer tents, beer huts, and beer buildings were located every few yards, Milwaukee's own Miller having a major presence on the grounds.

"Oh baby, there's a barbeque place." Tatiana said as we passed the in-festival police department, a white building.

The path opened up to a huge seating area with a large, north facing stage. About 15 to 20 different food stands circled the area, with dozens of picnic tables in the spaces outside the 25 to 30 rows of bench seating. Hundreds of people were milling about near the eateries, which were both well-known spots from the city, nationwide franchises, and mom and pop spots that earned their way onto the ground through connections and contests held by the organizers. A few hundred sat on the benches, focused on the stage.

I saw where Tatiana pointed, a pinkish little building that said, "BAR-B-Q Pit". It was in the opposite end of the crowded clearing. We walked directly in front of the stage, a space of about 20 feet separated the seats and the gates protecting the stage, specifically made for foot traffic. When we cleared the stage area, as if on cue, the crowd began to cheer as a band of older folks walked on stage and a black lady with an accent from beyond the States began addressing the crowd. Tatiana and I stood in a long but swift-moving line as the band kicked into a suave jazz ballad heavy on the strings, while the dame sang in a smokey voice. There were mainly black folks in the line, and as Tatiana and I swayed to the music, some others did too.

"They are good!" Tatiana said in my ear. I stood behind her, my arms wrapped around her torso, her hands on my forearms.

"Yeah, they are. You a heavy jazz fan?" I asked as we moved with both the music and the line.

"Actually, I'm fine with any music as long as it is kind to my ears. What about you?"

"I'm not ever vibin' wit' Polka, but outside of that, I feel the same way. When I was a teenager, not long after I moved wit' my moms, I used to play my laptop on her porch wit' radio speakers all the time. That's how I got popular, 'cause I'd be mixin' cuts and people would come to chill. I loved to DJ, and I stayed doin' it for my friends." I told her as we neared the ordering window.

"Really?" she asked, excitedly adding, "That is rather sexy! Were you good?"

I snorted a bit then said, "Good enough to always have people sweatin' me to do they parties."

"Wow, why did you quit?"

"Um, I don't kno', I jus' moved away from it as I got older. I wanted to do radio. Like 860am. They my fave 'cause they don't get caught up in focusin' on the Top 40 R&B and Hip-Hop, but play old cuts, new ones, plus they ain't afraid to throw in a song not on the radar " I told her as we reached the window.

We both ordered our lunch then went to an empty picnic table to the right of the stage. "Maybe you should start an internet radio station. With how people basically live on the web, plus podcasts and things, that would give you a chance to get back into it." She suggested, then picked meat from a piece of rib on the basket of barbeque in front of her.

"Could! We got the money, don't we!" I said with a sly smile. I chewed on some huge, barbeque sauce-soaked potato wedges as Tatiana chuckled.

She nodded, swallowed, then as I bit a piece of rib, she said. "Yep. And you would be in total control plus, with Facebook plus all the other social media sites people use, you could build a global audience in a matter of months. Imagine that!"

I smiled at how easily she believed in me without seeing a lick of my true ability or lack thereof. "You've got grandeur in mind I see." I said, then ate more of the delicious barbeque.

"Why should I expect less? I've seen you do some very intriguing things. Also, your mind works in unique ways which have easily astonished me. How could I doubt you?" She inquired her eyes locked on mine.

I had no answer for that.

When we finished our food, we walked north on the path that had brought us to the area we had decided to eat. We came upon a thoroughfare where kiosks of different artwork were being showcased, displaying the creations of sick kids in the Children's Hospital. The hospital was the #1 Children's hospital in the nation and located on the western edge of Milwaukee County. The different pieces were intriguing, some downright incredible, and all made by babies not old enough to fathom the intricacies of life, many of whom would never get the luxury to explore it on this side of existence.

Such a notion hit Tatiana and I quite heavily, contemplating the fact that some of the most pristine of souls whose art we were admiring lay in a hospital bed with a life-stealing illness and wouldn't grow to know the joy of a first kiss, or the gift of being swarmed with internal butterflies when with someone they liked. Reading one bio of a girl who was 8 and had a smile that could light up a ballroom pushed Tatiana to tears.

"You okay bae?" I asked her softly, while holding her. The tears she shed burned my heart for a second time that day.

She wiped her eyes in that way only women who wear makeup know how to do, then answered, "They're so young Chris, barely beyond being toddlers, but are going through so much! I..." she paused, sniffling, then continued, "I don't know how a parent can handle that!"

She had me on the verge of tears too as I walked her to a nearby bench along the jagged, white rocks that lined the edge of the lake in that area."I can't imagine havin' to go through it, but they have no choice. They gotta face it cause they love their babies! I pray that any youngsters we spawn are healthy, but if otherwise, we will be strong and devoted to them no matter what, got me?!" I said as she sat on my lap, her arms around my neck, as her eyes locked on mine. Her face brightened and her smile began to return. "I pray they are healthy and never get shot!" I added, which made her laugh, and punch me softly.

"You know, you're great for me!" she confessed, then pecked me on my lips. We donated a few hundred to the hospital and put a reminder on my phone to donate a chunk of figures later down the road.

To the north, beyond a huge alcohol tent was one of the other larger stages. The stage faced the lake. About 100 yards separated by rows and rows of metal benches, a walkway, then some picnic tables that sat on the grass which connected to the rock barrier along the water's edge. The stage was occupied by a country band. Maybe 3,000 people listened to The Band Perry sing their hit song, "If I Die Young". Tatiana and I stood in the overcrowded area, listening to the ballad. The band jumped to their newest hit, "You Lie". Tatiana began singing the faster song, a 20 oz of Coke now her makeshift mic. Both her and I shared a chuckle at the line in the hook which spoke of someone lying like a guy with slicked-back hair that sold a ford.

Coincidence...maybe.

"You and I are the minorities here. You do see that right?" I whispered as we listened to the band sing yet another song with a catchy hook.

Tatiana smiled, then said, "Hello!!! We are always the minority. Can't help that!"

I laughed at my own folly in words, then nudged her with my shoulder. "You kno' what I mean, smart ass!" I told her, enticing a laugh from her. I continued, saying, "I feel like that old Sesame Street skit where they'd sing that sing, 'One of these things are not like the other, one of these things aren't kinda the same'. Ya kno'?" This time she laughed so intensely, I felt kind of foolish. She was bent over gasping in laughter, holding her stomach as tears trickled from her eyes.

"Oh God boy." she said while trying to regain her composure. I simply stood there with a contorted look to match my confused feelings. "Oh God Chris, you are too silly!" she said when her laughter subsided.

"Seriously though, I really like them. A friend who happens to be a white girl from, as she coined it, 'the backwoods of nowhere near anything worth speakin' on' sent me a link to their YouTube page and I was hooked! As I told you—I love good music!" She explained. "What do you think? Like them?" Tatiana added.

"A long time before their song hit mainstream stations, actually. Caught 'em on an AM health doctor's show and I saw where they were headed. Sometimes singers or songs just jump out at me and I kno' they are goin' somewhere. This was one." I told Tatiana. She smiled at me. We stayed in that area and listened to the band until they finished their set.

CHAPTER TWENTY-ONE

We walked south along a shoreline path, white boulders and grass on our left separated us from the water. We passed a tattoo tent, the "Survive Alive" mobile home used to teach kids about fire safety, some various stands peddling things and a huge kid's play area.

The play area was epic, with many different stages, platforms, slides, tubes, wacky bridges, nets, and swings. Kids moved like ants in a chaotic scramble. Beside that sat an area holding a stage with a riser of seats facing it, where a puppet show was being held. As we walked past, we could hear the children and parents laugh. Behind that building was a bathroom. On the other side of the restrooms was a basketball court with bleachers on both sidelines, about 25 rows high. Music played from the speakers spread out around the area.

About 300 people, mostly teens and young adults, were in the area, some in the bleachers or standing around, talking, dancing or just watching what was going on. They were of all races, though mostly black. One guy maybe in his mid-twenties had a mic in his hand as he walked towards the center of the court. He stopped and addressed the crowd.

"Anybody else looking to sign up for the V-100 and SummerFest Free throw and Three Point Shootout needs to do so now. Registration ends in 10 minutes. It's $30 per event but Grand Prize for winning each event is front row seats at the John Legend, T.I., and Melanee Fiona concert tonight, with backstage passes." He said.

I saw the line by the registration table and said, "Tati, come on."

"You want to watch?" she asked as we stepped onto the area beside the court, excusing our way through the people hanging around chatting and the others who were on the court shooting baskets.

"Nah ma, we can watch basketball on TV. I'm winnin' us them backstage passes." I told her.

"Really?" she asked, looking at me with a raised eyebrow, skepticism in her eyes.

When we reached the registration table, I pulled out $60 from my wallet and gave it to a mixed dame who was seated at the table beside a Hispanic brother. I signed a form after answering a few questions and was handed a bag that had a V-100 hat, T-shirt, water bottle and some posters of T.I., Melanee Fiona, and John Legend. "Stick that number on your shirt, okay?" The lady said with a smile while handing me the number 19 on a piece of paper with a sticky side to it.

I handed the bag to Tatiana as we walked away from the table and found a place in the second row of the left bleachers.

"Are you serious Chris? You really know how to play?" Tatiana asked with a hopeful smile.

"Ma, I'm from New York City! Ballin' is nearly essential in my upbringings!" If you can't play ball in the BX, you get banished to like Maine or Vermont!" I told her.

She looked at me blankly, so I elaborated.

"That's like goin' from livin' in Waukesha ya whole life and bein' moved to...the OLD Westlawn! You gone hate it!"

"Oh." she said, then pushed me.

I smiled then continued, "They used to call me 'Swish Chris'." I took off my polo, handed it to Tatiana who stared a bit lustfully at me in my muscle shirt, and handed her the contents of my pockets after snapping her from her trance with a clearing my throat.

She chuckled, then said "Best luck!" She gave me with a quick peck before I walked onto the court.

About 10 minutes' worth of shots later, the cat with the microphone was back on the court. The Rap and R&B, deadened as he spoke. "Okay, okay. Everybody, please clear the court so we can get things started." he said and we began putting the balls on the racks sitting near both hoops.

A judge's table was on both sides of the court, with 2 people at each. The master of the ceremonies walked to the half-court circle. I sat by Tatiana, drinking some apple juice she had put into the water bottle.

She was all smiles as I drank. "You can really shoot. I wasn't sure of how sincere you were. I thought you were just being cocky!" she said.

I told her, "Oh, but I was ma!" and winked. She just laughed.

"Alright everyone, welcome to this years, 'V-100 SummerFest Shoot-out'. We were able to acquire a special guest to sit in on things. Y'all probably know him. He's a bit of a celeb. Give it up for T.I.!" the MC said.

The area went crazy with screams, though the women made most of the noise, as the rapper emerged from a building, with 2 beefed up bodyguards a few steps behind him as he neared center court. On the sidelines where the rapper had come from were a few other cats with chains and watches too icy to NOT be with the rapper. Those guys surveyed the scene, not the rapper.

T.I.'s jewels sparkled as though they held their own light source within. It was quite unreal in how the glimmered as he waved at everyone in the stands and all the other areas. He was handed the microphone and said, "What's up Milwaukee?" Everybody yelled for a few seconds. He continued, "I'm happy to be here! I wanna wish e'er'body the best a luck! I'll be seein' the winners later on. I'll do some autographs after the shootout." He waved, handed the mic to the MC, then walked to some empty chairs. His guards sat in the row behind him, while the other cats in his entourage walked his way from where they had posted up and sat on his side and behind him. They formed a buffer zone between him and the regular folk.

"Alright everybody! I'm Vontay Vibe and I'm about to kick this off. First place prize is front row tickets to tonight's T.I., John Legend, and Melanee Fiona concert. One grand prize winner per tournament will get a pair of tickets plus backstage passes for a meet and greet with all 3 artists, plus a $100 Green dot gift card. Second Place will get a $75 Green dot gift card. Third Place will get a $50 Green dot gift card. All the shooters, come to the court." The MC said.

I stood then stepped on the court after a hug and kiss with Tatiana. She whispered in my ear, "Good luck, I love you, do your best!" during the embrace.

"Here's how this is going down. We are starting with the free throw contest. 2 players will shoot at a time, one on each end of the court. The top go to the next round, and the tops from that round go forward until there are 2 who go head-to-head for the tickets. The 3 point shoot out will go the same way. On the free throw contest, you'll have 45 seconds to do your thing. When the buzzer sounds, its done! We will pick players at random for the start to face off in the first rounds for the brackets. Everyone else will relax on the sidelines. Good luck people!" Vontay Vibe explained then walked off the court. He reached into a hat, pulled out two pieces of paper with numbers on them, and the first two competitors took their places and got to it.

I sat beside Tatiana, watching the other players do their thing. I was in the second-to-last duo to go, and I was both excited and nervous when the spotlight was on me. "Next up we have 19 and 6. Step to center court 19 and 6!" Vontay Vibe said.

I stood, and Tatiana squeezed my ass as I began walking away, causing me to jump. I looked over my shoulder as a few people nearby laughed. I smiled while shaking my head at Tatiana. She mouthed, "I love you, be great!" while smiling.

"Shooting on the east end we have #19. What's your name #19?" Vontay inquired, putting the mic in my face.

"I'm Chris!" I said.

"Alright, we got Chris. #6, what's your name?"

"Monty." said a dark-skinned, pudgy brother.

"Okay, okay, we have Chris and Monty. Can y'all make some noise for Chris and Monty?" Vontay said and the crowd cheered. I shot a smile at Tatiana who clapped and yelled. "Let's get it then brothers!" Vontay added, and I headed to my free throw line.

I was jittery as I stood on the line, the crowd loud on my left and right. I shook my whole body, but it didn't help so I bounced while practicing my form. "Ready? Set. Go!" I heard, and a referee passed me a ball. I aimed, shot, then caught the next ball, aimed, and shot. I did not watch to see if the balls went in, didn't worry about that in the least. I simply let off as many shots as possible, figuring if I made half but shot twice as many as my competitor, I'd be good.

When the buzzer went off, it seemed like only a few seconds had passed. The crowd was cheering as I looked at the judge's table. "Okay, okay, that was completely one-sided!" Vontay said while motioning for me and Monty to meet him at mid court. "Sorry brother Monty, but as Boys II Men once sang, you've come to the end of your road, bruh! Our final score, 23-13. Chris will be advancing to the next round. Dang homie, your shots were quite fluid, like rain! What do you have to say about that?"

I grinned, shrugging like Curry after hitting a halfcourt buzzer beater or Jordan in the '92 NBA Finals. I walked to Tatiana with people in the crowd patting me on the back or complimenting me. "Wow! You were great Chris! You only missed a few. It was incredible!" Tatiana exclaimed, handing me the water bottle.

We kissed then I sat beside her. "Thanks ma!" I said after a long drink.

In the 2nd round, I was in the opening duel, and I completely bombed. I went from 23 baskets to 12. I was watching the path of the shots and slowed down. My concentration was devastated, and it was disastrous. I was eliminated by more than my pride will let me acknowledge. "Chris, don't worry! Shake it off! You will get them in the next competition. You have a great shot and I know you can do it!" Tatiana said, when I came to the sideline with my head down, being the cheerleader, all good women become just when their men need it. I watched the winner, an athletically built white cat with a pretty Hispanic dame on his arm, shake T.I.'s hand, snapping pics with the rapper, and receive his Grand Prize. I hated the stench of failure that I wore.

I decided to use the nasty feeling being defeated had put within me like rocket fuel in a Maserati—I was ready to blaze shit! I felt it in my every cell. "You, okay?" Tatiana asked as I sat there staring at the empty court.

"I'm good bae!" I told her, watching the shots I let loose drop through the net, though it was only me visualizing it in my head beforehand.

"You sure? You look...I don't know, odd. You...you're zoning out and tuning in, huh?" Tatiana said, picking up on whatever my aura emitted.

"Doin' my best to!"

"Then you can be proud, and regardless of what I will be proud of you too! You will be my superstar no matter what!" she said, and I couldn't help but smile.

I looked at her and said, "You're amazin' ma, I truly adore you sweetheart!"

"Likewise!" she said bashfully, and I leaned in for a kiss.

There were 16 people in the 3-point contest. The crowd had grown to fill both bleachers, plus the sidelines behind both hoops had a few rows of people standing there also. Surely quite a few tweets, texts and posts had been sent saying T.I. was on the sidelines, which explained the growth in popularity of the shootout.

"Alright people, it's now time for us to kick off the 3-point shootout " Vontay Vibe said as he walked to the center court circle. "Here's how we play this. There are 5 marks on the courts with 5 regular balls worth 1 point plus 1 money ball worth 2 points. Shooters get 90 seconds to do their thing. The 8 winners from the first round of head-to-heads will meet up in round 2. The 4 winners from there go to round 3 and then the final 2 will go duel for the passes and tickets." He finished.

I was in the second pair of shooters for the first round, and when I walked to center court, I felt like I could drop shots from halfcourt without effort! "Okay, here we have..." the MC began, placing the mic in front of my competitions face.

"Josh." the lanky, white cat with a funny looking blondish-brown goatee said.

"Number 8 is 'Josh'. Got that, got that. And here we have..." Vontay began, putting the mic in front of me.

"I'm Chris, the winner!" I said sans an inch of doubt. The crowd both cheered and ooh'ed.

"Well okay then, somebody's playing prophet, huh!?! I guess we will see. He did light up the net during the first round of the free throw contest, so I guess we will find out. Take your positions!" I was at the west half of the court, watching the crowd. I felt relaxed and focused. Music started, then I heard Vontay Vibe say, "Ready? Set. Go!" I grabbed the first ball and was in motion. The first shot felt good flying from my fingertips, and I felt great!

In the background, the crowd was loud, the music smooth and I heard the MC and T.I. commenting on the shots. I heard it, but it went on as if a second dimension had developed and was just beside my own. When I let the final ball go, I watched as it flew through the air and slash through the net like wind through a lace curtain. I walked off the court with the clock still ticking and my competition still shooting. I didn't check numbers but stood on the sideline watching Josh toss up 3 straight bricks as Tatiana handed me, the refilled water bottle. The buzzer rang, and I looked at my score.

"And we have our final scores with Chris blazing the net at 23, while Josh racked up 15. Round of applause for our shooters please. Good job brothers. The next players will be..." Vontay said.

Tatiana was giddy as she spoke, saying, "Baby, you were PHENOMENAL! Oh my god!" she said, handing me the water bottle.

"Thanks, mami!" I said, loving her energy.

"You are so cocky! I swear, you just ooze narcissism when you want to!" She said with an admonishing grin.

"Confidence, knowledge of what I can do. That's just me standin' firm in my abilities!"

"Whatever!" she said then kissed me.

I drank while watching the other cats do their thing. When the last players from the first round cleared the court, I leaned to Tatiana and said, "Watch this." I stood, walked to the court where 4 referees were shooting around. I grabbed a basketball from a rack.

Other players were not yet on the court, and the ref's looked at me oddly as I started in a sprint from one side of the court towards the west hoop. As I neared the free throw line, I tossed the ball high on the backboard, took three steps, jumped and caught the ball in it's rebound with both hands. While soaring towards the apex of my jump, I moved the ball over my head, cocking it in my left hand as I flew towards the hoop, then slammed the ball through the rim with authority. I landed gracefully, with my momentum taking me a few steps out of bounds beyond the base of the basket. The crowd went crazy!

After that I was really feeling myself and walked to Tatiana while waving my arms upward trying to amp the spectators up even further.

"That was wicked!" Vontay Vibe exclaimed, adding "Let's get round 2 in motion. That fella right there, #19, Chris, is actually in the first pair of shooters for this round. He will go up against #7 Mario. Come on guys, get in place." I jogged to the west court and stood by a rack. I was completely lit, and the crowd was going wild too. Girls on the sidelines were waving at me and yelling out my name. A few shorties blew kisses and winked. I had a feeling that I might have been having an orgy if I was single. I chuckled at the notion as I heard the MC say, "Ready?" I took a deep breath, then heard, "Set. Go!"

I felt good as I snagged a ball and started shooting. I had a great rhythm, and I truly liked how the balls cut through the air. I could nearly feel them connect with the rim as I released each shot. When I got to the final rack, I watched the final four shots fall directly through the cylinder. I walked away when I was done, going to Tatiana who stood amongst a crowd of cheering ladies. Tatiana gave me an extra V-100 T-shirt she had somehow acquired to wipe sweat away with, then hugged me. "You made the same score as last round baby. You did great!" She handed me the water bottle and I took a long swig.

"Told you! We goin' to that concert tonight ma! Front row, backstage, we there! Watch!" I said.

The MC said, "We have the ever-consistent Chris who clocked in with 23 points, and Mario with 20. So, Chris, you go on and Mario, you go...somewhere else! Next two up are..." I ignored the rest of his words, not realizing how close a call it was. I didn't watch the next shooters. I sat there beside Tatiana, visualizing my shots again, blocking out the world around me. The MC said the scores, then a momentary pause in the action came before the final round.

A kid of maybe 18 who looked Hispanic and dropped 24 points in that round was my final opponent. "Can we get #19 and #2 on the court for the championship round, #19 and #2." Vontay Vibe said. The two of us came to the half court where the MC waited. "Alright people, this is it! One of you will be at the concert later, mingling with celebs, while the other will be somewhere other than that. Who will be where, is the question?" he said, snatching a few laughs from the crowd. "On the east rim, will be #2. State your name, #2."

"Jose, the REAL winner!" the youngster said, his voice barely out of the octave for girls. He shot a snarl at me that was reminiscent of Simba when he first tried out his growl as a cub. I smiled at the kid.

"Oh, ho ho! I see that Jose is taking the competition up a notch. He did drop the most points so far in this contest, so his swag is valid!" Vonday said, then turned to me. "On the west rim we have #19, who has most definitely made his name known, but we will give him face time."

"I'm the delusion demolisher, and the champ, Chris. When this round is finished, number 2 will still be number 2!" I said with a smile.

"Ouch, that was deep, with big words and all! Let us begin, because I'm sure we all wanna see how this plays out!" the MC said, then stepped back.

The kid shot a 'Fuck you buddy!' glare that made me chuckle. I waved my arms upward to get the crowd more psyched. It felt like a concert with how loud and excited people seemed. I reached my starting point, stared at the rim, and noticed that it looked a little larger than usual. I shook myself loose, then took some deep breaths to ready myself for action.

"Okay shooters. Ready? Set. Go!" I heard, and the background vanished. I grabbed a ball, aimed, and shot. I felt like I had magic on my side because even though I was not watching them drop, I knew something good was happening. My full focus was on form the feel of the ball in my hands. I did hear the crack of the net every now and again, but I did a great job of imagining the happenings more so than anything. I watched my last 6 shots fly through the basket as if they were laser guided.

When I finished, I went and stood at the center court circle. The crowd noise and all returned like a roar of the ocean as it hit my ears.

The kid was still shooting when Tatiana ran onto the court, nearly tackling me in her embrace! "You did it Chris, you won!" she screamed excitedly.

The buzzer sounded as I said, "Relax Tati, it just ended!" I figured she did not understand the rules.

"No, you have won! You only missed 7 points. He was beyond that before he reached the 4th rack. You have won!" she explained, hopping up and down in her heels, staring at my eyes as she held my hands.

"Seriously ma?" I asked, astonished by the statement. Tatiana nodded, all smiles. I scooped her up and spun her around. She squealed in laughter.

"Alright ladies and gentlemen." Vontay said as he walked to center court. "We have an undeniable victory here. A total debacle. Chris, staying true to his word, demolished Jose, scoring 25 to 19. Congratulations to Chris, who is here with..." Vontay continued.

"This gorgeous goddess is my beloved Tatiana!" I said with pride as she beamed on my arm!

"Congrats to the two of you! You now have backstage passes and front row seats for tonight's concert, and a $100 Green dot gift card!" Vontay said as T.I. walked up to us. He shook our hands, snapped a few pictures, then we were handed laminated cards on nylon cords that hung around our necks. I was also handed the gift card. Plenty of pictures were taken and then we left, deciding we would get our autographs later. People shook my hand and snapped pictures, high-fived and patted me on the back as we left the area. I did not put my polo shirt back on for a while, deciding a cooling off was in order.

"That was so great AND I filmed it all!" Tatiana said proudly as we walked a path right near the water.

CHAPTER TWENTY-TWO

As we walked in the direction of the grounds where carnival rides and games were set up which was the far southeast corner beside the Amphitheater, my phone rang. It was inside Tatiana's purse, so she fetched it for me. I answered the call blind since the ID showed, "Blocked" and heard Drama spit, "You and that bitch think y'all celebrities now, huh nigga? One of my boys saw you and I'm on my way there right now pussy!" He sounded (as had become the norm) eager to put a bullet in me.

"Yeah yo, I crashed them cat's on the court. You any good son, I kno' you's a midget but—"

"Nigga, FUCK that bitch ass shit! This ain't a social call! I'm 'bout to kill you and that bitch, today!" he yelled through gritted teeth it sounded.

"Ain't you tired of wastin' ya time, bruh? We kno' you can't do shit while we in here. Too much security, too many witnesses. That's why we here. So, chill, and come Tuesday, you and I can go back to havin' fun. I really enjoy shootin' at you and ya flunkies, yo! I never knew much 'bout guns but them bitches sure are fun to let clap!" I said as we kept walking. Tatiana glanced at me nervously as I talked. She began giving me dirty looks, obviously not liking my cockiness, so I decided to cut the call short.

"You and that black ass—"

Drama started but I cut him short, saying, "— 'bitch are dead!' Yeah, yeah, we get it. We'll holla then, deuces!" I said, then hung up.

"You sure he can't get guns in here?" Tatiana asked me as soon as I ended the call.

"Unless they get rubber, ceramic or maybe stainless-steel pistols, which are all hard to find, ma." I told her, enveloping her in my arms.

"God Chris, I hate this!" she said in a near whine.

"Bae," I began, guiding her over to a huge white boulder on the shoreline. The waves crashed a few feet beneath us as I faced her. "Listen, he can come up here, but he won't find us, and he won't do shit! We will go to the concert, enjoy ourselves. Tomorrow we will be somewhere far from him. Tuesday, I promise you I am puttin' an end to this for good, one way or another! Then we live it up!" I finished, showing a genuine smile.

She searched my eyes for a bit then smiled. "Okay, let's enjoy today as we have been!" she said, pulling me back on the pavement, in the direction of the rides.

As we neared the area that had the rides, Tatiana saw a tent that sold Spanish dishes. "Ooh yey!" she said with glee, guiding me towards it.

"We just ate like 2 hours ago." I pointed out as she pulled me into one of the lines.

"So! I want a churro!" she said defensively.

"Oh." was all I could say to that. They played a Salsa song on the nearby speakers, and Tatiana swiveled her hips on my midsection seductively. It was a lovely experience that had me losing my composure.

"Yo, you bes' quit befo' you have all these women seein' MY churro!" I said into Tatiana's ear.

She laughed, then asked, "Exciting, aren't I?" Her grin was just as sexy as her movements. She pushed harder on me.

"Okay watch!" I said, which earned a laugh from her. She quit and pecked me on my cheek. We both got churros, then went to the rocks and watched boats out on the lake.

"What are you planning regarding Drama?" she asked, then bit her Strawberry filled churro.

"I'm not sure. I'm lettin' my ideas simmer in the back of my head till it's time to lift the lid and see what shit looks like." I said after chewing my vanilla cream filled churro.

"I cannot wait until Wednesday, I swear!" she said. I just smiled.

The area that held the Carny rides and games was maybe 150 yards long by nearly 50 yards wide. It was packed with people, mainly younger folks. It had a small roller coaster, a bungee drop, a fun house, a golf shot game where you had to hit a hole in one on a small island about 125 feet away to win a brand-new Ford F150. It was $25 per shot, but I doubt if anyone ever won. There were 2 whirly, dizzy type rides, one that simply spun you upside down while taking you in the air, a handful of kiddie rides and a Ferris wheel.

Tatiana and I bought a half-dozen sheets of tickets for the rides, then hopped on the Ferris wheel. We kissed like teenagers the whole first rotation. The last few go-rounds we took in the sights of the lakeshore, snapping pictures. Then we did the rollercoaster, which was a waste of time in how boring it was. We followed that up with the bumper boats. That was fun, no lie! For starters, I had never been in a boat on water wanting it to crash. Simply never been a fan of such a notion. But this was a blast! Tatiana was quite brutal with her boat. She knew how-to pick-up speed in the pool and smash me hard enough to give me whiplash! I made sure I sprayed her properly with my water gun for her effort! It was truly awesome to experience on such a nice evening.

    We went into the funhouse next, believing it to be just something new to experience...until we got inside of it. The inside had to be magicked into a larger size, like those tents in the Harry Potter world because it definitely did not match the external dimensions at all! We got lost 3 times, and it took half an hour to find the exit...after we got lost seeking the way back to the entrance. "Thank god we sober! We never would've gotten outta there if we weren't!" I said as we walked away from it. "Shoot, I was ready to call in a rescue squad anyway!" Tatiana joked.

    We followed that up with the bungee drop, which strapped you into a cage, lifted you super high in the air, let you freefall, and allowed you to bounce up and down like a Yo-Yo for a bit. It had Tatiana screaming like crazy, and I most assuredly recorded the whole thing without her consent or knowledge. She did not open her eyes or stop making incoherent sounds of fear until they opened the cage and let us free. As we walked past the people waiting for their turn on the ride, I said, "Sorry for screamin' like that. I was crazy scared!" People laughed at me. Tatiana wrapped her arms around me as we walked away.

Win me a bear!" Tatiana said in the cutest little voice as we passed a carny game stand. She gave me that look only women are able to do which makes a man want to do whatever was requested. Damn was her look extra sexy as she stood face-to-face with me.

"I'll do my best!" I said, kissing her on the forehead.

We walked to a game with a star paper target and rifles lined up. "What ya gotta do to win?" I asked the guy behind the counter.

"Shoot out all the black portions of the star. If there is not black on the paper, you win!"

I shrugged, handed the guy 2 bucks and he handed me a rifle. It was a rapid-fire BB gun and spat the balls out crazy fast. I aimed and held the trigger. When it ran out of ammo the first time, I was not even somewhat close to my goal. Nor was I the second, third or fourth tries, but I did gain ground. By the sixth try, I was determined.

After $16 and about 10 minutes, I accomplished it to Tatiana's delight. She squealed in glee before she chose a 2-foot-tall pink and white bear, saying, "Thank you! Thank you! Thank you!" happily as we walked away.

"Your welcome bae! Them damn barrels was slanted to the left." I said. She squeezed me and the bear in a hug.

We vacated the carny area, following a walkway west, passing tents that had polka, then Native American music blaring while people mingled inside them. We reached the V-100 volleyball pit, where the MC from the shootout was on stage. People played volleyball in a sand pit right in front of the stage. Tatiana pointed out John Legend up on stage. He was on a chair next to the MC and a lady I had never seen before. The radio station's music played over speakers, and below the stage just out of bounds of the volleyball court, a crowd had gathered. Those people were mingling, some dancing, while others just watched what was transpiring on stage.

The music stopped and an in-studio DJ could be heard over the speakers, "We're gonna do a live check-in at the 'Only for the fit, V-100 beach volleyball sandpit' on the SummerFest grounds. Vontay Vibe, you there?"

"Yeah, we're here Reggie! I'm down here live with the ever-so-popular John Legend. Say something for the people John." Vontay said, enticing a cheer from the crowd.

"What up Milwaukee, how's it goin'?" John Legend said suavely, grinning at the dames lined up in front of the stage, causing females to squeal. He chuckled at the reaction.

Tatiana and I watched the MC and the singer talk, then left, not much interested in standing around to hear people talk.

We kept walking on a path we originated on upon first entering the grounds, but on it at a place a few dozen yards from where the entrance was. We came up to a building with sets of open, glass paneled doors. Inside I saw rows of videogames showing on TV screens, an EA SPORTS banner hung above the doors. Being a video game nut, I was about to veer into the spot when Tatiana's squeal stopped me.

"Look baby, it says Corinne Bailey Rae will be on the Miller Lite Stage at 6!" she exclaimed, pointing to a sign on a light pole that showed the days acts. "Oh my god!" she continued in a near panic. "It's already 5:45! Where's the Miller Lite Stage Chris?" she stared at me expectantly, and when I shrugged, she nearly fainted.

Tatiana grabbed my hand, pulling me as she weaved us through the crowds of people, saying, "We have to find a map Chris!"

"Bae, chill! I'll ask an employee where it's at." I told her and saw a guy in a blue SummerFest T-shirt. I asked him the location, then Tatiana and I were in motion, headed to the same stage where the jazz group had been on in the middle of the grounds. Unlike it had been earlier, with Corinne Bailey Rae ready to hit the stage, the area was packed! It was standing room only with every bench seat taken, and even the spaces for food vendors, which was all picnic tables, were packed.

"Tati come on " I said, when I saw a vantage point not being exploited yet. She followed me as I slipped through the people who watched the warmup band rock a catchy tune. A restaurant had a second-floor patio that was directly flush with the stage, but behind the 25 to 30 rows and the walkway. We went up the stairs and paid the fee for 3 drinks, then sat at a table near the plexiglass railing.

"Perfect!" Tatiana said as she slid her chair beside mine and placed her left hand into my right one. I smiled at her as our first order of drinks came. Corinne Bailey Rae walked on stage to a chorus of cheers. She talked to the crowd for a few moments, then kicked off a bluesy ballad that seemed to reach into my core. She went on to a sad love song that caused Tatiana to stand and pull me to my feet. We danced that song, and a few more, only stopping to drink our drinks while she was telling the crowd about her next song. We stole kisses as we let the music dictate our moves, while other spectators clapped for both Corinne and us. Nearly an hour and change later, Corinne took a bow, thanked us like her music was anything but a gift to our ears, and left the stage.

When the concert was done, Tatiana was all smiles, showing pics of Corinne while talking of the music. "God, I love her! She has such an angelic voice! I loved the one... 'Like a star'. Ah, that song just...I can't even explain it! And her accent totally elevates her sound!"

"Yeah, that is a bad ass cut!" I said, as we passed the kid's playlot, headed towards the lake. We grabbed some pizza from a Rocky Rococo's in a space on the northeast end of the grounds beside a beer tent. It was just past 7:10 and we had to be at the Amphitheater by 7:30 for our meet and greet backstage.

CHAPTER TWENTY-THREE

We reached the gate for the Amphitheater, showed them our passes, and were allowed into the area. Tatiana and I walked past an open-aire cafe, with people milling about at the tables and service windows. The lines weren't too long since it was quite a bit before the concert was slated to start. We walked past a few vendors selling shirts, CDs, and other artist memorabilia. "Want somethin'?" I asked Tatiana as we passed it.

"No thank you." she answered, adding, "I'm ready to go backstage!"

We walked up a covered path with a rail in the center, dividing the breezeway. There was a sign directing people to one side of the railing or the other for their seating area based upon the color code on their tickets. A set of beefed-up security personnel stood by where the space opened into the amphitheater, right beside ushers who were waiting to scan tickets allowing entry into the seating area.

We showed one usher our passes. He scanned them, then said, "Please stand over here." He pulled out a 2way radio, said something, then told us, "Someone will be here in a second, okay?"

Tatiana and I both nodded and stood beside a door marked, "Restricted" in white block letters. People in line stared at Tatiana and I as if we were in trouble. A few gave us looks as if they knew we were caught trying to sneak in and we were about to get exactly what we deserved. "I am so excited!" Tatiana said, hugging her bear while bouncing.

"Yeah ma, me too!" I told her, mirroring her vivacious smile.

Moments seemed to drag as we waited. Then, a pert, black woman with a kind face and platinum hair walked out the door. She had a phone in one hand, a 2way radio in the other. She smiled at Tatiana and I, then said, "Hi! I'm Trisha. I'll be your chaperone backstage " She held out her hand after putting her 2way radio into the same hand as her phone.

"I'm Tatiana and this is my boyfriend, Chris." Tatiana said, introducing us as she finished shaking Trisha's hand and I began.

"It's a pleasure to meet you two! Please, follow me." Trisha beckoned and we walked into the doorway. "You will enjoy this!" she added as we trailed her down a short hallway. Tatiana and I pulled our phones out, ready to snap pictures at a moment's notice.

"I heard you really put on a show out there today, Chris." Trisha said as the hallway opened up to a spacious area with people moving about with items on carts and pulleys. "Congratulations!" she added as we walked.

"Yes, that was my hubby!" Tatiana said with pride as we turned into another hallway.

"The free throw kid is upstairs already. I had my assistant take him and his girlfriend around. T.I. and his buddies said you were out there like a superstar!" Trisha said with a chuckle. "I hate I was stuck here fixing a mishap because it sounded like a good show." she added, as we reached an elevator about 20 feet down a hallway.

"Yeah, it was a blast!" I said sheepishly, as we waited.

"Ha, he is being so humble now!" Tatiana began as the elevator dinged open and two pretty women excused their way past us. I chuckled as we stepped into the cart.

"Oh yeah, I heard he was out there being crazy cocky! But you got that whole 'long hair don't care' swag, AND a gorgeous sister on your arm, plus you did win so why not!" Trisha said as we rode up to where I held no idea.

Tatiana and I smiled in response. Then as the elevators dinged open again Tatiana said, "It'll be on Instagram and Facebook later."

We followed Trisha into a wide hallway with doors on both walls. People were everywhere, some on phones, others in small groups. As we passed them, some acknowledged us while others ignored Tatiana and I. Some doors were opened while others were not. "Yeah, I taped him, and it will be online by morning. I'll hashtag it 'Summerfest shootout' so it's easy to find." Tatiana said as we followed down the hallway.

"Alright, let me check in with Jon first." Trisha said, then knocked on a door in front of us. Seconds later it opened, and a lady greeted us. She and Trisha shared some words then we were welcomed in. There were couches on three walls, and an empty vanity table beside a room that looked like a bathroom. "You two have a seat in here, and I'll be back. You want anything to drink or eat?" Trisha asked.

"Got alcohol?" I asked.

"Nuveau and all." Trisha replied with a smile.

"Can we get a bottle of that please?" I said smiling back.

"Anything else?" Trisha asked with a smile.

I looked at Tatiana who said, "No thank you!" Trisha told the other lady to get us the drinks, as they both left the room, closing the door behind them.

"This is so unreal!" Tatiana said excitedly as we sat in the room.

"Feelin' like a celeb ain't you?" I asked with a smile as I surveyed the room. It had track lighting but was basically bare on the walls except for the amphitheater logo scripted across one wall.

Tatiana grinned at me and nodded. The door opened and, on a tray, the lady who opened it had our bottle, two glasses, and a small bucket of ice. "Here you are!" she said with a soft southern accent. She sat the tray on the coffee table in front of us, smiled after asking if we needed anything else and being told we were good. She left when we thanked her.

Tatiana and I took pics of us with glasses of Nuveau, which we both posted on our social media pages. Shortly after that, the door opened, and John Legend was led into the room by Trisha. He walked in with a relaxed smile, and we stood to greet him.

"No, sit sit. I'm not a dignitary. Just a brother with a very nice voice." He said with a chuckle. "How are you two feelin' today?" he added as he shook Tatiana's hand then mine.

"We doin' great!" I said, then we introduced ourselves, and began conversing. The singer was really down-to-earth, laughing easily as we talked. He allowed us to take a boatload of pictures and even sang a few lines from 'Ordinary People' at Tatiana's request, which I live streamed as she nearly melted into me. An assistant brought in a shopping bag full of signed items, then John was gone. Tatiana and I went through the bag, seeing T-shirts, all his CD's, pics and a few other things.

The other assistant sat silently on the couch opposite of us checking her phone, as Tatiana and I talked about the encounter.

Minutes later, Trisha returned with the rapper T.I. The rapper beamed at Tatiana and I as he entered the room.

"Hey, how y'all doin'?" he stated, his Atlanta accent quite pronounced. He was in a different outfit from what he had worn earlier.

As we stood, he said with excitement, "Oh yeah bruh, you was destryin' them other guys on that court earlier!"

Tatiana shook his hand as I said, "Thanks yo, I was heated that I choked on the free throw contest!" I shook his hand then we all sat down.

T.I. chuckled then said, "Your lady right here nearly knocked you over when she ran up on you!" We all laughed at that.

"I was happy!" Tatiana said with a mild defensiveness, while smiling.

"Wait, Chris and Tatiana, right!?" he said.

"Yep, that's us!" Tatiana told him.

"When I saw you on the free throw line the 1st round, I was like 'damn dude a robot droppin' them shots like that'!" T.I. said

"Then I choked." I admitted.

"Yeah, but T.I., you should have seen him on the sidelines. I did not know what he was doing until he looked me in my eyes and was like, 'I'm winnin' us them passes!' Then I knew he was determined!" Tatiana shared with the rapper, who listened raptly. She beamed while finishing, saying, "His eyes spoke a truth word could not touch!"

"You got a good shawty right here bruh, sista's like this one is rare. Take care of her, a'ight?!" T.I. said, adding, "I gotta ride out, but I'll see y'all when I'm on stage. Okay?"

We took some pictures, then T.I. shook our hands and left. Trisha followed him out. The assistant who had vanished mid-meeting came back with a duffle bag full of things from T.I. It wasn't limited to just basic memorabilia. He even had a pair of Samsung Galaxy tablets, which completely shocked Tatiana and I. The assistant watched as we examined to tablet box. "He really likes to give people more than they expected!" she told us, smiling.

"He definitely did his thing wit' this!" I told her, Tatiana nodding in agreement.

It wasn't long after Trisha left when she was back, this time with the beautiful Melanee Fiona in tow. Melanee was gorgeous-gorgeous! Not that phony, make up and fake everything type gorgeous, or that snap chat filter type gorgeous. No! She was that good genes, sexy lineage, pretty parents type gorgeous, the au natural variety of beauty! And her perfume was intoxicating.

Hi!" Melanee said, all warmly, continuing, "how are you two?" She held her hand out to shake. "I'm Melanee, as I'm sure you two know. It's a pleasure to see such a beautiful couple. Girl, I am so jealous!" she finished, her whole demeanor friendly and joyful.

"Looking to trade? You take him and I will take your success, money, and freedom to do whatever!" Tatiana said after we introduced ourselves.

"Okay girl, where do I sign?" Melanee responded, then let out an adorable laugh, as she sat directly to our right. She was wearing a nice dress that was classy, but still had a special kind of pizzazz that made it jazzy. "Tatiana, this life is NOT as fun as you think. I can hardly find a man who doesn't simply see 'the singer Melanee Fiona'. I need a guy who sees Melanee, the Toronto girl who loves amusement parks, chili dogs, football and painting."

"Wow, we have so much in common! Tati, is she signin' wit' a pen or digitally?" I joked.

Melanee laughed a high-pitched, adorable sound. Tatiana gasped, then pushed me. I held her bear up as a shield, grabbing it from where it sat beside the couch atop of the bags of things the others had furnished us with. "Shush! You know that is not happening! I love you too much boy!"

Tatiana said. I wrapped my arms around her from beside her and kissed her on the cheek.

"I love how precious you two are. This feels like real love! How long have you two been together?" Melanee said with the most heartfelt of smiles.

Tatiana curled her arms atop mine, pressing herself tighter into my hold then answered, "7 months last Friday!" without hesitation and drenched in pride. She added, "It feels like longer though, as if this isn't the first time, we have been united. Plus, we spend so much of our time together. Yet, it always feels brand new daily!"

I chuckled eternally but held Tatiana firmly while smiling.

"That's so beautiful! Did he buy you that bear? It is so beautiful!" Melanee asked

"Here, it's so fuzzy!" Tatiana began, holding the bear out towards Melanee, then added, "He actually won it for me!"

"Aww!" Melanee cooed, with Trisha in the background saying the same while Melanee hugged the bear.

"Pro'ly would've been cheaper had I bought it." I said with a snort of a laugh.

"Yeah, but it is cherished more when it is earned. Boyfriend/girlfriend rule." Melanee pointed out, then said, "So, are you two making plans for the future?"

"Actually, I could see us wit' a house, a baby, his and her everything. So, marriage could be on the horizon." I said, a bit more sincerer than I expected to have felt in but a few days.

Melanee's eyes lit up like a sparkler. She clasped her hands over her heart, then said, "Aww! You're okay with that, right girl?"

"Yesss!" Tatiana exclaimed.

"Okay! Aww!" Melanee repeated then laughed.

My phone and Tatiana's rang almost simultaneously. I saw it was my mom and hit 'ignore', and Tatiana did the same on her phone. We both apologized to Melanee who waved us off with a smile.

"So, what is the best thing about Tatiana, Chris?" Melanee asked.

"Honestly? Nearly everything! She's the first dame I've ever met who showed me that I'd be missin' out with her not near me. Like, I don't wonder if I...am doin' right wit' her 'cause I can feel that I am. When we apart, it's like movin' through a gel how time slows down. Whenever we reconnect, it's like fireworks and tingles. She is what love was made for, and I can't let that go!" I answered.

Tatiana turned my way and pulled my face to hers for a kiss as both Melanee and Trisha "Awwed" in unison. I saw that a few tears had fallen from Tatiana's eyes when we pulled apart. Tatiana smiled at me then reached into her purse and pulled out a teeny Kleenex packet.

"Can I have one girl? That was so beautiful!" Melanee said while fanning her face, trying to keep her tears from messing with her makeup.

Tatiana handed her the pack and Melanee stopped the waterworks.

"Tatiana girl, you keep him! He's a true sweetheart!" Melanee added.

"I am girl, he is all mine!" Tatiana said with a smile.

"Yeah ma, like 5 minutes ago you were out to trade me fo' a few million and fame." I said in faux anger.

"Yeah, yeah." Tatiana said dismissively then pecked me on the cheek.

"I'm going to write a song about you two. You are what a couple should be. I pray that you two make it to forever! As...as a matter of fact I am going to give you my real Facebook page. You send me the pictures we are going to take, and I will sing at your wedding!" Melanee said, her face all joy and pride.

"Really?" Tatiana asked excitedly.

"I promise! You two made my day! I am a hopeless romantic and you two really did it for me!" Melanee replied, smiling brightly our way.

I was shocked and happy all at the same time. "That...that would be...Wow!" was all Tatiana managed to say.

"Thanks Melanee, that's wonderful!" I added

"No pressure though!" Melanee said, holding her hands up. We all laughed.

"Nah, that jus' means we won't be eloping in Vegas or Hawaii." I confessed, earning chuckles from everyone.

"But you can honeymoon there!" Trisha pointed out.

"Good idea!" Tatiana said.

"Well, I really would love spending more time with you two, but the show isn't long off. I do have to get prepped." Melanee said, genuinely apologetic.

"It's fine. We understand." Tatiana said and I nodded in agreement.

We took pictures, the girls shared them on their phones, then exchanged Facebook info. Melanee bade us goodbye with hugs and best wishes. As Melanee and Tatiana embraced, Melanee whispered something into Tatiana's ear. They released smiling. The assistant handed us a bag of Melanee Fiona goodies. I put them all into one bag and Trisha escorted us out of the room. I sipped the bottle of Nuveau as she led us through the backstage area. Trisha and Tatiana talked the whole way. When we made it to the restricted door, Trisha hugged Tatiana and I, then said, "I hope you two really enjoyed this!"

"Trisha, this has been the best day I've had in a forever ma, no lie!" I admitted.

"Yeah girl, this was fantastic!" Tatiana said happily.

"Great! You two enjoy the show! Bye!"

"Bye Trisha!" Tatiana and I echoed as we stepped out the door right beside people in line and ushers eying us curiously. I downed the last of the Nuveau.

"Bae, I'm goin' to run this to the car, a'ight?" I said, then pecked her on the cheek.

"Okay, be quick." She said after giving me a hug

I jogged down the ramp, duffle bag in hand as I avoided those now coming to claim their entrance into the amphitheater.

As I got my hand stamped for reentry into the SummerFest grounds, my phone rang. I pulled my Bluetooth earpiece out and said, "Hey mom."

"Hey, you, called earlier after I saw you post some new pics and do that live stream!" she said, a smile in her voice.

"Yeah Ma, I kno'. I was in the midst of conversin' wit' Melanee Fiona still so I couldn't answer. Sorry!" I said as I jogged west on Chicago Street.

"How'd you pull that off?" she inquired, as only a mother could. I made it to the Shelby and put our bags into my trunk.

"Long story short, I won us some backstage passes, and we got to meet Melanee, T.I., and John Legend." I explained as I jogged back towards the entrance.

"'We...'? Who's the plus one?"

"Her name is Tatiana."

"Well, when am I meetin' this 'Tatiana'?" she asked in a way she knew would not irk me even though it was the first of her 3-point play on a guilt trip.

I decided to cut her short as I neared the street directly across from the grounds. "Eventually mom, let's not do this dance right this moment." I said earning a chuckle.

"Alright baby boy, I'll give you that. I'm actually calling because we are doing the 4th at your Gram's tomorrow. You have been summoned." she explained as I went through the metal detector.

"Can I get back at you on that?" I asked, not really wanting to spend the holiday with family when Tatiana and I could do so many other things.

"Yea, yea, yea. Do so or I will blast you on Facebook, Instagram and Twitter!" she threatened, earning a laugh.

"A'ight antique one, I'm gone! Love ya mom!"

"Love ya back, baby boy!" she returned as I ended the call steps from where Tatiana stood patiently.

CHAPTER TWENTY-FOUR

"Hey! Why is your Bluetooth on? Drama call again?" Tatiana asked after our kiss filled reunion.

"Nah, it was the other woman in my life." I said as we were led into the amphitheater's lowest section of seating, which was all yellow.

"Um, explain!" she said as we were led to the front row, throwing me an arched eyebrow look.

I chuckled, then said, "My mother." She rolled her eyes in response.

Tatiana and I had not simply front row seats, but were in the dead center of the row, about 8 feet from the stage. As we sat, Tatiana leaned close to me and said, "This has been a great experience."

"And it's only 'bout to get better!" I told her, then slid my arm around her.

The cat who won the free throw contest and a Mexican shortie sat just to my left. As the speakers played some music just to keep the audience engaged, he asked, "Did you two get a lot of shit from them too?" He was sporting a huge grin.

"Hell, yeah yo! Melanee even volunteered to sing at our weddin'." I told him excitedly.

The dude and his dame burst into laughter, looking at me like I was crazy. "Yeah, right man, she hardly even spoke to us. She acted as if she was shy. Or maybe she just being all 'Hollywood', thinking she was better than us!" he said with an attitude.

Tatiana sucked her tongue in disgust, but said quite calmly, "She was nothing like that with us! She was so friendly and kind, truly down-to-earth. We had a great time. I have her real Facebook information."

The guy's girl had a cute accent, but she spoke with a snotty tone as she said, "T.I. and John Legend were both very nice, but Melanee Fiona was all distant, like she didn't want to be there. I... I don't know, but I was a big fan of hers and now I don't like the bitch!" The girl shrugged then took a sip of beer from a plastic cup in a snobbish way.

Tatiana shot me a look which I took to mean, 'It was probably just them!' I just shook my head.

I went to a nearby concession to grab us some goodies to chow down on and when I had sat back down, the show began. A comic kicked things into gear and the brother was hilarious! He had an African accent, and some wild stories. He enjoyed saying 'motherfucker'.

John legend kicked off the show, starting a ballad from off stage, with no music playing. As he stepped on stage, the women began to squeal, and the screams did not let up the whole time he was on stage.

He slipped seamlessly back and forth between songs, even summoning Melanee Fiona to the stage for them to sing their duet, and having T.I. jump on one of his tracks, surprising the audience. John Legend really came out and connected with the women in the place. He ended with a few songs that had couples in the spot dancing, Tatiana and I included. It was a great show.

During the intermission, I went to grab some more drinks and some cheese fries. I was still tipsy but could have gone for a few puffs of a blunt. I came back and Tatiana was on her phone, smiling. The comedian was back on stage, tossing out wicked jokes that had those in the audience who watched him laughing loudly. Tatiana laughed, but at whomever was on the phone, then handed it to me. "Who is this?" I asked her, holding the phone.

"Talk and see." she replied with a grin.

"Hello?" I said.

"Hey Chris. How's my ex doing?" I heard but did not immediately recognize the voice.

"Um, I didn't kno' Tatiana had an ex-girlfriend, but I guess that'll give us somethin' new to converse 'bout later on." I said, quite seriously. Both Tatiana and the mystery voice on the phone laughed, with Tatiana tossing a jab to my thigh.

"What? I'm talking about you, duh!" the voice said.

"Oh." I replied, then put a face to the voice and chuckled. "Shit, Tasha?"

"Yeah!" she replied, then let go of giggle.

"Oh. Well, I'm proper ma." I said unsteadily, my intoxication and my mild nervousness kicking in. "I'm doin' proper." I repeated, a bit clearer

"And you're 'doing' my one-time best friend, but I'll let that go. You enjoying the concert? I see two have great seats!" she said, though it didn't carry any negativity...it seemed.

"Shee-yeah, we right up front, under the stage." I told her, an awkward stutter in my brain-to-mouth processor.

"I know, I saw you when you sat down." she told me. "Look to your left!" I looked down our row but saw no familiar face. "Not in your row. A couple behind you." she said, emitting her adorable laugh, which ate at my stomach and memory.

I glanced over my shoulder and saw her throw a wave in the air. She sat about 12 seats over and 5 rows back. "Good seats!" I told her, facing forward again.

"Not as good as yours. AND you had backstage passes—that had to be a lovely experience!" Tasha said.

"It was, it was. Well, here's Tatiana! Take care!" I said, prepping to dig into the food. Tatiana was already eating.

"Wait. You don't want to talk to me?" She quizzed, a hint of melancholy in her words. I glanced at Tatiana, but she was watching the comedy routine.

I chuckled, though I was not paying attention to the funny man. "Maybe a few years back I'd have given 3 toes, one finger, and a front tooth to talk ya ear off. Right now, though, I'm good, and even though I was the one who broke up wit' you, I regretted it every single day after! If you'd have forgiven me and granted me that second chance, I begged fo'...I don't kno'. But I'm too Gucci wit' Tati! Plus, you and her are friends not us, so..." I said, allowing the weight of those words to float across the space between Tasha and I.

I handed Tatiana back her phone and realized that she had been eying me for a few moments. As she took it, her eyes met mine and I looked towards the stage as she said, "Hey girl."

She conversed for a few moments longer then ended the call and asked, "You, okay?" Her face showed compassion that reached my soul.

"Yeah bae." I answered, smiling at her.

Tatiana hesitantly said, "We will talk about it later, okay?" She had seen through my charade instantly. I simply nodded.

T.I. came on the stage and the crowd went berserk. I'm talking all out apeshit! He and 2 cats were all over the stage as he spat his songs, with all the ferocity of the lyrical animal he is. His hype men kept the crowd amped with their antics. It was fly to see him flow through his catalog of music, even having John Legend come out and sing his chorus on their song 'Slideshow'. During his final song him and his boys pulled out wads of cash and threw the figures into the crowd. The bills were 1's, 5's, 10's and 20's but nobody complained about catching free money at all!

The intermission that followed T.I.'s performance was the one Tatiana and I used for bathroom breaks. When we got back, the same comedian was tearing it up on stage. We sat and watched as he did his thing. He finished, walked off the stage, then the whole place went pitch black. A murmur went through the crowd.

"Do we have any lovers in the house tonight?" we heard Melanee Fiona ask, enticing screams from the crowd. "Yeaaah, I hear you. Ladies, does your man do you as he should?" Melanee asked, to yet another shower of screams from all the women in the crowd. Suddenly a pink spotlight shone down on her as she stood in the center of the stage. The effect was rather girly, but the light made her look angelic.

She walked to the edge of the stage as a few more lights shone down on her, then asked, "Do we have any ladies in here who believe they have that forever kind of love?" More screams from the crowd came in response. Her music began in the background as she continued speaking. "I have never done this before, but tonight I met a beautiful pair of lovers that actually left me wanting what they had!" Melanee said with a chuckle, as the crowd again screamed.

"Chris!" Tatiana said with an excited squeak into my ear as she clutched my left arm and bounced in her seat.

"Tati, I kno' ma, relax a bit." I said to her, because she was barely able to stay in her seat.

Melanee continued speaking, looking out into the sea of faceless screams with a lovely smile. "As a matter of fact. Tatiana, you and Chris please stand up for me please."

Screams erupted all around us. Even Tatiana's squeal seemed louder than normal. She had buried her face into my neck and was tapping her heeled feet in the ground as I sat there stunned by Melanee's actions. I didn't even move. I simply stared at Melanee who looked directly at

Tatiana and I smiling. We stood and a pink spotlight splashed us with its beam. Tatiana was giddy, shaking with excitement as I held her with my arm around her slender waist.

"Chris, Tatiana, you two come up here! I have a special seat for you two tonight!" Melanee said with the grandest smile she had yet to lend us. Tatiana and I didn't move. Again, Tatiana hid her face, this time using my chest as her hiding place. "Come on!" Melanee beckoned with her hand and a chuckle.

"Tati, let's go!" I said into Tatiana's ear as the crowd went crazy for us. I noticed two beefed up security personnel walk to the opposite side of the riot fence blocking us from the stage. I helped Tatiana by picking her up and hoisting her over the fence, the security helping her from the other side. I looked back at the other couple who spoke so sourly of Melanee and waved before I hopped the fence myself. We were walked to the stairs just to the right of the stage.

All while we walked, Melanee was saying to the audience, "I met them, and I saw love that you expect in lovers who have been together for years and years. I was touched and jealous of how tight they were."

When we got on stage, Melanee said, "Come over here." She stood in the center of the stage and with my hand holding Tatiana's, we went to her. Melanee gave us both hugs, then said, "Everybody, this is Tatiana and Chris."

It felt amazing to have the whole arena screaming for us. Tatiana once more buried her face into my neck after we waved, and Melanee laughed. "See, aren't they adorable?!" Melanee said and I felt my face go flush. She leaned our way and said, "You two sit over there!" I looked at where she pointed and saw a loveseat on the other side of the stage. It was in a position where we could see perfectly, I found out after the fact.

"Thank you, I love you!" Tatiana said, loud enough to be heard on the mic in Melanee's hand.

Melanee laughed, then said into her mic, "You two are so welcome! I love you back girl!"

As Tatiana and I headed to the couch, the pink light stayed on us. We sat cuddled up, facing Melanee as her music got louder. "This is my 'True Love' concert." Melanee said to screams from the audience. She began to sing, and Tatiana had her phone ready to record. As Melanee sang, she would toss us smiles while we enjoyed the concert.

During one song Melanee sang, Tatiana and I stood and slow danced, our eyes locked on each other. It was a lovely feeling, and when I leaned in for a kiss, it sent beautiful bolts if electricity through my core. Melanee did a pair of duets with John Legend, and T.I. rapped on one of her songs before the set ended. It was a true gift to be so close, to feel like a part of the show while her music carried such intensely emotion. When she sang her last song and thanked the crowd, it felt like the end of something too dynamic for us to have experienced.

Tatiana and I were walked backstage after Melanee, where she waited with her backup singers, all toweling off. "Surprised you two, didn't I?" she asked with an effervescent smile.

"Yes girl, you made this a MILLION times better!" Tatiana said happily. She gave Melanee a hug.

I hugged Melanee then she said, "I was so moved that I wanted to enhance this for you two." She beamed at Tatiana and I.

"Excellent job Melanee, you definitely did that!" I said, earning a chuckle. I added, "This will make for the best posts ever!"

Everyone there laughed at me. Tatiana hugged my arm and pressed against my side. "Well, I just wanted to say goodbye to you two. Remember what I said though. Give me the date and time and I will be there for your wedding, I promise!" Melanee said, then waved as we all parted ways!

CHAPTER TWENTY-FIVE

Tatiana was still floaty as we left the amphitheater area, going through the pictures on her phone as I did the same. We talked in excited tones, walking towards the water's edge because the fireworks were set to be discharged in a matter of minutes. People were all awaiting the begin of the display, standing in rows, facing the barge out on the lake where the pyrotechnics would be cast from. Following the fireworks, the day was done, party over, everyone was cleared out.

We walked on the path until we neared the basketball courts and went to the top of the northern bleachers. I stood behind Tatiana, who was up against the railing. I had my arms wrapped around her as we waited. "Baby, this has been the best day ever!" Tatiana shared as we looked out over the waters, seeing the dozens of boats bob in the inky blackness of Lake Michigan, also waiting for the show to begin.

"Yeah ma, this was way beyond what I expected to experience today! I'm so glad you gave in 'cause I would have not missed this for nothin'!" I told her while I slid my thumb up and down the smooth skin on her left side.

She chuckled, sighed, then kissed me on my cheek. "I love you, Chris!"

"Love ya back Tatiana!"

A single spark started the Big Bang and colors began to boom then blossom like flowers in the black night skies above us. The fireworks display lasted nearly half an hour, the explosions so close we could feel the concussions and the colors seemed to rain down upon our heads. Ooh's and aah's littered the area as we watched the show. When the finale of multiple explosions happened overlapping in a flurry of color and sound, everyone watching clapped and cheered unifiedly.

From that moment the exodus began. My phone rang as Tatiana, and I made our way across the basketball court towards a path that would take us to the gate we had entered the grounds through. "Hello?" I said, putting my Bluetooth into my ear and answering it without touching my phone

"Bitch nigga, you and that slut do kno' we waitin' fo' y'all, right?" Drama said with a grin I could feel through the line.

Tatiana and I walked in a huge crowd of people all headed for exits. I looked around but saw no one watching us. "Yo, you kno' that unless you outside the Sheraton in Glendale, you can't be waitin' on us, right? We left SummerFest after the concert. You shoulda been there—"

"Pussy nigga quit lyin'! I had niggas watchin' you and that bitch, plus my other niggas waited outside every exit. You and that bitch ain't left or y'all be dead already nigga!" Drama spat.

Tatiana asked soundlessly, "Is that Drama?" I nodded but smiled. She was scared, I could tell. I grabbed her and held her tight as we walked with the crowd, getting closer the exit gate we used.

"So, you plan on havin' one of your goons shoot into a crowd wit' police on every corner, by every parkin' lot and on ev'ry nearby block? Do the dummy wanna end up in prison fo'ever or shot the fuck up? That is stupid as hell!" I pointed out, as I walked, keeping my head on a swivel as I continued my check for signs of danger.

As we neared the gates, I saw on the other side a cat staring intently at the people who walked past him, checking his phone periodically. He stood on the ledge of a raised flower bed, giving him the ability to look down upon those who passed. I pulled Tatiana to a stop and the throng of people simply moved around us without missing a hitch. Drama laughed and said, "He a soldier, he be a'ight!"

"And he gone snitch on yo' ass the the second he get in that interrogation room! You gone go down right wit' his ass, idiot! I'm out!" I said, then ended the call. Tatiana was looking into my face as we stood there, fear like a veil covering her face.

"Bae, we gotta split up." I told her, my hands holding hers.

She shook her head emphatically. "No Chris, I won't leave you!"

"Listen, there's a nigga standin' out there lookin' fo' you and I together. I want you to go and stop a cat who's leavin', a dark-skinned cat wit' a group and flirt with him heavily. Be all up on him. When I call you, have him and whomever he wit' hold up while you talk. I'll tell you what to do from there, okay?" I explained.

She was near tears but nodded and said, "Yes. I love you Chris!"

"I love you too Tati! Grab the car and meet me on the intersection by the Italian Community Center, okay?" I said, then kissed her.

"Okay." she said then walked back into the crowd of exiting people. I watched her for a few moments until she disappeared. I looked around for my own set of ladies walking together. I had not found any by the time Tatiana came walking towards me with 3 dark-skinned guys and a white girl.

I called her and she had the whole group pause. "Jus' walk out. I've not found the cover I need yet. I'll be watchin' over you, and if he spots you, I'll distract him, okay?"

"Yep!" she replied, then ended the call. She got closer to the main cat she had been chatting up. He put his arm around her and whispered something into her ear which she laughed about loudly, laying her head on him. As she passed me, seeing her on the cat like that sent a bolt of jealousy shooting through my core. As they passed me, Tatiana threw me a wink and smile so smooth, I was sure that no other person could have caught the gestures had they been watching.

I kept my eyes on her as the group left the gates, prepared to cause a ruckus of some fashion had the cat looking for us spotted Tatiana. He paid her a millisecond of attention as he did all the other faces, continuing to scan the crowd, a scowl on his young face. When I saw that Tatiana was a safe distance away, I walked back deeper into the grounds.

I noticed a gaggle of white girls, 3 blonds and a redheaded beauty. I approached the redhead and pulled out the heaviest Puerto Rican accent I could muster and said, "Hola mami, how are jew doing?"

Her friends all smiled at me, matching her expression as they all stopped walking. We stood near a beer hut as the blaze-haired beauty replied, "I'm fine, how are you?"

I held out my hand and she grabbed it as I revealed, "I'm doing excellent. I am Xavi."

"I'm Theresa." she replied, shaking my hand. She added while smiling gorgeously, "Nice to meet you Xavi!"

"The pleasure is truly mine! With a lady as angelic as jew, it is but an honor!" I said, smiling suavely. Her girls were now standing a few steps away, watching and whispering while staring at me.

"Wow, really?! I'm 'angelic'?" Theresa asked, skepticism in her emerald-colored eyes.

Kicking my conversation into high gear, I smiled, then said, "The fire of the God's captured in your hair, the envy of those lesser entities caught in the color of your eyes...mami, jew epitomize what impeccable is. If jew aren't angelic, then I will proudly sin to stay where you are!"

She laughed in mild surprise, then fanned her face with her left hand. "Okay then, I can accept that!" she said.

"Might I walk with jew ladies, give us a chance to learn more of each other?" I asked her. Then, I looked at her girls and added, "jew lovely ladies do not mind if I accompany jew while talking with jor flawlessly beautiful friend, Theresa, do jew?"

One of the blonds who wore glasses and was fairly thin in body type snatched Theresa by the arm, pulling her away from me a bit. The friend said something to Theresa, and the two girls laughed. Her other girls poked their heads into the huddle, and they all whispered then laughed. Theresa broke the huddle, coming to me and saying, "You may walk with me if you would like. I'd enjoy that!"

I offered her my elbow, and she was taken aback momentarily by the gesture. I gave her a reassuring smile, and she slipped her pale, thin arm into the opening, hooking her elbow in mine. She shot me a darling smile and we began walking.

"Where are you from?" she asked as we all walked towards the exit gates.

"I was born just outside of San Juan, Puerto Rico, but moved to this city 6 years ago. My job moved me up here." I told Theresa, as her girls looked in on our conversation. They were on our left, which was great positioning for me since the cat who waited beyond the exit was on the left side of the opening.

"What do you do for a living?"

"Web design, app creation, a little bit of tech support. Basically, anything dealing with the internet. I work for a small firm a few blocks from here on Water Street." I lied.

"Wow! That is so awesome! I'm studying Mechanical Engineering at the Milwaukee School Of Engineering." she returned. I was quite impressed and showed it in my wide-eyed look.

We were passing through the exit gates with hoards of people, her girls just in front of Theresa and I. The cat who was waiting, surveyed the scene, scanning faces. He saw me, looked at Theresa, then moved on with his eyes. "Jew are the one doing something exciting!" I began, as we moved out towards the street which came to the entrance area then curved north. "What does that entail?" I added as we crossed the street.

Our group headed west up Chicago Street, passing a motorcycle parking lot where the roar of Harley-Davidson bikes echoing off the underpass above as they started up and drove away was nearly deafening. "It's basically the study of fundamental aspects of how more complex engines of our society work. We also focus on ways to improve both design and efficiency." she explained, nearly yelling to talk over the motorcycle engines.

"That is magnificent! Jew must be as brilliant as you are beautiful!" I said, glancing over my shoulder at the cat who was still posted on the ledge of the flowerbed, seeking Tatiana and I. His back was too me and the girls.

"I guess." Theresa said modestly, then pressed her side against mine.

I saw that Tatiana had the car parked on the northeast corner of the next block, idling, but I kept walking and talking with Theresa to avoid any suspicion.

When I was about ¾ of the block away from the character looking for Tatiana and I, my accent vanished as I said, "Theresa, I apologize for lyin' to ya but my name is actually Chris."

The group of dames were all looking at me in shock, but Theresa had an extra bit of confusion showing. I stood facing her and stared in her pretty eyes than added, "I meant what I said! You are beautiful and obviously brilliant, and if I was single, I'd love gettin' to kno' you better. I only lied 'cause that cat back there with the black shirt and shorts on..." I pointed the cat out over her shoulder. "Dude was waitin' to shoot me and my lady. You jus' saved my life! I gotta run now, sorry!" I finished, pecking her on the cheek, then jogged away towards Tatiana.

"Xavi—Chris...wait!" Theresa yelled as I crossed the street, but I waved without slowing down.

I climbed into the car with Tatiana. "You okay mami?" I asked Tatiana after I kissed her. She eased into traffic, which was both heavy and sluggish.

"Yes, but that crazy nigga tried to kiss me! I was like, 'Sorry cutie, call me!' then walked away." she said, tossing me a mild look of irritation.

"Well, I had a pretty redhead, and 3 blonds escort me outta the gates." I said, which earned me a look that left me feeling unsafe, so I fixed my statement. "Excuse me, they escorted 'Xavier' out. Chris had stepped away for a bit."

She smiled then said, "Great clean up job!"

I chuckled.

We drove to our hotel's parking lot, directly behind the Pfister's rear entrance and pulled into a second story space. "Imma call Drama so he can send that poor boy home." I told her as she cut the engine.

"No! Do not call him. Let his little flunkies wait on us all night!" Tatiana directed as she popped the trunk open.

We exited the Shelby, and I grabbed the bags out the trunk as we laughed.

Tatiana and I shared a shower, then went right at each other, making love like it was the first time we could get our hands on each other in months. We constantly switched positions and worked to push each other beyond ecstasy until well beyond midnight. When we finished, she asked as we lay in the darkness, "Chris, why does your phone almost only ring when Drama calls? I'm sure you have friends and whatever that call you, right?"

I chuckled, realizing I was either about to lie or reveal one of my trade secrets. I sat silent for a few seconds, then decided it to be a nonissue. Trade secrets are eventually exposed to the light of day one way or another. "Actually, it rings quite often." I admitted

She had her head on my chest but raised it to look at me. "I've not heard it ring regularly at all." she said.

The streetlights from below our window coupled with the nocturnal Downtown glow illuminated our room just enough for us to see each other in the darkness of our suite. "Call my phone." I said with a smile.

She grabbed her phone from the nightstand on her side of the bed and called me. We both watched as the face of my phone turned on and it rang. She looked at me and said, "Really!?!"

I laughed, then said, "Okay, okay. It rang because you are programmed to ring. Hold on." I grabbed my phone, tapped on the screen for a few seconds, then said, "Call me again."

She did and we both watched as it vibrated in my hand. She chuckled, then asked, "You just ignore people when they call?"

"They can leave a message or text." I told her.

She laughed, rolling her eyes, then said, "Why don't you answer? I don't mind. I do not talk a lot on the phone, but I would not be ignoring calls."

"It's just that I've been wit' you and I don't feel like conversin' with dames who bore me. As to my boys, it's a holiday weekend so they doin' they own thing. If they tryin' to get togetha, it's an all-boys event. Best to jus' ignore that for now." I explained.

She kissed me and I felt butterflies erupt on my stomach. When she pulled her lips from mine, she said, "I'm not stealing you from your friends. Do not think I am that way."

I nodded.

"What about your parent?" she asked after we had been silent for a few moments.

"It'll ring for them." I told her absently, dozing off into a dream.

"Oh." was the final thing I heard her say before I was lost in a dream.

CHAPTER TWENTY-SIX

The a.m. sun blazing through a window at 7:30 woke me. I looked around, adjusting my eyes to the bright surroundings. Tatiana was beside me, knocked out. She was a lovely chocolate angel, her hair like a dark fan, flared all over the pillow. I slipped out the bed silently and went to the bathroom, nude, and handled my functions.

I came out, found my Newport's, and lit one as I walked to a window. I looked down on Wisconsin Avenue east as I puffed my cigarette. I didn't have a plan about what I wanted to do for that day yet. I really held a desire to do something supremely special with Tatiana, taking her away from all the craziness that I had introduced into her world. I walked to the small refrigerator beside the minibar, snatching an orange juice, before going back to the windows, watching the holiday traffic.

After a few moments of city watching, I grabbed my bag of clothing, and dragged it over to the couch. I picked out my outfit for the day, then laid it on the back of the couch. I returned the bag to a corner, then phoned downstairs for breakfast! I put on boxers from the night before that were beside the bed, then took cash out my shorts to tip the person who would deliver the food.

My phone shrilled and I ran fast to answer it before my sleeping beauty was bothered by the noise. "Hey mom, what's up?" I asked, walking away from the bed where Tatiana snoozed peacefully.

"Hey baby boy, how you are doing today?" my mom inquired, extremely cheerful at that early hour on a summer holiday.

"Jus' started the day minutes ago ma, but I'm proper! How are things down there?" I asked as I sat on the room's recliner.

"Good, everything's good! You're off for the day, yes!?"

"Yea ma, why?"

"Everybody was planning on meeting at your Gram's place BUT we changed that idea and decided to do the whole Lakefront thing. I've not seen you since Mother's Day, and you can meet my boyfriend, Owen." my mom said, really pressing me.

"Really ma, guilt trip?" I said while I thought of how Tatiana would feel. I knew this would not fall under the heading of 'Special', but I also knew that Tatiana and I would have many days of adventures. My whole family came to holiday events governed by my Gram's so it would give Tatiana a chance to meet my family.

"Silly son, guilt is a motherly mandate, and I will forever use it however I see fit!" my mom said then laughed.

"Lemme phone you back ma. If I do come, my girl is coming' too!" I stated firmly.

"That would be great! Is she the pretty one in those pics? How old is she? Where is she from and how did you meet? What—"

"Mom, mom, ma! Stop! Chill! I'll call you back in a few minutes, a'ight?" I said with a smirk, cutting her off.

She laughed softly, then said, "Okay, okay baby boy. I'll be waiting. Oh, and one more thing."

"Yeah ma?"

"When am I getting grandbabies?" she asked with a chuckle.

"Goodbye mother! Love ya!" I said, rolling my eyes even though I know she could not see it.

I shook my head while smiling, remembering how my mother was always a bundle of fun. As a kid, I always knew that dad was the stern, rigid parent while mom was the one who made life a party. Those two differences were what made it a blast to move with my mom even though I missed the NYC lifestyle.

"Who was that?" Tatiana asked sleepily

I looked her way and saw that she was still in bed, not having moved a centimeter. "You awake or jus' talkin' in ya sleep?" I asked with a grin she did not see because her eyes were still closed.

"Half and half currently." she replied which made me smile wider.

"Breakfast is on its way. That was my National Inquirer of a mother requesting my presence in Chicago for a family holiday function." I answered.

Tatiana sat up swiftly, the cover flipping off her upper torso, revealing her naked breasts. She yawned then asked, "When do we leave?" She smiled then stretched.

"Didn't say we'd show. Told her I'd call her back an' let her kno'." I answered, staring at Tatiana's perfect breasts.

Tatiana crawled out of bed and put her lace underwear on as I stared, catching beautifully erotic mental stills of her body. "Do you want to introduce me to your family?" she asked, walking towards me with a look that was both sexy and serious all at once. I had a feeling that a lot hung in the balance of my reply.

"Seriously, you think I'd be hesitant to bring a beautiful, educated, tough, sweet, funny, loyal, heartfelt lady around my family Tati?" I asked.

She shrugged as she lowered herself onto my lap, wrapping her arms around my neck. I chuckled, raising an eyebrow, and asking, "Have you NOT been payin' attention since Friday?"

She emitted a smile that shined like the sun outside our room's windows, and asked, "So, when do we leave? Or do YOU not want to see your family?"

I inhaled deeply, then released the audible breath. "I wanted to do somethin' excitin' and special!" I explained.

She was still smiling as a knock at our room door sounded. "It will be a lot of fun and quite exciting for me! And so special too! Plus, it will beat being shot at and chased!" She noted.

"Okay, let me grab the door. It's our food." I said, and she allowed me to stand. I walked to the door as she put on my polo shirt from the night before. I opened the door and handed the guy a $20 after signing the bill. "Thanks!" I said, then pulled the cart inside our room and closed the door.

"So, we are going, correct?" Tatiana asked as I maneuvered the cart near the coffee table.

"I'll call my mom in a bit, and we will leave once we are dressed, a'ight?" I told her, earning an excited squeal from my lovely lady.

We shared a bath, repeating our tub lovemaking but going at it with a higher passion. I can't say why, but we seemed to hold a richer hunger for each other that morning and it was only satiated by our new level of intensity, pressing us to a climax that was dynamic.

Clean and dressed, I called my mom. "Hey baby boy! You and your girl coming?" my mom asked when she answered her line

"Yeah ma, we're headin' your way. My girl is quite excited!" I explained.

"Good! I look forward to meeting her and seeing you again. She not white right, cause you know how I feel about white girls!" my mother said, causing me to laugh loudly.

Tatiana poked her head out the bathroom door to see why I was laughing so raucously. "Seriously ma?" I started, once I regained composure, adding, "You half white! Ain't that a bit twisted in a self-hatred kinda way, lady?"

She laughed, then said, "Shut up, that is NOT a factor here, nor does it change my feelings!"

"Whateva mom, I'm not tellin' you anything more about her! You'll see her an' you will love her, no matter her skin tone!"

"Okay, okay! We are all going to meet at South Shore Beach. You know where that is?" my mom said.

I thought for a bit, then replied with, "Isn't it up past 57th street? No matter, GPS will kno' how I get there."

"Your girl got a car, or did you buy one?"

"My white girlfriend got one. Be sure to save us a parkin' spot. You kno' how that lakefront stays packed on summer holidays!"

"Your cousin will have that taken care of. I will make sure of that!"

"Okay ancient lady, I will see you in a bit!"

"Yep, love you!"

"Love ya back ma!" I replied then ended the call.

Tatiana and I were headed south from Milwaukee at 9:30 that morning. I had the Mustang flying down the interstate, hitting 100 while still within city limits. The radio was on V100 blaring whatever rap and R&B songs the DJ decided to play as I weaved through the holiday traffic. "Chris, why are you driving so fast?" Tatiana asked about 15 minutes into the trip.

"Two reasons actually. Fast cars are meant to be driven fast and highway drivin' is so borin' ma!" I told her while switching lanes to pass a minivan.

"So, you do know what you are doing then?" she inquired, looking over at me.

"Yeah ma, we proper!" I told her.

"Okay then." was all she said after taking a deep breath an exhaling audibly. I chuckled internally.

"What did Melanee whisper in ya ear yesterday?" I asked her just as we passed the city of Racine. Traffic was less heavy as we passed country farms.

Tatiana smiled then answered "Nothing." in a way that let me know whatever Melanee said was something!

"Seriously ma, tell me!" I pressed, now very curious.

"It was a woman thing." she said, still smiling.

"Whatever jerk face!" I said, making her laugh.

"Aw," she began, reaching over and pinching my cheek while continuing, "Now Chris is pouting. Poor baby!"

I pushed her hand off my face and said, "Oh yeah? That's why I told my mom you a white girl!"

She let out a shocked chortle then said, "What?!? You told your mom that why exactly?"

"Pull up YouTube." I told her while smiling.

"Why?" she asked, grabbing her phone from her purse.

"Jus' look up 'Dave Chappele'."

She was typing as she asked, "What does that have to do with you telling your mother I am white? Okay, I have his stuff up, what am I doing now?"

"Search for 'black, white supremacist'." I told her.

"Huh? Okay, here it is."

"Watch it, then I'll explain because you'll have a clearer understandin'." I said, making her face contort in confusion. I heard the video play.

The comedy skit was about a blind black kid raised by a racist white couple who taught him to be a white supremacist. The man grows up to be a high-ranking clan member, never knowing that he himself is black. At one point during a Klan's meeting, he decides to remove his hood, and an audience member says, "He's a nigger!" The supremacist goes apeshit, when he realizes they are talking about him. He spazzes out on the cat who called him nigger. It is all out hilarious!

Tatiana laughed at some parts, while saying "Nuh-uh" and "That is so wrong" at others. When it was done, she asked, "Are you saying your mom is black but hates black people?"

"Yeah, because that makes a whole lot of sense." I said sarcastically, earning me a cut-eye stare from Tatiana. That might have included a punch had I not continued talking in a different tone. "What I'm sayin' is that she white and black but act like she don't want me with a white dame. I told her you were white jus' to fuck wit' her."

"You are an ass! She better not hate me because of you!" Tatiana said with a nervous smile.

I laughed at her concern then looked her way saying, "Relax bae, she is not like that. It is jus' an ongoing joke between us. She is really cool! And how many bad women wanna be grandmothers?"

"I hope she likes me!" Tatiana said softly.

I looked at her then asked, "Why?"

"She'll be my mother-in-law!" Tatiana replied, looking at me like I was slow.

We came to the tollway at the Wisconsin-Illinois border in Gurnee Mills, Illinois. I paid the $2 toll while saying, "Yeah, it ain't like she goin' to be in ya face 24/7. We live 90 miles away ma!"

"So! She will want to see our babies!"

"That's true. All 8 of them." I said, just to get a reaction out of her.

"What? 8? Never happening!" She replied with chuckle.

"A'ight, I'll settle for 6." I quipped, making her laugh again.

"Please! I may go for 4, but that is pushing it! I do not plan on having a ton of babies. I love kids, but I can barely handle you pushing into me. That is way too much pain having baby after baby pop out. I want 3 myself. What is your number?"

I paused in contemplation as we flew past Gurnee Mills mall, then Six Flags Great America. After a few moments, I said, "Honestly, I never considered a number. I only ever really wanted a son to carry on the last name and a daughter to walk down the aisle. After that, we can do more if you want or stop. It is your call!"

She smiled at me and said, "I love that plan! Let's go with that."

CHAPTER TWENTY-SEVEN

After the 2nd tollway, I pulled off the highway just past an advertisement for a fireworks depot. We were a few dozen miles into Illinois, but not yet close to Chicago. "What are we doing?" Tatiana asked me as we rolled down the exit ramp.

"Gas and there's a fireworks store up here. Gotta be sure we have plenty of them for later!" I told her as I rolled into a gas station beside the fireworks store.

"You want something?" Tatiana asked, climbing out the car when I parked beside a pump.

"Uh, you kno' those white powdered doughnuts?" I asked her.

"The little ones?"

I nodded as I too stepped out the car. "2 packs please mami." I said, adding "and some strawberry milk, thank you!" She smiled over her shoulder and waved in confirmation. I watched her sway, her long, slender chocolate legs in pink short shorts was such a sexy vision. I waited until she was at the counter before I began to fill the tank.

She walked back to the car with a huge smile on her face, a bag in her hand. "What's up?" I asked as she neared me.

"The girl behind the counter said you were staring at my ass. She said exactly, 'your cutie-pie boyfriend was watching your butt as you walked'."

I laughed as I held her door open, then said, "I was actually starin' at ya gorgeous legs, lovin' how your skin tone and the color of ya shorts contrasted."

Her smile grew wider than a Hummer as she asked, "Can I believe that?"

I shrugged, smiling, and returned, "If I was checkin' out ya ass, why would I lie? I could say so. You'd jus' smile and kiss me!"

She shook her head while chuckling, then flipped her hair over her shoulder saying, "Okay, but you do like my ass, right?" She had an eyebrow raised as if she might be posing a sincere question.

"Sexiest ass I've ever seen!" I told her.

She kissed me, then said, "Thank you!" I grabbed her ass, making her cut her eyes at me as she climbed into the car.

In the firework store, I snatched up all types of cool explosives, really taking advantage of the buy 2 get 1 free sale they did all the time. We roamed the aisles of the place, grabbing boxes of this and that from the shelves like this was the last Independence Day ever.

"Are you serious Chris?" Tatiana asked and I put three large packs of tanks into the nearly overflowing cart.

"Yeah ma, they got some awesome shit, so why not? I mean, e'er'body gone be there an' we want them all to have somethin' to enjoy." I grabbed a package of baseball-sized explosives to mimic the show we saw the night before, then added, "Plus, me an' my mom are junkies for this shit bae. You'll see!" Tatiana just shook her head in awe of how much had accumulated in the carts.

We left the store with 4 bags and 2 big boxes of fireworks. As we loaded the things into the car, I told her, "Oh, by the way, when I say 'e'er'body gone be there', I'm talkin' 'bout nearly e'er'one spawned from my granny's body, which is a large number of folks." I said then closed the trunk.

"That is fine. I have never been around a big family, so this should be a lot of fun!" she said as we both climbed into the car.

"What's your family like Tati?" I asked as we flew through the outskirts of Chicago on the freeway.

She sighed then said softly, "My family is me plus my friends. As I told you, my Granny passed and my mom...she...she abandoned me as a baby. My granny said my mom was 27 and doing drugs, which sent her to jail. She found out she was a few weeks pregnant while in there and stayed in the whole time she was pregnant. My Granny said that was why I came out so healthy, and drug-free."

"And gorgeous, very, very gorgeous!" I said, without thinking.

She smiled at me then continued. "Anyway, my mom had me about 10 days after she came home. We lived with my Granny for about 2 months, then my mom went out one day and did not come home. She called my Granny and told her she wasn't sure when she would be home. My mom...she never came home. My Granny said she was never going to put me into the system, and she raised me. She also explained that drugs stole my mom.

"My Granny, she said my mom may have been stolen mentally. She believes it was the pain and shame that kept my mom away. My Granny said my mom probably wanted to come back but couldn't due to the hurt she had built within me." Tatiana was silent for a bit, staring out the window, her face focused on the land we passed.

I didn't know what to say so I chose silence. After a few more quiet moments I reached over and weaved my fingers into hers. "I'm sorry to hear that bae, truly!" I told her, not sure if it was the right thing, nor feeling the courage to share deeper sentiment. I felt so sad for her, and worse for asking.

"I think I met her a few times." she confessed with a bittersweet cadence.

"Really?" I asked, shocked.

For the first time since this topic was brought up, Tatiana looked my way. Her eyes were glistening with the threat of tears, but she had a sincere smile on her beautiful face. "A lady, the same one about the same age my mom would be during that time seemed to pop up in places I went to regularly. This lady would share with me a brilliant smile that felt so familiar. I have not had an encounter with her since I graduated from high school." Tatiana explained, then looked out over the hood at the road ahead of us. She added, "I... saw her a few dozen times, especially near my birthday. She never spoke to me. She'd smile and hold eye contact for a bit before walking off."

I sat in contemplation of how that had to feel for her but couldn't fathom the internal ache of her life based upon such an experience. I felt bad, and I wanted to heal whatever pains she held from her past, even though I knew I couldn't change yesterdays for her. "Tati, you kno'..." I began, then paused, wondering if I was a man strong enough to say what I felt, and relay the depth of which I meant things.

She turned to me, eyes still sparkly with the threat of tears but a smile on her face. "Yes?"

"I love you! We met but days ago, but I truly love you! I can't say what is on the horizon for us with certainty. I wish I could, for your sake alone 'cause you're somethin' so special, on planes and in ways that most people don't even know exists! Regardless, what I want you to know is that I'll be beside you as a friend if ever you and I part ways, you will always be able to reach my way and depend on me. I promise!"

She began to cry, but her smile was so brilliant it made the sunshine beyond our car seem dim in comparison. She leaned over my way and kissed my cheek. "Don't worry Chris, I will make sure we are happy, and you will be my hubby always! I promise!" she said, and I felt my heart swell. I couldn't stop smiling.

"You are the only one I have ever told about the lady whom I believe was my mom." Tatiana admitted as we reached the city, and traffic forced me to slow from 100 to 75. She was in the midst of GPS'ing the exact location of the park.

"Why did you keep that to yourself?" I asked her as I navigated the slower traffic with no intentions of cutting down my own speed any further.

"It was my...it felt like a secret, a game of sorts, and I believed that she would eventually come up to me and reveal herself." Tatiana explained.

"I'm honored you felt close enough to me that you'd share such a personal thing wit' me."

"Chris, when we met...I knew, I just knew. Even if none of the crazy things that we have been though happened, I am positive that I would still be all about you! These things are NOT why I love you. And none of it is why I trust you, believe in you, and look forward to all that we will be!" she said, and I felt myself grow inside regarding her and I.

For a bit I had no words to return, so I remained silent. "That...that is really a huge thing ma. Thanks!" I finally managed to say, staying focused on the road ahead. I knew that if I looked her way...well, I just kept my eyes on traffic.

"I love you, Chris." she said in a way which made it seem like my being her secret-keeper was a no brainer.

"I love you, Tatiana." I said back, all smiley faced.

"The Park is south of Downtown, but before the Museum of Science and Industry. The map says we can take the highway right to it." Tatiana told me as we rode south into the city.

"Do you want me to take surface streets? If we do Lake Shore Drive, you'll get some proper views of the skyline. You can snap pics." I told her.

We were a few miles before the northern end of Downtown, about to pass North Avenue. She chuckled then said, "It just dawned on me that I am out of Wisconsin!" I smiled in her direction as she continued, saying "We have been talking and I completely pushed that out of my mind! I feel like a blond!"

"Don't sweat it love. I've not been all that focused on location either—jus' you and playin' Speed Racer. I wouldn't have said shit had the buildin' tops stabbin' the clouds not reminded me." I confessed.

We exited the freeway on Division Street, heading East. Tatiana took pictures of the not-too-distant skyscrapers as well as the architectural makeup of the basic blocks of Chicago. We cruised through the city, Tatiana even having me pull over a few times to get pics of us on older bridges. I loved being the one showing Tatiana the landscape.

On Lake Shore Drive, I drove us south, not at all moving fast so Tatiana could snap pictures of the city like a paparazzi, oohing and aahing. I threw out tidbits of places I had background info about, or personal history with. She was so excited to see the city, and I loved her jubilance.

When we neared the park, I pulled out my phone and dialed my mother. "Hey baby boy! Where are you and your girlfriend at?" she said upon answering her phone, her tone all happiness.

I laughed then said, "We close lady. Where exactly are you's parked? Can you get me a specific marker?"

"Hold on. Okay, you got your GPS thingy, right?" she asked after her own laugh.

"Yeah ma, why?"

"Owen showed me how to get my precise longitude and latitude. Let me pull it up." my mother explained.

"Bae, be ready to GPS what I tell you, a'ight?" I said to Tatiana who nodded in response.

"Baby boy you there?" my mom asked.

"Yeah, tell me what ya stalker of a boyfriend has taught you." Then added "Ouch!" after Tatiana punched my right bicep. I tossed Tatiana an angry look, but she rolled her eyes in reply.

"Whatever nigga! Here's my info, son!" my mom relayed some coordinates, and I repeated them to Tatiana.

"I have it mapped Chris." Tatiana said with a bit more glee than I expected.

"Great! A'ight mom, my white girlfriend says we have your location. We'll be there soon!" I said into the receiver.

I heard my mother suck her teeth as Tatiana pushed my arm. "See you two in a bit."

"Yep ma, love ya!"

"Love ya back baby boy!" my mom replied, then the call was over.

"You really are pushing this whole 'white girl' notion, huh? Why not tell her I am not white?" Tatiana asked as we neared the turnoff that put us on the street which drove through the park.

I shook my head at her as I grinned, saying, "She observant! She'll notice the difference!"

"Chris, will she be mad?" Tatiana asked with a straight face.

"No, but if she is, so!"

"'So!'?" Tatiana repeated with an exasperated look.

"Yeah ma, 'so!'. She needs to quit bein' all picky for me! She only says that 'cause of one shorty I dated when I was a teenager that she wasn't fond of! Her bad!" I said with a smile. Tatiana did not further that topic.

CHAPTER TWENTY-EIGHT

We drove down a two-way street then went under Lakeshore Drive, until we reached an intersection. We turned right and drove down a street that cut through the lakeside park. It was a very wide laned two way with cars parked perpendicularly to the traffic on both sides of the street. "Baby, the GPS says they are not too far ahead." Tatiana informed me as I slowly rolled southward on the lane.

The area was alive with people on both, the lakefront side and the side that was up against the Lakeshore Drive causeway. People grilled and set up their picnic areas on both sides, while kids were everywhere playing and just lounging. "Over there, it shows." Tatiana told me, pointing to the left side of the car, which was the lakefront side of the street.

I had Tatiana call my mom. "What's up wit' that parkin' spot?" I asked when she greeted me.

"Ya cousin A.J. is taking up 2 spots. I'll let him know you're here." my mother said.

"A'ight ma. I see his Rover. We'll be here waitin'."

"Okay, see you in a second." my mom said before hanging up.

I pulled up behind a sparkly, pearl white Range Rover, all chrome-accented with huge rims. People honked and I waved them around me. "Wow, that's nice!" Tatiana said, looking at the truck. I saw my cousin jogging in our direction.

I leaned out the window and yelled, "Hurry up nigga, befo'e ya windbag city people try lynchin' my ass!" My cousin smiled, flipped me two middle fingers, then hopped into his truck. Within a few seconds he had pulled his car into one spot allowing me the chance to ease in on his passenger side.

As I climbed out the car, my cousin was walking around the front of his vehicle. I went to open Tatiana's door, and we met my cousin at the bumper of the Shelby. " My mafucka New Yawk! What up cousin?" A.j. said, with a smile before we embraced in a hug. When we let go of each other, he looked at Tatiana and said, "Aye, you can't be comin' round here with model's nigga! It ain't fair!" He added with a chuckle.

"Yeah, you kno', you got the money, the beautiful family, the whole happily ever after shit! I got to have some way to even out the game B!" I said as we all stood around. "Tatiana, this is my cousin A.J. A.J., this is my bae, Tatiana!"

"Hello beautiful lady! It's a pleasure to meet you!" A.J. said to Tatiana, his smile genuine. He held out his hand in her direction.

"Nice to meet you also." Tatiana replied, shaking his hand while matching his warmth.

"Man, ya momma said you was bringin' a white girl. Not sure if you noticed, but" he lowered his voice into a loud whisper while leaning my way with his hand blocking his mouth, "this one ain't white!"

We all laughed as I grabbed Tatiana's hand and we began to walk in the direction of my family, my cousin following suit. "He said he did it to mess with his mom." Tatiana explained as I surveyed the scene. It was beautiful out, sunny, and early 80's with a slight breeze coming off the lake. Families had set up with blankets, lawn chairs, and tables all around. The Park was a combination of happy summertime sounds—music, laughter, and firework blast, and the excited squeals of children having fun.

"She still acts sour sometimes 'cause of that pair of white girls from the summer you spent in Milwaukee wit' us, bruh!" I told him as I spotted the area our family had claimed as basecamp. He and I laughed while Tatiana arched an eyebrow and gave me a curious grin.

Over by a huge tree, I saw everyone, about 50 feet from the concrete pier that was level with the water which made up the shoreline in that section of the park. A barrel grill sat beneath the tree, with 3 picnic tables not far away. A trio of aunts moved things from coolers to the tables as one of my uncles did the prep work for the grill. His wife sat at another table laughing with their oldest daughter. Teens and young adult cousins were spread out in the area, some tossing around a football. Others were in little huddles talking and doing what folks do at family gatherings.

Kids were everywhere. Some played with remote-controlled vehicles, some drones buzzed around, and trucks raced on the grass. Others played by the pier under adult supervision. The rest sat on blankets in the shade, focused on tablets and phones. I saw a group of my uncles playing dominoes at a card table, drinking beers, and talking shit. I saw

A.J.'s wife, Erika with 2 of my other cousin's wives and I waved her way. She and the other women waved back.

"Uncle Chris, Uncle Chris!" I heard and saw A.J.'s two daughters flying in my direction on stick figure legs, coming from the direction of the pier. Both of the tree-limb thin beauties leapt into my arms, and I squeezed them.

"Lexi, Ya-ya! How are my favorite little ladies doin' today?" I asked after pecking them both on the forehead. Alexi, or Lexi was their baby at 7. Eya, or Ya-ya was 9, the oldest. Both girls had a flawless combination of their parent's physical features, though each girl looked more like one parent or the other.

"We are great!" Ya-ya exclaimed as we all walked in the direction of my mom, sitting on a chair beside my grandmother, under a tree not far from the grill.

"Yeah, we are doing so awesome! We are going to set off fireworks later!" Lexi said excitedly.

"You waited for me to show befo'e blowin' things up? Is that what I'm hearin'?" I questioned with a chuckle.

"Yes!" Lexi said gleefully, smiling at me angelically.

"Not by choice though." Ya-ya admitted, her honesty a beautiful trait. "If they let us, we would have been setting them off."

The adults laughed.

"I would have told them to wait for my uncle Chris!" Lexi said, then stuck her tongue out at her older sister, while laying her head on my shoulder.

"Yeah, because everyone would have listened to a BABY!" Ya-ya shot back, sticking her tongue back and adding an eyeroll.

"Okay then princesses. Meet my girlfriend, Tatiana." I said as I placed the girls on the ground. Politely the two girls introduced themselves to Tatiana, incorporating a cute curtsey into the exchange. Tatiana introduced herself in return, mimicking the curtsey. "Check it you two. Go play for now, and in a little while I will present you wit' an awesome, amazin', superb surprise, okay?!" I said to the girls.

"Alright!" Lexi said, clapping and hopping in place.

"Okay Uncle Chris!" Ya-ya said, equally excited in her own reserved manner. Both girls bounced away to where the other kids were hanging out on the pier.

"Mommy, Nanna!" I said as we neared my mom and grandmother.

My mom hopped up, all smiles as she hugged me. "Hey baby boy, how was the drive?" my mother said after a hug and peck on my cheek.

"Fast! If we had not stopped for gas and pyrotechnics, we may have been here 45 minutes ago." Tatiana answered with a chuckle.

"Oh no girl, you let HIM drive on the highway? You cannot do that 'without' life insurance, plus a combination of good seatbelts and great airbags!" my mom said, and everyone within earshot laughed.

"Without life insurance, plus a combination of good seatbelts and great airbags' ha ha ha!" I mimicked in an irritated voice and Tatiana punched my arm. Hard. I shot her a look and she shot me one that threatened more abuse if I did not behave.

"Thank you! He's too old for me to do that to his ass anymore! I'm his mother Kyra." My mom said smiling at Tatiana, her hand extended.

"It's an absolute pleasure to meet you! I'm Tatiana." my girlfriend said, shaking my mother's hand.

"You got fireworks? A lot?" My mom asked, a sparkle in her eyes as she grinned at us.

"Yep Kyra, he had us get boxes and bags full!" Tatiana said, now seeing what I'd said earlier.

"Really? Uhm, let us go see these alleged materials, shall we?" my mom posed, with an epic smile.

"Come on, I'll help." Tatiana said, then held her hand out to me asking, "Keys please?" I handed her the car keys, then recruited a few of the nearby teens doing nothing to help retrieve the merchandise.

"Damn, your mom made a friend fast!" A.j. said with a laugh as we watched my mom and Tatiana talk happily as they walked away.

"Hell yeah. Looks like they'll be havin' fun together. Who got the weed? Do we gotta shake down lil' Rob them, or are you holdin'?" I asked, referring to a few younger cousins who kept weed on them like it was clothing.

"I brought a few blunts worth, so we good!" A.J. said.

"Yo, lemme greet the elders, then we can go blow, a'ight?" I told him.

"Yeah, I'm a snatch a beer so I'll walk with you." he said as we walked to our grandmother, hugging and kissing her after she commented on the "pretty chocolate lady" I had brought with me.

From there, we swooped in on my aunts, all cooing while bombarding me with hugs and cheek kisses like I was a newborn baby. I then dropped in on the uncles, shared a few chuckles with them and A.J. before he and I walked to a part of the pier where no one else was.

A.J. rolled a blunt, talking as we stood, sipping beers. "How long you and Tatiana been a couple?" He asked as we lounged, sitting atop a concrete barrier.

"2 months." I answered, holding to the lie Tatiana and I agreed upon.

"She mus' be somethin' 'cause yo ass keep ladies' miles and miles away from the fam!" my cousin said with a snicker.

"Yeah nigga, she'll be the one bringin' the next lil' ones to our family tree bruh, watch!" I told him, staring out onto the lake, watching the boats roll on the waves.

"That's cool bruh. It's time you settled down!"

"What yo? Jus' 'cause you and Erika started young don't mean we all should." I teased, chuckling.

"What's wrong with marrying your high school sweetheart and first love?" A voice asked from behind us.

I turned and saw a smiling Erika, A.J.'s wife and children's mother. I gave her a hug then answered, "Nothing at all ma! You kno' I've been hella jealous of you and him since forever! I been seekin' that insane love you's got! How's he been actin' lately? I don't need to kick his ass, do I?"

Erika laughed as she cuddled up with her husband. "Yeah right! My husband is always good to me. He knows better!" she said while dipping her raven-haired head onto A.J.'s shoulder. He rolled his eyes.

"Yeah, yeah, yeah." A.J. said, and we all laughed.

"I see you did not come say hi to me with your plus one. She's pretty and the girls like her." Erika said with a smile.

"Sorry but my mother hijacked her before I could." I told her.

"That's because she wants a daughter-in law and grandkids." Erika explained. "So, tell me about her."

"How 'bout you do what women do and talk to her." I said, earning a crass look and a middle finger. I laughed, then added, "But fo' real, my mom got explosives, so she needs parental supervision Err!"

Erika laughed in agreement, then walked towards my mom, Tatiana, and a now growing group of people around the cache of fireworks. A.J. and I continued smoking the weed, talking. We were joined by other cousins who produced joints, vape pens and blunts. After a few minutes, we were over a dozen strong, huddled haphazardly, smoking, and joking gleefully!

Tatiana enjoyed the family as she, my mom and anyone else nearby exploded pyrotechnics. Erika, my mom, 2 aunts, 3 uncles and more kids than a small elementary school all had fun blasting things. I walked over to make sure they were saving the bigger things for nightfall, and saw they mainly used the things intended for the earlier festivities. I helped with the lighting of things for a while, then came lunchtime.

We all demolished the sea of food that had been prepared for the gathering. It was great watching Tatiana interact with the family. She was so happy and friendly. She melted into the fray with ease.

After the food, we played a game of touch football that was only the older cousins and younger uncles and aunts. It wasn't a long game because it was a long time since we had played and most of us were blazed off the weed. Tatiana tackled me in a way that was not friendly at all, then pecked me in the cheek as I lay there stunned while the family laughed and talked shit about me. Then the youngsters played a much more entertaining game of football, which we enjoyed because they played hard.

When the sun slipped low in the western skies just far enough for the skyline to give off long shadows, my mom was back to the fireworks. "Mother, give it a chance to get a bit darker." I said, attempting to stall her.

"Baby boy, we got more than enough with what D.D. and Monica brought. We gotta do them all tonight and remember that people have to work in the morning, so being out all night is not an option." My mother told me.

Tatiana added, "Yes Chris, and we have to drive home plus get up in the morning." She wrapped her arms around my neck and kissed me sweetly.

"Okay, okay, let's do this then!" I said smiling.

As my mom and some other adults set things up on the pier, I pulled Tatiana aside. "Huh?" she asked innocently, smiling at me.

"I kno' why you did that!" I told her with a grin.

Tatiana wrapped her arms around my neck, staring me in my eyes while smiling lovingly, and asked, "Did what babe?"

"Play dense if you wanna, but I'm not blind lady!" I told her with a smile.

She chuckled, dropping her forehead to my chin. She looked back into my eyes, smiling sweetly, and said, "I love you, bye!" and walked away.

We set off the fireworks as soon as it got dark, continuing until we had gone through everything we had. The whole family plus folks who were nearby were either watching or helping us blow shit up. Pics and posts were happening all throughout the day and continued up until the second we were leaving.

Erika, A.J. and their girls made Tatiana and I promise to go spend a weekend with them at their summer cottage in the Wisconsin Dells. My mom made us promise to do dinner in Chicago with her and her boyfriend soon and often. Before we left, seemingly most of the family had connected via Facebook, Twitter and IG.

As we sat in the car preparing to leave, I could tell that Tatiana didn't want the gathering to end. "You a'ight mama?" I asked as I pulled into the lane, following the flow of traffic. We moved at a lax pace, outside the car, all around us fireworks exploded in the skies.

"Huh? Yes, I'm fine!" she said, looking at me with a beautiful smile as we followed traffic to the expressway.

"E'eryone loved you today!" I told her as we reached the freeway and headed north.

Her face lit up like the explosions in the airspace beside the highway we drove on. "You think so?" she asked, smiling at me.

"Bae, mos' definitely! If non-family folks had been present, you'd have held the introduction title of 'daughter-in law' by my mom. E'eryone else adored you too sweetheart! You's family now, believe that!" I told Tatiana.

She beamed like a ray of sunlight as she said, "I have never been to this type of family gathering. It was so different, but everyone treated me like they had known me since birth. I never once felt like I was an outsider, or in the way. I felt like family, and I loved it! I am so happy you brought me along!" she leaned over and kissed my cheek.

"I'm glad about it too! I loved seein' you in this type of situation. I do not think I have seen you so joyful. You seemed...free and so charismatic. Watchin' you today showed me more of who you are than any other time we been together. I saw that you are who I saw you as, and I love it! You are so beautiful Tati, I swear!"

She stared at me, smiling for a few moments, then said, "I love you so very much Chris!"

We made it to the hotel just past midnight because I couldn't speed under the cover of darkness. The places patrolmen hid I couldn't see clearly at night, so I respected the speed limit! I was also high, and Tatiana had weed in her purse so we couldn't afford being pulled over.

The risk didn't outweigh the reward. In our room, we made love slow and long, savoring every second like it was all that mattered to us. We gave each other all we had. It was another bout of bliss and when our bodies quit, we talked about our future. We began sharing what type of home we desired having.

"Tati." I said right near the edge of sleep.

"Yes?" she answered in a sleepy tone.

"I'm glad I forgot to buy milk."

She chuckled, then said, "Go to sleep boy, you are tired!"

"I love you woman!"

"I love you too!"

CHAPTER TWENTY-NINE

Tatiana woke me the next morning with breakfast laid out. "Baby," she cooed, "it's time to wake up. Check out time is 11:30. It's nearly 10 now." I opened my eyes to her smiling face, dressed in my shirt from the night before and socks, looking as edible as any morning meal.

"Okay ma, I'm woke." I said in a scruffy voice as I rolled out of bed and walked to the bathroom nude. I stretched and yawned while standing behind Tatiana as she washed her hands. I hugged her, kissing her neck in greeting.

As I slid my hands under hers in the running water, she said, "Good morning."

"Great one to be wit' someone you love!" I said, turning the water off as Tatiana dried her hands on a towel beside the sink. She turned to face me as I dried my hands off too. She kissed me then I slid my hands down to her waist and lifted her onto the edge of the sink! I felt her center, bare pressing upon mine and became excited immediately. I kissed Tatiana deeper with the idea of sex before breakfast.

Tatiana must have felt where we were headed because she pulled away, her delicate fingers on my chest as she said, "Chris baby, let's eat first." Her eyes were still closed, and her bottom lip found its way between her teeth so sexily it was hard for me to rev down.

"Yo, we great at multitaskin', so I was figurin' we kill 2 birds' wit' sex and eatin'." I posed, which earned a laugh from her.

"Yeah, because that will work. I can barely think with you inside of me, so how am I going to eat?" she asked with a grin.

I shrugged and she pushed me back enough so she could slide off the sink. She led me by hand out of the bathroom and into the living portion of the hotel room. We ate in front of the TV, talking mainly about the highlights of the night before. Neither of us touched the topic of that day's events.

I didn't because I had no idea how I was going to bring things to a close. I think Tatiana didn't want to talk of it at all. The food was absolutely delectable, and we savored each morsel. Add to that the great conversation as the clouds filtered the sunshine that slipped through the room's windows, and it was a great scene. The weatherman said we'd see off and on showers all day, but the temps themselves were on the steamier side of things.

Tatiana and I shared a bath, continuing our routine of lovemaking. It was great as we maintained our slow pace in the hot water, working each other with magical efficiency. When clean and sexually satisfied, we left the tub to dress for the day.

"Chris, where will we put our things while we do whatever it is you plan on doing to end all of this?" Are we simply leaving it all in the car?" she asked as we packed everything into our bags.

I sat on the edge of the bed as she sat cross legged on the floor a few feet away. "Why not? I mean, then we can make a decision 'bout what next and jus' go! No goin' to grab shit—jus' bounce! You a'ight wit' that?" I told her as she folded a dirty shirt and pushed it into a bag.

"I am fine with that." she said. After a few moments of silence she asked, "So, what IS the plan?"

I snorted a chuckle, then leaned back on the bed, my elbows holding me up as I stared at the ceiling above and confessed, "I have pieces of it in place, but I'm still puzzled on the whole picture ma."

She stood, her long legs in short shorts so sexy. She took two steps then crawled atop me. She gazed into my eyes while smiling and said, "Alright, let us put a plan together, together." I nodded while smiling, sliding my hands up her thighs then lower back.

We kissed. When our lips parted, I said, " First, I wanna hit up the DMV, get the car registered. Since we goin' to have guns in it, that'd be best!"

We checked out and drove west up Wells Street 9 blocks to the Department of Motor Vehicles Downtown offices. We both went into the facility which was packed at 11:30 on a Tuesday morning. We spent the time waiting to discuss the things I thought we'd need! Tatiana tossed in better alternatives and options than I expected. By the time we left the DMV, we had the temporary plates and the first half of our plan formulated.

We went to an Old Country Buffet located on the far southwest side of the city, just a pair of blocks from Southridge Mall, off of 74th and Layton. Sitting in a corner table near the window, we ate lunch while devising the 2nd part of our plan. "What all do we know about Drama, babe?" Tatiana asked then forked some macaroni and cheese into her mouth

"Beside the fact that the nigga would love to see us dead, an' would feel twice as elated doing it himself?" I asked with a chuckle, before scooping a piece of chicken dumpling and mashed potatoes into my mouth.

She nodded chewing while I stabbed some broccoli with melted Cheddar. "Yes, which means he will show up wherever he believes we are, correct?" She said after swallowing.

Covering my mouth I admitted, "That's true, but if we lure him somewhere, what then? I mean, jus' tryin' to play like it's high noon at the O.K. corral won't work 'cause we'll be outgunned ma."

She pondered that while chewing on a piece of battered fish. I ate a hot wing while awaiting her response. "You are right, which means we have to set him up in a manner that will get the police interested!" she told me.

I took a sip then said, "I'm not sure how we can get them involved in a way that—wait! I can rob a bank, leave the cash in a hotel room, get Drama there along wit' the police! He goes down for that an' is out of our hair!"

Tatiana started laughing when she heard "rob a bank" killing my enthusiasm before it had really blossomed. "Boy," she began, expelling a pity filled chuckle, "you are NOT robbing a bank! I mean, really bae?"

I shrugged sheepishly. "Tati, it'd work!" I told her, less positive of that now than I was mere moments before. I did my best defending what I knew was a dead issue.

"You might be right, but you are not doing it. I cannot have you taking a chance that would lead you to prison." she explained with a patient smile.

"I kno' but still, umm..." I said, trying to figure out a better idea.

"So, we know that luring him somewhere is step one, right?" Tatiana said, acting as if the last statements did not happen.

I swallowed then said, "That be on point lady, but where and how do we get him gone?" I rolled spaghetti on my fork after speaking.

"I got it baby! I think I know what will work!" she exclaimed, with as much excitement as Edison must have had when he got that very first lightbulb to work without exploding or fading. She told me her plan, her eyes aglow in conviction and glee. When she finished, we were both all smiles.

"Tati, you are a fuckin' genius!" I said, adding, "No lie!"

She beamed at my praise, saying sweetly, "Thank you! Remember that in the future when you disagree with me!" I chuckled and toasted her on that.

We finished our meal, then began to put the plan into play.

Tatiana drove us 2 blocks south to Southridge Mall. We hit up a RadioShack, purchasing the needed electronic items we'd need for our plan. From there, we went to a cellphone kiosk and bought a prepaid burner phone. After that, we went shopping for new clothes and some other less important things to be sure our plan would fall properly. We left the mall with everything we'd need to end the whole ordeal.

CHAPTER THIRTY

Tatiana drove us north on the busy, six-laned 76th street. It was 3pm and we were scheduled for an open house on 65th and North Avenue. It was actually a very nice place based upon the virtual tour on the company's website. I looked at a few other houses as she drove us to the mall, but the one I chose was the only one where the realtor would show the place on such short notice. I really thought hard on the future as Tatiana, and I talked. I had the feeling Tatiana had similar thoughts dancing through her head like a B-boy.

I pulled out the prepaid phone and dialed up Detective O'Malley. He answered in a gruff clip of a voice saying his name and title. "Yeah detective, I got some info on that armored truck heist and if you'll hear me out, I can get you a live confession...IF you want that." I said, calm and cool.

The dick spoke as though he was only mildly interested in what I planned to share. "Who is this and what ya have for me?" he asked.

"The 'who' is irrelevant. Do you want the person or nah?" I said in a testy tone.

He sighed then said, "Go 'head, I'll be sure to have it looked over." His voice almost impossibly seemed even less intrigued.

I chuckled at his attitude, then told him to remain on the line and to stay silent no matter what. The cop inhaled then said, "Come on with it, I have a load of files on my desk here kid!"

"I'm serious as fuck! Say nothing' till I address you, or you'll fuck shit up!" I stressed to him.

"Alright, alright! Jesus holy mother." he said as I clicked over to do a conference call to the kid's phone. I answered it then called Drama on 3-way. I put the phone on speaker and pulled out a digital voice recorder we had bought at RadioShack.

Drama answered on the second ring. I already had O'Malley on the line as Drama said, "Bitch ass nigga, you and that black ass bitch back in town I see."

"Nigga, how you figure we back in the city? We could be callin' you from San Diego, bitch! But whatever! I'm jus' curious 'bout somethin'." I said, trying to bait him without being overt about it.

"Don't trip. I'm the only one who rapin' ya bitch! We won't run a train on the bitch. Then I'm offin' her in front of you, and doin' you last." he said, finishing with a maniacal laugh that was rather unpleasant.

"So, you say, so you say. But no joke, I have been wonderin' how did you kno' them gold bricks would be in the armored truck you and ya boy's hit? Or did your dumb ass, blockheaded niggas have a lucky break and stumble upon them? I mean, you niggas ain't the brightest mafuckas 'round!" I said, then laughed just enough to anger him. If Drama was the guy, I imagined him to be, I figured doing that would trigger his ego just enough for him to be reckless.

"What?! Nigga, I did kno' the gold was in the truck! My boy Levar had a connect on that end, but I put the plan together and handled it like a goon s'posed to!" he replied, all arrogance.

"Yeah yo, I saw how you and ya boys get down, shootin' up my wifey's apartment out in Westlawn and shootin' at us at the hotel by the airport. That was wild and you had us scared to death." I told him.

He laughed in a triumphant manner before saying, "Hell yeah, but I can't wait to catch you and that bitch. You won't get away, and imma enjoy rapin' her black ass right in front of you!"

Even though there was no way I was allowing him to put a hand on Tatiana while I was still breathing, his words pissed me off in a major way! "A'ight son, but how did you niggas dodge them cops? When you flew up Lisbon, they were on ya nuts like pubic hairs! I figured you fuckboys were caught up like Usher!" I said with a chuckle, once again hoping his vanity would still be on overload.

"Shot them fags. Well, we shot AT the ones who hopped out and chased us on 42nd. When me and my boy Train hit the alley that cut from Lloyd to Spaulding and jumped out the whip, them bitches was right behind us. Train hit a yard first, then I followed him. Them bitches bent around the corner of a house, running and pop, pop, pop. Train let loose. One fell. The other pulled his ass back around the corner." Drama explained excitedly, finishing with a self-satisfied snicker.

I didn't know if Drama was in route to our location, but even being in motion I still wanted to get off his radar. "Yo, you crazy! I'll holla later!" I said, then hung up and quit recording. "O'Malley, you catch all that?" I asked, focusing back on the policeman.

The cop spoke with fire in his every syllable. "Son, who the fuck was that bastard?"

"Check this. I recorded the call so it's all on tape–" I started but O'Malley slashed my words like he had a machete in the jungle.

"You called that piece of shit, so tell me his number, NOW!" the detective said.

"Yo, O'malley–"

"No, you listen. You tell me who the fuck that was and give me his number now or I will have this call traced and hit you with Aiding and Abeding plus obstruction. Felonies!" he yelled, sounding nearly rabid.

I chuckled then said, "Yo, don't threaten me! This a burner phone, so tracin' it will be a waste. Now, give me a way to reach you 24/7 and not only will I give you him, I'll get you e'er'thing you need to send him away for a century plus, got me?"

The cop was so livid, I could feel it through the phone, but he spoke in a calmer tone saying, "I... here is my cell. Call me at that number only with his info or else!" He relayed the number, and I ended the call, turning the burner off just in case the copper got crafty.

To give Drama a stationary target momentarily, I had Tatiana pull into a gas station, and I dialed up Drama on the kid's phone. "Nigga, what the fuck, you bored?"

"Yeah, bored! I got a question yo. How the hell you kno' where we at all the time?" I posed, simply to toy with him.

He laughed at me then said, "Told you I gots people everywhere! I'm like a ghost. I see through walls and shit. You can't run, imma always find you. You should just stop tryin' cause I'll find you...real soon too, watch! Bet on that!"

I snorted a laugh and directed Tatiana to drive west for a little bit. "Yo Drama, where you at? We can meet up. I don't mind throwin' shots at you fags. My boo wanna lay you fuckas down too! Can we do that? Tell us where you's at!" I said as Tatiana drove.

She turned north on a busy 92nd street as Drama chuckled. "That black ass bitch 'bout that life, huh? Tell that hoe I wonder how loud she will scream when I'm fuckin' her in the ass!" he said, enjoying himself much more than any normal person should be.

I laughed, more at him than with him before saying, "Yo, she is a screamer too, no lie!" Tatiana punched me and threw me a menacing glare, but I kept talking. "I hit her from the back the other day and bastards next door called the front desk on us!" I finished, earning two more hard jabs from Tatiana's little fist.

Drama laughed then said, "I can't wait to catch you and that bitch!"

"Since you obviously spooked to meet us somewhere, I'm goin' to go. We gotta go look at this crib we 'bout to buy wit' ya money. I'll holla later, deuces!" I said, then ended the call before he could speak.

Tatiana was talking the second I hung up. "Do not EVER do that again Chris! He is talking about raping me and you are laughing, telling him how I am in bed. That is out of line!" she said, tossing me an angry look as she drove.

"Tati, mami, listen. I will have to be dead, absolutely done before I let him get close to touchin' you! I will always, always, always spend my last breath protection' and providin' and lovin' you! I said what I did to fuel his desire. I want him so antsy to come after us. That is how we keep him under our control ma. Dude will only touch you when I don't exist!" The conviction compounded with the look on my face gave Tatiana the solace she sought because she relaxed.

She was back to normal as we made it to the location of the house being sold. Tatiana and I sat in the car going over our cover story again. It was the scheduled time, so we left the car, and walked hand-in-hand to the two-story, single-family home. The front door was open as we entered the fenced in front yard, which was clean and properly maintained, but small. I rang the bell and said, "Hello?" into the space beyond the door.

The click of heels on hardwood floors announced a female before she said, "Hi, come right in!" The realtor came into view. Tatiana and I both entered, being met in an open living room by a thin white woman with hazelnut hair and a wide face.

She smiled at me and Tatiana as we said, "Hi!" in unison.

"Hi, how are you two?" she asked, holding out a well-manicured hand for us to shake.

"We are fine! How are you?" Tatiana said, shaking the woman's hand. I shook the woman's hand next.

"I am great, thank you! I'm Allyson. I spoke with your fiancée earlier, I believe." the lady said as we all stood in the entrance.

I now spoke saying, "Yes, that was me. I'm James. This is my beautiful fiancé, Kia."

Tatiana seemed giddy at the word and flashed the cubit zirconium we purchased at the mall for this occasion. "Wow! That is

gorgeous!" the realtor said, sharing in the joy all females seem to get from the prospect of an impending wedding.

Ecstatically Tatiana said, "Thank you! He popped the question 2 weeks ago and I am still floaty!"

I chuckled at that. The realtor said, "Congratulations! Hopefully this will be the home you two start your family in." Both Tatiana and I smiled wider as the realtor began telling us about the place.

We started in the living room, walked through a dining room equal to the size of the living room but was pushed off to the right a bit due to stairs that came down from the second floor. Past that was the kitchen, which wasn't large but carried all the amenities of a gourmet cooks playground. A pantry and laundry room was connected to the kitchen. Down a hallway was a bathroom, on the wall just behind the pantry/laundry room area. "As you see," the realtor began, "the downstairs is very practical and open. The numerous windows allow a lot of natural light in. It isn't a huge place, but more of a home for a family just beginning their journey as you two are."

She walked us to a side door in the kitchen, which opened to a mudroom, and the back door, leading us out into a medium sized backyard. "This is a yard made with kids in mind. A little tyke would have a blast back here! The wooden fence presents your family with privacy. The garage holds 2½ cars, and has places for tools, as well as a workbench." the realtor told us as we walked somewhat swiftly through a slight drizzle that fell on the path leading to the garage. We scanned the interior of the garage, then returned to the house.

The realtor led us up to the second floor, the stairs ending in a hallway which went the whole length of the upstairs. A total of 5 open doorways were on the left and right sides of the hallways, with doorways bookending the front and rear of the hall. "Up here we have the master bedroom whose windows face the front of the house." the realtor told us. She showed us the master bedroom facing the front of the house. "Here is the other bathroom." she said, opening one of the 3 doors along the sidewall.

She then showed Tatiana and I what was behind a door not far from the bathroom. "This is the second largest bedroom. It's—"

"Oh, sorry!" I said, cutting her off as I pulled out my phone that had begun to ring. "I have to take this. I'll go downstairs. Finish please."

I said and was halfway down the stairway before either of the women could react or protest.

As I walked down the stairs, I heard Tatiana explain apologetically, "He's a top exec at his internet solutions company, so when work calls, it means something went sideways and he has to problem-solve."

I spoke loudly, as if explaining protocol while I unlocked a window in both the kitchen and dining room as fast as I could. Then I simply paced the dining room, pretending to talk down to someone who had royally screwed up.

As the ladies came downstairs, I was saying, "And so help me God Donnie, if it isn't up and runnin' by business hours t'morrow, you will be collecting unemployment, got me?" With that I tapped the phone pointedly, pretending to end the call.

Tatiana spoke up as she walked to me. "James, stop being a big meanie to your subordinates!"

I pecked her lips with mine, then said, "I'm sorry bae! They jus' screwed up the syntax for sector 6, which made 15 company's computer systems nearly go offline completely. That could cost the company nearly 6 figures if they do not have it corrected by the morning."

"I know, I know." Tatiana said in a consoling tone as she wrapped her arms around my neck. "You have a tough job." She added, kissing me again on the lips. She moved on in subject, asking, "Baby, what do you think about this house? I love it!"

"Oh yes, I'm lovin' it too! It'd be exactly what we would need to bring the baby home to." I told her, rubbing her baby-tee covered tummy.

She was all smiles while saying, "I totally agree with that!"

The realtor was all smiles too as she said, "Due to the shape of the market right now, this house is set to go at an incredible price. 117 thousand. It is great structurally, in a great neighborhood with parks, schools in the Wauwatosa school district, entertainment venues all around, plus stores within walking distance. It has Central air too! It is easily worth 150, but the slump in the economy has things a bit shifty, so..." the realtor trialed off, allowing her words to hang in the room like balloons filled with helium.

When she finished, I told the realtor, "We have another place to checkout befo'e makin' up our minds. Is it cool if we let you kno' by noon t'morrow?"

"That would be absolutely great!" she said. We shook her hand then left the place.

CHAPTER THIRTY-ONE

Tatiana and I drove eastward, down North Avenue to 43rd street, then headed south for 3 blocks. At the intersection of Lisbon Avenue and 43rd, we hung a left onto Lisbon, continuing in an eastward direction once more. We parked half a block from my apartment building, as the rain fell in sprinkles outside the car. "Chris, why not let me go in by myself? We did not see the kid out and he is the only one who can identify me." she said as we sat in the parking lot of a tire shop on the corner of 40th and Lisbon.

I was going to deliver the money orders we had purchased for the other residents in my building as Tatiana held me from exiting the vehicle. "Tati, what if they pop up? I'd rather be the one they chasin'." I told her as rush hour traffic trudged by us. No one was outside who did not have to be, it seemed, as the rain picked up right before our eyes. A group of kids sat on a nearby porch, seeming to hold a vigil for the return of clear skies.

Though we had seen no one shifty, I refused to allow Tatiana to go into the building. I'd rather lose my head than lose my heart. Sensing my titanium stance on the issue, Tatiana relented. "God Chris, you are so stubborn! You go, but you better keep your phone on and take a gun!" she stated with a mild hint of irritation.

I gave her a hug and kiss, then climbed out of the car with one of the guns inside my jacket pocket. I hit my Bluetooth as she phoned. "I'm here sweetheart." I said, walking with both my hands in my pockets, hood up, fitted cap and shades covering my face.

"Good! I'll be ready to go immediately." she said, and I heard the car engine start up as I walked with my head down.

I went to the front door and noticed that the lock was broken, and no key was required for entry. I slipped into the dim hallway and stepped to the stairs, tapping each one gingerly before I climbed up, to make sure they did not have any residual grease from the WD-40. The hallway smelled like smoke, but not overwhelmingly so. It was more of a tinge.

I knocked on the first door I found after listening for a few seconds and hearing the unmistakable squeal of laughter that young children emit. The door was on the left side of the hall. "Hold on, I'm comin'." a female voice said before I knocked a second time. "Who is it?" the voice asked from the other side of the door.

"Chris. I'm your neighbor." I said politely.

A brown-toned, girlish looking lady opened the door. She had on a black T-shirt, loose on her thin frame and jeans that accentuated her thin hips and thighs, plus her hair was in a rag that some gangs use to identify their affiliation. Hers was pink. She wore pink socks also. Though she had scowled upon opening the door, her features softened into a warm smile when she saw who I was. "Oh hey! Don't you—didn't you, I mean—live in the burnt apartment?" she said kindly.

I had never even seen her once in or near the building, but she had noticed me. I regretted not meeting her somewhat because she was quite pretty in a pure kind of way you rarely stumble upon. "Yeah ma, I—" I began, but stopped as an adorable baby girl crawled up behind the lady, then used her legs to climb into a standing position.

The lady picked the baby up, kissing her. "Sorry. This my baby girl Deysha. What was you sayin', um..." the lady said.

"Chris. I'm Chris." I said, smiling at the beautiful baby, all pudgy rolls with 4 front teeth. "I wanna give you some money. You mind if I come in?"

She had a look of confusion in her face but let me inside. As she closed the door, I sat on a futon couch in a living room the exact same size as my old one. "You got some money fo' me? What fo'?" she asked as she sat the baby on the not-so-clean looking carpet in front of a few toys.

"That fire was my fault, and I got some money so you can move to a new place." I told her.

Her skepticism was almost tangible as she stared at me like I had sprouted 3 extra eyes and a second mouth. "Nigga, I'm 19. I got a baby by a man who I ain't seen since I was three months pregnant. I got a momma and daddy who don't allow me to come around wit' they grandbaby cause I accidentally got pregnant wit'out bein' married and refused to have an abortion. I got no job, no skills, and my welfare benefits barely get me through every month. I'm goin' to school, but I kno' don't shit come fo' free, so what's the catch?" With that said, she folded her thin arms across her chest, and gave me a tough, daring grin, as if challenging me and expecting that she had blown up whatever scheme I was there about.

It struck me as extremely cute because though she portrayed a tough exterior, I saw that she was just as scared as most teen moms unsure of what life held in store for them. I chuckled and pulled out 2 money orders. I sat them on her coffee table, then said, "No catch, no garbage. You take these and please find a proper place for you and ya precious daughter, okay ma?"

She reached and picked up the money orders. Her eyes went larger than baseballs, and she covered her mouth with her free hand. "Oh god, are you...is this fo' real?" I nodded and she began to cry, her eyes going back and forth, scanning the money orders and my face while I simply smiled. "Thank you, I... oh, thank you so much!" she said, looking at me, her eyes now a soft, warm brown.

"You's are welcome. I gotta go, but please take care a'ight pretty lady?" I said, standing to leave.

"Wait. I always wanted to ask you but was scared. Are you single 'cause I'd love to make dinner fo' you."

"Yeah, I am taken. She actually waitin' outside."

"Oh, well...thank you so much!" she said, with mild disappointment.

"You are welcome! Take care of that baby 'cause she is so gorgeous!" I said, walking out her door.

The woman smiled, saying, "I will! Bye!" She stood in her doorway as I walked down the hall. I heard her door close as I knocked on the next door, a few feet down the hall on the same side. I realized that I did not get her name.

I knocked a second, then third time with no answer so I slid a money order under the apartment door before moving on.

I passed my old apartment door on the way. The entrance was boarded up heavily and the smokey smell was quite intense as I moved on. I walked to a door a few feet from my old one and knocked. A tiny voice asked, "Who is it?" It was a feminine voice—that was all I could tell.

"It's Chris ma'am. I used to live right across the hall." I said in a polite, soft voice.

I heard the click-thump of locks being disengaged, then the door opened partially. "Yes baby?" A small, elderly black woman with a soft smile asked kindly.

"I am so sorry botherin' you ma'am, but I wanted to give you this money to take care of any damage caused by the fire in my apartment the other day." I said.

She gave me a patient smile that was all any child or grandchild ever wanted from a parent or grandparent, then said, "Chris, it wasn't your fault! Those nasty hoodlums the police found with guns were the ones who started that fire. You keep your money young man, I'm fine!"

"Ma'am please. They were after me and that's why I want you to take this. It'll help if you wanna move." I told her and handed her a money order.

She looked at it, still smiling patiently then said, "I'll keep it because its impolite to turn down a gift, but that wasn't your doing son, so do not let it sit on your conscience, alright? Thank you kindly."

"Yes ma'am, I won't! You are quite welcome! You have a great week!" I told her before walking away. She waved and closed her door.

I walked to the last door and knocked. It was in the same side as my apartment, only a few feet away from the back stairwell. I knocked a second time and a gruff male voice asked, "Who is it?"

"Chris, from next door." I answered, stepping back from the door a few steps.

A tough-looking, African warrior type brother opened the door with the aura of a bull hoping to charge at a matador. "The fuck you want?" he questioned as if I had just interrupted his hibernation, mating, last meal or all three at once. I was a bit spooked by how the shirtless mound of man stared at me, so my right hand casually found its way into my jacket pocket, and around the handle of the compact pistol.

"Yo, I wanted to give you this money order for any damage the fire in my place may have caused you." I told him. I held the money order out with my left hand, and he eyed the paper like it had an invisible tripwire that would be triggered as soon as he touched it.

Finally, he cracked what could have been a smile, took the money order and said, "Okay then." With that, he closed the door in my face.

"Okay then." I repeated as I headed to the front stairs, after standing in the hall in stunned silence for a few moments. I walked out and Tatiana waited at the curb for me.

I climbed in and Tatiana pulled away.

"That girl in there, your neighbor...you and her ever hang out?" Tatiana asked as we drove south on the highway, headed to a gun shop I found that was located on the far southern edge of the city.

The gun shop was located on 27th and Cold Spring, just beside a graveyard. I chuckled then said, "Actually, I never even seen the girl befo'e. If I had, I may have tried to get at her. She was pretty."

"Aww, too bad!" Tatiana said in false sorrow.

I laughed, then said, "Queen of mine, do stop! You kno' I'm yours!"

Tatiana looked at me with a blank face, feigning innocence as she asked, "What?"

I snorted comically, shaking my head slightly, then said, "Whatever." She smirked adorably, then looked at the road ahead.

I used the internet to identify the guns I had been using: a Glock 9-millimeter and a .45 caliber. Tatiana pulled us into the gun shop's parking lot, and I went inside, leaving the gun I had taken with me in my building in the glovebox. I purchased 2 boxes containing 50 shells for each gun, plus 2 extra clips for each gun. I did this solely for the sake of having these things on hand. I had 2 bullets in the Glock, but the .45 was empty. I wasn't sure what may or may not come to be later on, but I wanted security, or at least the idea of it. I jogged back to the car with my purchase and Tatiana drove us north again.

She took us to the Walmart in the Mid-Towne shopping center and we both went in, grabbing the final things we'd need in order to finish our plans. From there, Tatiana drove us to get dinner. It was 7pm and we were starving. After subs at Subway on 65th and North Ave, Tatiana and I put a plan together that we hoped would bring this whole situation to a close.

The rain had picked up and a few cracks of lightning began to show itself in the storm-darkened skies as we drove east on Lisbon Ave from 49th street. Tatiana dropped me off at the bus stop on 41st and Lisbon, then drove around the east side of Washington park, calling me as she reached the opposite side of the park, 4 blocks south on Vliet Street. "I am about to turn on the kid's phone. I will 3-way Drama, after I call the burner phone, okay?" Tatiana said, music playing low in the background.

"Perfect ma, do that." I said and ended the call. Seconds later the kids phone number popped up on the prepaid phone's ID. I answered.

"Hold on." Tatiana said, and moments later I heard a ringing on the line. I was watching Drama's house, seeing which car he would use when he left his place.

"Pussy nigga, you kno' where I fuckin' live. Why don't you slide through so we can handle this?" Drama said upon answering his phone.

I chuckled, seeing no movement outside of his house. "Yo, where's the fun in that? I'm still tryin' to figure out how you always kno' where me and the wifey at. That is mad eerie!"

Drama laughed sardonically then said, "Told you, I'm like a ghost."

"Which don't explain much." I said, pausing to light a cigarette. I continued, saying, " if you kno' where we always at, why not catch us when we sleepin'?" I saw 2 cats; Drama and another guy leave the house and climb into a blue Mini Cooper.

"Less fun! Chasin' is excitin'. It's like huntin'!"

"Yo, you ain't doin' shit BUT chasin' us. You like Elmer Fudd chasin' Bugs Bunny or Wile E. Coyote chasin' The Road Runner. You never catch ya prey and in the end, nothin' but shady shit happens to ya! I'm curious though." I said, then chuckled as I watched them pull off north, then hang a right headed east on Lloyd Street? "What did you do wit' the whips that I torched?"

I could feel anger fly at me through the phone as he spat, "Bitch, I had them junked. But I scooped a new whip and I'll be takin' that out on that black ass bitch when I catch y'all."

I chuckled, then said, "Yeah, but that Mini Cooper you pushin' now is mad fly!" I texted Tatiana from my phone to hers to kill the power on the kids' phone when I spoke the next line.

Drama's laugh was nervous when he spoke this time. "You...you saw my new car huh?" he asked.

I had begun to walk west up Lisbon towards 44th where Tatiana was going to meet me when she turned off the kid's phone. At the moment she was driving west up Vliet Street. "Yeah yo, I jus' watched you and one of ya boys pull off. I'm at your crib right now wit' a gas bomb. I love fire! Don't you? Bye Drama!" I said, then Tatiana ceased the power.

On my phone I called her. She was giggling as she answered. "Bet he is speeding back to his place as we speak." she said.

I was jogging towards the meeting place as I said with a chuckle, "Hell yeah, he pro'ly wish that park wasn't between him and his crib! Where you at?"

"Just turning onto North Ave, headed in your direction bae. I will be there in seconds."

"A'ight ma, see ya soon!" I said and relaxed on the stoop of a corner store. Tatiana pulled up a few ticks later and we drove to the alley of the house we had gotten a tour of earlier.

CHAPTER THIRTY-TWO

We both walked into the backyard as if we belonged there. I made sure no one was watching me as I raised the kitchen window. I climbed in and opened the backdoor for Tatiana. "Ma, let's set e'er'thing up as fast as possible, a'ight?" I said. She nodded and we went to work. We put in place little electric lanterns that allowed us just enough light to see by without turning on the regular room lighting.

We prepped the dining room really fast.

On the floor, we sat up an airbed and put a blanket over it. We sat a small flat screen on the floor beside the bed, plugged it up but did not turn it on. I went to the living room and put a small HD camera opposite the door. The camera was the same color as the walls, and I faced it towards the front door. I placed another camera in the kitchen, atop a cabinet, facing the backdoor.

When I returned to the dining room, Tatiana had just finished putting the duffle bag full of new clothes we had purchased at Walmart beside the bag, detailing everything and making the room look like we lived there. I sat down an ashtray and tore a few cigarettes, lighting the shortened end just for effect. "Tati, let's go get the gold, a'ight?" I said after we both surveyed what we had put in place. It looked acceptable, so we left, headed to the storage unit.

We grabbed 2 gold bars, and once again painted paperweights the color of gold bars. With hands still gloved, I put the bars into a bookbag we had purchased and jumped into the car with Tatiana. We returned to the house and k sat the bookbag beside the bed, leaving the now empty box of bullets next to the bed. Tatiana laid out some empty food wrappers and empty pop cans. I sat a roll of toilet paper in the bathroom and placed a bar of soap on the sink.

I phoned detective O'Malley on the prepaid phone as we made sure the finishing touches were in order. Tatiana turned on the TV and put it on a channel playing video clips from YouTube. "O'Mally." The dick answered on the second ring.

"Yo, I phoned you earlier wit' the cat who knocked over that armored truck Friday on the line. Check it, I'm 'bout to give you his info, where he'll be in a few minutes, what the fuckers will be drivin' plus where he has the gold bars. Got me?" I said as I made sure the front door was locked.

"Definitely! I'm all ears son!" the cop replied.

"Hold up a sec." I told the detective, then clicked over calling the kid's phone. Tatiana answers, then called Drama. We sat the kid's phone on the floor next to the bed and waited for Drama to answer. "O'Malley, say nothin'!" I commanded.

"Okay." came the dick's reply.

Tatiana and I walked out the backdoor, leaving it slightly ajar. "Bitch nigga, you back after that shit you pulled earlier? What up pussy?" Drama spat at me, then laughed harshly.

I climbed into the car with Tatiana, and she drove us around to the front of the house, parking in the driveway of another house that was for sale towards the end of the block. The rain fell in sheets, muting the orange glow from the streetlights on the block. We were 7 houses down the street, on the opposite side of the street. Through the tinted windows of our vehicle, no one could see what we were up to.

"Yeah Cameron, me and the wifey are in the place we purchased thanks to you. I figured I would call you an' say thanks!" I said gleefully.

On a tablet we had purchased, Tatiana had pulled up the program that allowed us to watch the wireless cameras we had set up inside the house. Tatiana was also looking things up online for our plans beyond this final situation. "Aw yeah? How sweet, cake ass nigga!' Drama said with an evil laugh in his words.

" Yo, you kno' what I find too fuckin' funny, Mister Bolden?" I asked in a chill tone.

"What, bitch nigga?"

"The fact that you's either shot at me or had ya goons blow the hammer in my direction, had ya whole squad searchin' fo' me and bae, yet you and never get ya hands near us! You really are like a ghost — you can't touch shit!" I told him and laughed.

He mocked my laugh in the unfriendliest of ways. "Good one, bitch ass bastard! I'll sho' you soon enough when I'm rapin' that black ass ho' and then killin' you both nigga, watch!"

"Now, Cameron Bolden, you kno' you can't find us. We sittin' here watchin' TV, lounging in bed, cuddled up. We not concerned wit' ya bitch ass yo. You not spookin' nothin'! You's a phony, a total fraud nigga and we kno' it!" I said cockily, hoping it would rile him up. I watched the house which was about half the block behind us.

"Don't even trip bitch! Soon enough I'm a sho' you jus' how real shit can get!" he said through gritted teeth.

I tapped Tatiana on her thigh and as rehearsed she leaned close to me and said in a whiney tone, "baby, hang up on him! You do not need to continue wasting your time talking with that worthless idiot!"

"Mami," I began, matching her smile, "I'm jus' provin' to him how powerless he really is. He may have shot at us a few times, but in the end, this fucker is low caliber on every level! I'm 'bout to end this call in a sec, love!"

"Tell that bitch I'm gone put dick all up her ass when I catch y'all! You gone watch too!" Drama said in a tone that emitted venom like a rattlesnake.

"Hold on, I'll tell her!" I said. After a few second of silence, I said with a laugh, "yo, she said you's pro'ly a closet fag and can't get hard unless you imagine she a nigga. That's why you so obsessed wit' fuckin' her in the ass and you want another dude to watch you fuck!" I finished with a loud laugh that I knew would have him seething.

I could hear his heavy breathing as he spat, "Put that how on the phone, NOW!"

Still laughing hysterically, I managed to say, "Nah, she don't wanna talk wit' ya yo, she's proper! You started the shit an' she finished!"

"Ooh, I can't wait to catch you and that bitch! I'm a destroy her insides watch!" He was speaking through gritted teeths, and I could nearly see his snarl over the phone like we were facetiming.

It kept me smiling. "Yeah, whatever. I got's to kno'—how long you been livin' on 41st, yo? I lived in my place fo' 2 years, but never saw you!"

"I been livin' in this crib fo' a year, but my whole life I been in this area. This my hood!"

"Why you put ya cousin on the block when you could jus' be keepin' dust in his pocket out of love? My cousin's would never be hustlin' like that if I was holdin' major figures!" I told him, simply trying to keep him on the line.

Tatiana showed me a picture of 2 jetskiers skimming the waters odd the island of Bermuda and mouthed, "That will be us!" I smiled and nodded, then went back to watching the street.

"My lil' bro-bro wanted to hustle." Drama said plainly, as if what he stated was natural.

"So, you have a kid on the corner sellin' dope on your behalf? That's fucked up!" I told Drama, then lit a Newport.

"Whatever pussy nigga, you don't kno' nothin' 'bout the game!" he spat condescendingly!

"Nigga, I'm from New York! We invented the game! Fuck you mean, talkin' stupid like that! But I ain't worried 'bout what you sayin'. You ever worry 'bout the police findin' the pistols you and ya boy used to pop the cop wit'? I would be!"

"Hell nah! My nigga 3-scoops won't ever snitch cause he a top-notch G, an' I lost the guns in the Washington Park lagoon! I can tell you 'cause you fin' a be dead real soon!"

I saw the Mini Cooper turn slowly unto the street, easing past the house we had set up. The car parked 3 houses away from the one holding the kid's phone. They did something in the car as I said, "Drama, how fast you gone run out if ya car alarm goes off?"

"Why?" he said in a distracted way.

"I'm across the street from ya place ready to cause some property damage." I explained nonchalantly.

"Oh yeah? Do your thing. I'll step out an' watch!" he said, laughing.

I put the now fully loaded Glock into my gloved left hand and watched as Drama and 3 other cats got out his whip. Two jogged through the neighbor's yard, beside the dummy house under cover of the heavy rains. When Drama reached the front door, I said, "Yo, imma go now. I'm out!"

"Nah, don't go!" he said, but I hung up.

"O'Malley, his home address is 2017 north 41st street. I'll call you wit' mo'e info'mation in a few!" I said then hung up on the detective too. "Tati, you kno' the plan, right?" I asked, kissing her as she nodded. I grabbed a bag of the needed supplies, then I stepped out of the car. I crouched as I walked past the parked cars on the street.

When I was a few cars away, Tatiana started the Shelby's engine and pulled out of the driveway. My phone rang, and I put my Bluetooth in my ear, answering, "Yep."

"Knock knock bitch nigga, we here!" Drama said with a cackle. I hung up on him.

The second vibration was Tatiana calling me. "Bae," she said as I answered, "one is in the house!"

"Okay. Stay on the line an' tell me when they on the way out! I can see Drama an' once he inside, I will put things into play."

"Alright." she said, going silent.

Staying low, I jogged over to the Mini Cooper, watching Drama. He was let in the front door by one of his goons. When he vanished from sight, Tatiana said, "They are in the dining room. They have not gone upstairs yet."

"Good ma, keep an eye on 'em." I said. I pulled out 3 rolls of duct tape taped into a cylinder and placed it over the passenger's side headlight. I put the gun barrel inside the cylinder.

"They all just went upstairs bae." Tatiana told me. I shot one, down into the center of the headlight. The pop was lower than a firecracker, but the heavy rains blanketed the noise as well.

I moved in a crouch and did the same thing to the driver's side headlight. I hoped that I'd be able to kill both lights but could not be positive I was successful. I was about to do the taillights when Tatiana said, "They are headed out!"

At that instance, I looked and saw the front door open, and Drama with his goons walk out. I couldn't run because they might have seen me. Plus, I really wasn't interested in doing that anymore! Drama carried the bookbag we left that had painted paperweights and a single gold bar. I rose up just over the hood in a shooter's stance and started to let off shots in the their direction. Then ducked behind the car near the wheel well.

A goon yelled and fell, as Drama and his other minions dived off the porch for cover. One cat moved with a hobble towards a car, as Drama ran to another car for cover. I watched from a new position to see what they were doing. "Chris, Chris, you, okay? Chris, speak to me please! Oh god, please!" Tatiana said in a panic.

"Tati, relax! I'm good, stay ready!" I whispered. I looked up and it rained shots in my direction, hitting the car I used as cover and the Mini Cooper beside it. I moved at a crouch to yet another position, saw the cats and let loose 6 shots in their area, hitting a car they all were behind. I then took off running with my head low into a nearby gangway on my side of the street.

The scratch of rubber soles across wet concrete compounded with my heart kick-drumming against my ribcage was all I could hear when I first began flying through the gangway. The path lead me between two houses, opening at a backyard that was all shadows. I breathed rapidly as I moved. As I neared what seemed to be a rather squat garage, the now familiar sound of rapid-fire automatic machine gunfire kicked off. Just before the tata-tat-tatatatat started, I found myself falling face first, not noticing a 4 step drop down at the end of the pathway. I landed on my chest, hands bracing as I crashed into the wet pavement, bullets slicing through the space my body would have been had I not fallen.

I heard running footfalls coming up behind me, and instinctively rolled over, and readied the pistol I had somehow managed to not let go of. A figure in a hoodie came into view at the top of the stairs. I let off the remaining bullets in the gun and saw the goon's torso jerk as he yelled in agony, just as he fell forward in my direction. I scrambled to the left, then got to my feet and he smacked into the concrete of the alley.

I took off, crossing the alley 2 houses down, then running through another gangway. I tossed the first clip and put the second into the gun as I moved. I ran through a yard and came out between a pair of houses as more spitfire sounded behind me.

I was already at an angle I did not think the bullets could track but kept in motion anyway to avoid finding out if my assumption was accurate. I burst out onto the next block and darted between 2 park cars before crossing the street. I entered another gangway just as more tat-tata-tatatat followed me, the bullets hitting bricks a half step behind me, bits of mortar hitting me on the back and raining down on me. I ran through the backyard and waited at the end, just around the edge of the garage in the alley watching from a crouched position. When a thin cat hit the opening to the backyard, I let loose shots in pairs, and saw the fella fall. Drama was behind him and returned shots my way with a thick pistol that sounded like a cannon.

I didn't pause to see what he would do. I ran across the alley, slipped through another gangway, came out on the next block where Tatiana waited and hopped into the running car. She pulled away without word nor hesitation.

As we drove down the one-way street at a normal speed, "Tatiana asked anxiously, "What happened bae? Are you okay?"

Out of nowhere, I felt this blazing burn begin on my right forearm. "Shit!" I said through gritted teeth as I saw a slash in my jacket that had blood around it.

"Oh Chris, you are shot!" Tatiana yelled in a panic as I took off my jacket. The searing was way hotter than anything I had ever felt in my life.

Through the pain I said, "Tati, drive. I am not hurt bad. Focus on the road!" I wiped away blood with my jacket simply to see how bad the damage was. I saw that it was a gouge the size of a sharpie marker, just above my wrist bone, about an inch long. It wasn't too deep, but it bled heavily, so I put pressure on it.

Tatiana was crying as she drove us north on 63rd street, looking over at me every few heartbeats. "Tati, I think I was grazed. I'm good! You don't have to cry. Make a left on Center, the next busy street."

"You need a hospital!" she proclaimed, worry comprising every syllable.

I smiled to relax her, then said, "We jus' need to clean and bandage it. That is exactly what the hospital gone do, an' then call the cops which will get me put in jail. Nah, we got this!" I then pulled out the prepaid cellphone from the center console and called O'Malley.

"O'Malley here."

"Yo, the fuckers who robbed that armored truck will be drivin' a blue Mini Cooper wit' busted headlights somewhere in the vicinity between 65th and 40th, from Burleigh to Vliet. The gold will be in a pink bookbag. He was jus' involved in a shootout on 65th, a block North of North Ave, and has guns in his car, along wit' drugs. You have all you need right now. I will do whatever I can to get you mo'e, but fo' now, I'm out!" I told the cop as Tatiana pulled into a Walgreen's parking lot on 76th street.

I had Tatiana take down a list of things I would need to treat the wound while I made sure to wrap my arm in the sleeve of my jacket. She jogged into the store to grab the items. I called Drama from the prepaid phone. "Yo, you nearly shot me bitch!" I said when he answered.

"Pussy, you popped two of my aces! You dead motherfucker! You dead when I find you!" he spat furiously!

"You been sayin' that fo'ever, bruh! Yo, where you at right now? We can finish this!" I said, then recalled the GPS app and pulled out my phone.

"I'm a find you and that bitch, watch! You two are walkin' memories!" he said in a rather enraged fashion.

"Oh, you mus' be on ya way to St. Michael's Hospital, huh? I see that is what GPS say for ya phone." I told him with a chuckle even though my arm was really hurting.

"Yeah bitch, my boy's need doctor's!"

"No sweat! You almos' had us, but our alarm went off! Too bad we had to leave our shit behind. You ain't have it wit' you so we can grab it now."

He laughed then said, "Got my gold back though nigga, got my gold!"

"Shit!" I said forcefully, then hung up. I called the detective back and gave him Drama's exact location and the destination he headed for.

Then I phoned Drama back. "Aye, I'm headed to your place an' imma wait fo' you there, cool?" I asked as Tatiana climbed back into the car. She tossed the bag of medical supplies into the backseat.

"Yeah, bitch. I wanna look over this gold, make sure you ain't tryin' to trick me again. Imma be there!" he said.

Tatiana began to drive us to the Sheraton Suites on Highway 100 and North Avenue, across the street from Mayfair Mall. "Good nigga, 'cause I'm puttin' holes in you jus' like I did wit' ya lame ass nigga's!" I told him.

I heard sirens in his background, then heard Drama say, "What the fuck?"

"Oh my, could that be the cops I hear?" I asked with a chuckle, then added, "Guess my call lettin' them know exactly where you were and where you headed worked out then."

"Nigga, you set me up? Fo' real, pussy ass bitch!?"

"Every step of the way!" I said, with a laugh. "Let's see here...you got recently fired guns, stolen gold bars, you actually told the lead detective on the case where you hid the gun that you shot a cop wit', you broke into a house—which is all on hidden camera—you confessed to armed robbery of an armored truck, which I recorded. You kinda done, my nigga! One more thing...only one of those bars are real.

The rest are wit' me an' my beautiful black ass queen!" With that, I hung up on him.

Tatiana still had a fearful look as she drove us west up North Avenue. I leaned back in the seat, closed my eyes, and smiled.

CHAPTER THIRTY-THREE

At the hotel, in our room's bathroom, Tatiana had the bottle of alcohol ready to poor into the gouge. We both stood over the sink, looking at the wound. "Chris, this is REALLY going to hurt!" she said, her face already contorted in sorrow. "Try not to move." she added, grabbing my hand.

"Go 'head ma, I can take it!" I said.

"Okay." she said sheepishly, then began tipping the uncapped bottle.

When the liquid hit the gash, I nearly yelled out from the blinding pain. I let free an internal growl as the burning trumped all other pain I had felt in my life. Tatiana blanketed me with a few dozen "I'm sorry's" but the pain was too rich for me to even try to say words. She cleaned the area with gauze, then put Neosporin over the wound. She placed fresh guaze over the area, then wrapped it with surgical tape.

"Thanks Tati!" I said when I was able to speak words again.

"You are welcome! I am sorry it hurt." she told me, with a look of genuine remorse in her eyes.

"You did what you had to. Its nothin' to feel bad about mama. Thank you again!" I told her as we put the bloody, used items into the bag they came in so we could toss it when we left.

Tatiana and I laid in bed watching the news. "Is it over Chris?" she asked softly as the fingers of my right hand played around her belly button.

"There's one more thing I wanna do tonight, an' then it is all over ma, okay?" I replied. She nodded then kissed me.

At 2 in the morning, Tatiana and I parked on the block behind Drama's house and walked right up to his front door. Tatiana had the Glock in her hand concealed by the darkness. I had the .45 in mine as she knocked. His house was a compact place: 2 floors, but not very long nor wide. I did not figure there would be too much space inside with how it looked from the exterior. I called the home phone the whole time we drove towards the place, starting from the second we left prepared at the hotel, and no one had once answered. As I did a lap alone around the exterior, I heard the phone ringing inside, so I was pretty confident that no one was home. Even as we stood on the porch, the phone still rang.

While Tatiana watched the pitch-black street behind us, void of streetlights thanks to knocking them offline with a crowbar to their power box half an hour earlier, I used the same crowbar to pry open the front door. Tatiana shone her flashlight into the open space. I put the crowbar away and we entered the house. Closing the door behind us, I turned on my flashlight. "Tati, we lookin' fo' his bedroom. We need to find whatever papers he had that let him kno' where I worked. If not, I'm torchin' this joint." I said matter-of-factly as we slowly walked around the place, guns in one hand, flashlights in the other.

There were no bedrooms on the first floor. Only a bathroom, living and dining room plus the kitchen and some closets. We went upstairs to an attic-sized space with two bedrooms, plus a tiny bathroom separated by the stairwell opening. We went right into the first room and hit a light switch. It had electronic equipment, a TV, dresser and bed. We examined all within our vision, then empties out the dresser drawers on the bed. We found nothing of consequence then moved on to the small closet. There was nothing in there of interest either.

We killed the lights and went to the other bedroom. It had a master lock connected to a heavy bar. I pulled out the crowbar and cracked the door open with relative ease. We hit the lights and found a room that was lavishly laced. It had a nice bed set, flat panel 4k TV with surround sound system, rows of fresh gym shoes laid out against a far wall, and a video game system on a stand under the TV. On the dresser, I looked through the items all spread atop it, cologne, jewelry, pictures and other inconsequential things.

Tatiana was searching another part of the room. "Found a gun and some weed...a lot of weed actually! Oh, some money." she relayed, as she came across items of interest. I pulled out the six drawers, dumping them one-by-one, but found nothing at all that belonged to me. "Baby, I found it! It is a paystub. It was on the nightstand with your pictures, and a few letters from someone in New York with your last name. Who is Annabella?"

I walked over to where Tatiana stood, and she handed me the items. "My aunt in New York, an' had his stupid ass went out to Brooklyn on some dumb shit, they would have ended his ass no problem. Her son's are all Bloods out there. She used to threaten me when I was a kid, sayin' she would have them beat me down if I fucked up in school." I said with a smile.

Tatiana snorted a chuckle as I put the pictures and other papers into the bookbag we had brought. "Bae, where is that weed and money?" I asked her.

She walked to a bin and opened the lid. 2 huge, vacuum-sealed bags of weed were exposed with another stack of cash. I took the cash and one bag of weed, placing them into the bookbag, then said, "I got plans for this second bag!" I put the second one on the bed.

We snatched all of Drama's jewelry for good measure, then killed the lights and went back downstairs, me carrying the weed. I took a chunk of the weed from the bag and put it on a plate we had snagged from the kitchen. I also put the Glock I had used to shoot at Drama and his goons earlier next to the plate.

As we left, I called the police using the prepaid phone. "911, what's your emergency?" a dispatcher asked.

"I saw 2 guys jus' go into my next-door neighbors place wit' guns. They kicked in the door, and I heard—oh shit, they shootin'! Get here!" I said, then gave the dispatcher Drama's address.

"Sir, please stay in a safe place, possibly a tub or basement or interior room." the 911 dispatcher said before I ended the call, right as we reached the car.

Tatiana started the car and asked, "Why did you set all that up?"

She pulled away from the curb, heading back to our hotel. "The police will enter, see the weed, the pistol and initiate their own search. They will have the probable cause needed to look into the place more thoroughly, find anything that is hidden within the house, which will add to the prison time Drama gets." I explained.

We got back to our hotel room and fell asleep immediately. For the first time since we had met, we slept in total peace, curled up together.

Over a late breakfast, Tatiana and I watched the FOX 6 newscast on the tablet we purchased. They announced that Drama was captured. They did not release his name, and used words like "alleged" and "believed to be" but Tatiana and I knew exactly what they could not say for legal purposes. We bathed, dressed, and prepared all the evidenced we collected on Drama. Later that day, we stopped at a post office to mail it all to Detective O'Malley.

5 DAYS LATER

I glanced over at Tatiana in her white, 2 piece bathing suit, laying in the white sands beside me, the contrast with her sable skin, all smooth like melted chocolate, making my hunger for her rise again. "Tati?" I said as we lay on the secluded resort beach on the island of Andros in the Bahamas, the morning sun just painting us in its rays.

She looked at me smiling in her bug-eyed Gucci shades and floppy sunhat, then asked, "Yes my love?" in an airy way that made me chuckle softly.

Euphoric due to the scene, and the fact that she was in it with me, I said, "Bae, I love your black ass!"

She laughed, sliding her arm, then the rest of her soft, slender body atop mine. Straddling me she said, "I love being your black ass queen!" Eyes closed we kissed, the crash of waves like a heavenly applause, a universal encouragement of our love.

When we stopped kissing, I smiled at Tatiana and said, "Best July ever!"

She smiled wider then said, "You are so silly!" before kissing me more!

EPILOGUE—ONE YEAR LATER

Tatiana and I lay in bed, not sleeping, simply listening in the twilight moments of the morning, knowing that any second, we will hear the waking sounds of our 6-week-old son. He is in his bassinet right beside our bed. Micah has a schedule he put us on since coming home, and we know it better than he does?

"You know it is your turn." Tatiana whispers playfully, knowing I am awake.

I smile, eyes closed still, and chuckle softly. "Yes, my lovely wife, I do kno'! I am but waitin' for our prince to stir!" I tell her, opening my eyes to meet her smiling face.

Tatiana and I have been married now for just short of a year, our anniversary being September 1st. We moved fast but neither of us have regretted our choices to-date. Actually, we both joke about how we should've met a while sooner because we lost some time to love each other!

When we returned from what ended up being a 4-week vacation, island hopping through the Caribbean, Tatiana and I bought a small house on the lower east side of Milwaukee, a few blocks away from the lakefront. We fixed up the Shelby, restoring it to its antiquated glory.

Since we had our finances in order, I took Tatiana's advice and began DJ'ing again. I put some mixes out, then started doing 2 hour shows via Facebook Live, where folks could call in or comment requests and it blew up. Within a month I was doing bigwig parties and fundraisers all over the town. With the help of my cousin AJ, we put money down to rent the airspace of a local Am radio station.

6 months after conception, it was the 2 most streamed station in the city, with top advertisements and music star endorsements. We decided to upgrade and purchased an actual FM radio station. Quickly, our station became the 2nd highest rated station in the state, with a webcast audience nipping at the heels of most syndicated radio shows. I run the primetime show, Monday through Friday, and I love every minute of it.

Tatiana finished school just before the doctor put her on bedrest during the final weeks of her pregnancy. She graduated with honors and as she crossed the stage, my mom, her acceptable boyfriend Owen, my cousin AJ, his wife Erika, their daughters, and some of Tatiana's friends all cheered insanely loud when she was given her certificate inside of Milwaukee Auditorium Downtown. She was in tears when she came to us afterwards, looking so educated in her cap and gown.

She has the papers ready to open her own daycare when our son is 2 months old. She has the site rented and furnished. She is currently getting a few more interviews done for personnel and is excited to get that in motion. I am glad to be the man standing beside her. She is such a beautiful being. Her daycare already has a waiting list, plus gets great exposure thanks to the fact that she sleeps with this guy who owns a radio station.

Drama was found guilty of a long list of crimes, both on the state and federal level. He will probably never know freedom again. Tatiana and I actually felt bad for him, so we sent him a long Thank You note, leaving out our names of course, and hooked him up with a few years on some pen pal websites for prisoners. We never found out what happened with the kid Ralo, but we hope he went on living a different life. As for the guys I shot on that rainy night. Thankfully, they recovered from the wounds I caused them. I know that at the time, I was playing a deadly game, I'm not sure how I would have felt about having killed someone. They did go to jail with Drama, but they were all a part of his enterprise, so that was good for us.

I fixed Micah a bottle and fed him while sitting in a rocking chair on our enclosed back porch, staring into the face of my baby boy. Beyond the huge bay windows, I could see the just risen sun over the lake. Micah ate with his eyes closed; his left hand wrapped around my index finger. Tatiana was in a kitchen behind us fixing breakfast for her and I. She was softly singing a song from Melanee Fiona's newest album called "Scripture". Melanee told us that we inspired it, and premiered it at our wedding, just as she promised. Melanee even allowed me to debut it on my show plus she was my very first celebrity guest.

Tatiana walked up behind the rocking chair asking, " Chris, you drank the last of the milk?"

I looked back at her smiling apologetically as I said, "Yeah ma, I am sorry. I forgot to snatch a carton last night on the way home. My bad bae."

She shook her head while smiling. "I will go get more. Last time you went on a morning milk run, you found a future wife, nearly a million dollars in gold bars, and got us shot at every single day for almost a full week. We will NOT do that again!" We both laughed. Then, she kissed me on the cheek before walking back into the kitchen. I looked back at Micah, who had opened his eyes to see my smile.

About The Author

This is Anthony's debut novel, but more is on the way. He is a lover of all things written and plan to release more novels and poetry books in the very near future so stay tuned. Anthony is originally from Chicago, Illinois, but moved to Milwaukee, Wisconsin as a child, and absolutely hated the place, then became indifferent until finally falling in love with the city!

He is the father of two beautiful daughters, Mercedes and Mia, who absolutely mean the world to him. In his words, "They have always given me purpose when all else has failed, and they have eternally been the brightest of stars during the darkest of nights! They are incredible, and I am honored to have them as my babies!" Talk about a father's love.

Anthony is currently pursuing a degree through the Milwaukee Area Technical College and is on the college's President's Honors List due to his 4.0 GPA. He looks to complete his degree and use it to further his writing career. Anthony may be contacted by mail or email using the information below. Go ahead, tell him about your thoughts on his writing.

Anthony J. Machicoté
PO Box 80221
Milwaukee, WI 53208
Ajmachicote@gmail.com

www.ingramcontent.com/pod-product-compliance
Lightning Source LLC
Chambersburg PA
CBHW071236160426
43196CB00009B/1084